"Ali Abdullatif Ahmida's volume on the Liby oral history. This narrative recaptures the fu known atrocity. The prose and the poetry of fo currents of regional variation are gripping and ing have been truly honoured here."

—*James C. Scott, Yale University*

"Based on oral, archival and published documentation, Ali Abdullatif Ahmida provides a damning condemnation of Italian colonialism in Libya and of the scholarship that so far has overlooked the scope and significance of the genocidal violence which enabled it. A genuine contribution to the literature on Libya, on colonialism and on studies of genocide."

—*Mahmood Mamdani, Columbia University*

GENOCIDE IN LIBYA

This original research on the forgotten Libyan genocide specifically recovers the hidden history of the fascist Italian concentration camps (1929–1934) through the oral testimonies of Libyan survivors. This book links the Libyan genocide through cross-cultural and comparative readings to the colonial roots of the Holocaust and genocide studies.

Between 1929 and 1934, thousands of Libyans lost their lives, directly murdered and victim to Italian deportations and internments. They were forcibly removed from their homes, marched across vast tracks of deserts and mountains, and confined behind barbed wire in 16 concentration camps. It is a story that Libyans have recorded in their Arabic oral history and narratives while remaining hidden and unexplored in a systematic fashion, and never in the manner that has allowed us to comprehend and begin to understand the extent of their existence.

Based on the survivors' testimonies, which took over ten years of fieldwork and research to document, this new and original history of the genocide is a key resource for readers interested in genocide and Holocaust studies, colonial and postcolonial studies, and African and Middle Eastern studies.

Ali Abdullatif Ahmida is a professor and founding chair of the Department of Political Science, College of Arts and Sciences, at the University of New England, USA. His speciality is political theory, comparative politics, and historical sociology. His scholarship focuses on power, agency, and anti-colonial resistance in North Africa, especially modern Libya.

GENOCIDE IN LIBYA

Shar, a Hidden Colonial History

Ali Abdullatif Ahmida

Routledge
Taylor & Francis Group

LONDON AND NEW YORK

First published 2021
by Routledge
2 Park Square, Milton Park, Abingdon, Oxon OX14 4RN

and by Routledge
52 Vanderbilt Avenue, New York, NY 10017

Routledge is an imprint of the Taylor & Francis Group, an informa business

British Library Cataloguing-in-Publication Data
A catalogue record for this book is available from the British Library

Library of Congress Cataloging-in-Publication Data
Names: Ahmida, Ali Abdullatif, 1953- author.
Title: Genocide in Libya : Shar, a hidden colonial history / Ali Abdullatif Ahmida.
Description: Abingdon, Oxon ; New York, NY : Routledge, 2021. | Includes bibliographical references and index.
Identifiers: LCCN 2020013573 (print) | LCCN 2020013574 (ebook) | ISBN 9780367468903 (hardback) | ISBN 9780367468897 (paperback) | ISBN 9781003031772 (ebook) | ISBN 9781000169300 (adobe pdf) | ISBN 9781000169362 (epub) | ISBN 9781000169331 (mobi)
Subjects: LCSH: Genocide–Libya. | Genocide survivors–Libya. | Concentration camps–Libya. | Concentration camp inmates–Libya. | Libya–History–1912–1951. | Italy–Colonies–Africa–History. | Italy–Relations–Libya. | Libya–Relations–Italy.
Classification: LCC DT235 .A4 2021 (print) | LCC DT235 (ebook) | DDC 365/.450961209043–dc23
LC record available at https://lccn.loc.gov/2020013573
LC ebook record available at https://lccn.loc.gov/2020013574

ISBN: 978-0-367-46890-3 (hbk)
ISBN: 978-0-367-46889-7 (pbk)
ISBN: 978-1-003-03177-2 (ebk)

Typeset in Times New Roman
by Swales & Willis, Exeter, Devon, UK

For Rifa'at Abou-El-Haj, Salim al-Kubti, Ali Burhana, and Abderrhman Ayoub

CONTENTS

ILLUSTRATIONS

Figures

Maps

ACKNOWLEDGMENTS

This book was supposed to be completed many years ago but it was delayed because of unanticipated illness and death in my family. My father, Abdullatif, and my youngest brother, Omar, both passed away three years ago. Also, I lost three dear friends: Muhammad al-Faqih Salih, Muhammad Naji, and Idris al-Mismari two years ago. I struggled with the pain of sudden loss and unpredictable feelings of the endless ups and downs of mourning. But slowly the book became a source of solace. It gave me purpose to learn about the larger pain and the struggle for survival of the Libyan people facing genocide and, more importantly, coping skills used by others for recovery and emotional healing. This delay surprisingly made the book more cohesive and polished, and in a way I am glad it took ten years of research across three continents, working to make sense of the evidence, and resolving the riddles and puzzles of the case. Ultimately, I was lucky to have my small wonderful family and my supportive and kind friends and colleagues who have helped me during the period of researching, fieldwork visits, and writing this book. In short, this hard book helped me endure, and heal. I express my heartfelt appreciation and gratitude to all who supported me directly or indirectly, especially the concentration camp survivors and their families.

I wish to thank several institutions and people who have given me support, valuable criticism, and suggestions during the last three years of working on this book project. I am very grateful to Joe Whiting, my Routledge editor. Joe saw potential in my original proposal and was patient and understanding of my requests for including maps and photos, and of deadline extensions for completing the book.

Chapter 2 was previously published by the journal *Italian Studies* (2005). I am grateful to Taylor & Francis for permission to reprint an updated version

of the article. Also, I am grateful to Ms. Stefania Ruggeni of the Italian Archives at the Ministero degli Affari Esteri: Farnesina Historical-Diplomatic Archive, for permission to publish a photo of Libyans in the concentration camp of
Slug [Seloug] in 1930. I also want to thank the Libyan Studies Center in Tripoli, Libya for permission to include copies of photos in this book.

In Libya, I continued to find support and assistance at the Libyan Studies
Center in Tripoli. I am grateful to my good friend Mohamed Jerary, the Director of the Center, and the Center's staff, especially Nasr al-Din Jerary, Mahmood el-Deek, and Layla Aburqaiba, who assisted me during my many visits
to Libya researching material for this book. At the Libyan Studies Center,
I was given valuable access to files of the original collected oral history project
and the historical archives. In Benghazi, I am very grateful to my friend Salim
al-Kubti, who was key to my introduction and access to many concentration
camp survivors and their families. Also, I am indebted to historians Abdalla
Ibrahim and Atiyya al-Fayturi, and Abdalali al-Awkali and Ali al-Rishi, who
facilitated my research and also drove me around to meet survivors and to
bring me to the historical locations of the five main concentration camps. My
appreciation goes out to political scientist Omar Elaffas and his family who
hosted me at their home and made my visits successful. I also want to thank
historian Yusuf Salim al-Barghathi, who shared with me his oral interviews of
many survivors who had already passed away. These friends and the survivors'
families welcomed me as one of their own. They were generous and gracious
hosts during many years of fieldwork research and visits to eastern Libya.
Thanks to Khalid Bashir and Abdallah Zagub for their help and generosity in
sharing with me the oral history and the documentations of the town of Hun's
forced evacuation and uprooting collected by the Association of "Dhakirat al-
Madina" ["The City's Memory"].

In Tripoli and Sabha my brother Salem Abdullatif Ahmida provided logis-
tical support in all my visits. Ali Burhana was most helpful in providing me
with cultural context and knowledge on how to understand Libyan folk poetry
and rural cultures. I am grateful to many Libyan university colleagues who
passed my survey questions to their students, especially Azza Bughnadura,
Zahi Mgheirbi, Omar El-Afass, Um-al-Izz al-Farsi, Hawadi Muhammad, Adel
Senussi, Mahmoud Abu Suwa, Malek Bushehhea, Ali Dukaly, Afaf al-Basha,
Mukhtar Karfa, and the late Muhammad Naji. In Italy, I would like to recognize the generous support of Anna Baldinetti, Eric Salerno, Federico Cresti,
Nicola Labanca, Angelo Del Boca, Muhammad al-Khoja, and the late Abubakr
al-Kilani. In England, I am indebted to Ken Kirby, the BBC producer who
helped me figure out the controversy over the film *Fascist Legacy* and the
cover-up of the Allies regarding Italian Fascism crimes and atrocities.

In Egypt, I am indebted to the late historians Raouf Abbas and Abdalazizi
Nawar, who provided access to the valuable and unpublished papers of historian Muhammad Fu'ad Shukri. These papers shed a new light on the Arabic

records of the Italian concentration camps. Thanks to Dean Ahmad Yusuf Ahmad for his help and support through allowing me access to read and copy some of the rare books on the topic hosted at the Arab League's Higher Institute Library in Cairo. In Tunisia, my dear friend Abderrhman Ayoub helped me get access to the Tunisian Archives and above all shared with me his wide expertise on orality, memory, and language which broadened my knowledge of the field of folk poetry and internment.

In the United States, part of my research for this book was completed while on sabbatical leave from the Department of Political Science, College of Arts and Sciences, at the University of New England. I was also supported by a grant paid for by the University. Many colleagues at the University provided supportive feedback and criticism that helped me during the period of research and writing of the book. I would like to express my gratitude to the former President Danielle Ripich, Dean Jeanne Hey, and my colleagues Brian Duff, Alex Campbell, Eric Zuelow, Alicia Peters, Stephen Burt, Halie Pruitt, and Stephen Byrd.

I would like to thank the librarians Sonya Durney, Barb Shartzlander, Brenda Austin, and Cady Atkinson, the creative media and computer specialist Neal Jandreau, and my assistant Mary Johnson at the University of New England for their assistance and support. Work-studies students Brittany Nadeau, Sam Schilroth, and Alyssa Roof assisted me in researching the state of the field of comparative fascism, and locating rare material and films on the subject. I am indebted to students in several of my undergraduate courses, especially the Political Science Senior Seminar, Empire and Genocide, Gendered Nationalism, and the Invention of Traditions, for their insights and feedback regarding the comparative study of genocide and their curiosity and enthusiastic reactions to the reading and thinking about the forgotten African cases, including Libya.

Thanks to Josh Pahigian, Patti Rutka, and John Mason, for proofreading and editing earlier drafts of the manuscript. They made valuable editorial suggestions. I appreciate the uplifting support of my two dear friends and colleagues Beth De Wolfe and Susan McHugh. They read sections of the manuscript and provided me with useful and critical feedback.

Khaled Mattawa made useful comments on the original draft of the book and translated the long folk epic/poem "Mabi-Marad" by Rajab Buhwaish al-Minifi in the terrible Agaila Fascist concentration camp (1930). Elliott Colla reviewed and edited the translation. I am indebted to Rifa'at Abou-El-Haj, Abderrhman Ayoub, Mahmood Mamdani, Jam Scott, and Peter Gran who provided encouragements and constructive comments on the original proposal and a draft of the manuscript. Joel Gordon, John Carney, Marnia Lazreg, Terry Burke, Chas McKhann, Ted Swedenburg, Lisa Anderson, Ruth Iyob, Abdi Samatar, Dan Chirot, and the late Ellis Goldberg provided helpful feedback on the manuscript. They brought to my attention current debates from a broad field of critical and reflexive anthropology, genocide studies, and scholarship, which helped me place the Libyan case in a larger context and to see the comparative and global implications of Libyan history. Finally, I would like to express my gratitude to three anonymous referees who made valuable points and asked questions that helped me revise the manuscript.

While many individuals supported me during archival data retrieval, oral interviews, and to articulate my arguments, responsibility for the final draft remains mine alone.

My small family saved me during the tough ten years of research and writing. My wife Beth continued to provide support and encouragement and my two children Haneen and Zach, who are now in college, lived with this book project half their lives. They rightly urged me to finish the manuscript and move on. I agreed and promised them that the next book will be on a light topic, cinema. Their delightful spirits have continued to remind me that books are not an end but are about real people and the larger world.

A NOTE ON THE TRANSLITERATION

The proper names of persons and places are spelled according to the Arabic transliteration system followed by the *International Journal of Middle East Studies*. Turkish names and persons and administrative terms are spelled according to Arabic translation, as most of the sources of this study were written in Arabic. Exceptions to this system of transliteration are the use of ga instead of qaf in Libyan Arabic and commonplace names or proper names that are widely used, such as "Fezzan" instead of "Fazzan" and "Derna" instead of "Darna." Additionally, I kept Mohamed if used formally and used Muhammad when it is not translated earlier.

GLOSSARY

agha   lord, master; commander of the janissary military troops. In Barqa, Cyrenaica, am 'agha is an aid to the head of a religious lodge

'alim   (pl. *'ulama*). scholar or specialist on Islamic law

'ayan   notables

'a'ilat 'a'ilah   family, household

badawi   pastoralist or nomad

bait   house, household

baraka   (pl. *barakat*). God's blessing; a person who is blessed with *baraka* is called *murabit* and *sharif*

Barqa   eastern Libya

barr   land

barr al-haramin   the land of the two holy places

bilad   country

Bilad al-Maghrib   from Arabic, the western region of the Arab Muslim world from Libya to Morocco

Bilad al-Sudan   lit., the country of the blacks; the name given by Arabs to the region south of the Sahara and between the Nile and the Atlantic Ocean prior to European colonialism

Cologhli or Kolughli   from Turkish Kolughlu, descendants of intermarriage between Turkish troops and local North African women

dhikr   (pl. *'adhkar*). Sufi term for chanting and repetition of certain words or poems in praise of God

din   religion

duwr   (pl. *'adwar*). division, turn; a division of anti-colonial tribal resistance in Libya during the colonial period

fatha or fatiha   start, the opening of each chapter of the Qur'an; prayer to gain the help or the blessing of God

fatwa   (pl. *fatawa* and *fatawi*). formal legal opinion given by an *'alim* or jurist of standing to a question given to him by a judge or individual

hadith   reported words and deeds of the prophet Muhammad by a reliable chain of transmitters and scholars of Islamic law. The Qur'an and the hadith constitute the major authoritative sources of Islamic law

hamada   stony desert plateau; among the largest in Libya is hamada al-Hamra, located between southern Tripolitania and northern Fezzen

Hudur   'urban folks'

ikhwan   brothers, brethren, members of a religious order

ijtihad   scholarly free interpretation of Islamic law by a qualified scholar of standing. The conventional view is that *ijtihad* was closed by the twentieth century and *taqlid* or conformity was in Islamic law. This static view has been challenged, as many scholars pointed out that even if conservative *'ulama* closed the gates of *ijtihad*, people still reinterpret the law in new ways

iltizam   tax concession on agriculture

imam   leader of prayers attached to a mosque; leader of the community or the state in Shii and Kharaiji Islam

isti'mar   colonialism

jabal   mountain

jabbad   peasant hired to irrigate a farm of a landlord in exchange for a share of the crop according to initial agreement. The sharecropper *jabbad* draws water from a well using a donkey

Jamahiriyya   from Arabic, the state of the masses the official name of Libya between 1977 and 2011

janissary   Ottoman military corps till the beginning of the nineteenth century

jihad   religious struggle against inner base impulses and desires, and also against the infidels who threaten the land of Islam

khalifa   (pl. *khulafa*). caliph, successor of the prophet, title of the ruler of the Muslim state

kuffar   'infidels'

lahma   in western Libya refers to clan or subtribe

ljtihad   rational and free reasoning Islamic law

marad   illness

Mi'ad   a tribal negotiating form

miriland   state land

mtalian or talian   (pl. *mutalinin*). "gone Italian," *harqi* in Algeria, a term used in Libya to describe Libyans who collaborated with the Italian colonial state as soldiers and bureaucrats

mu'alim   (pl. *mu'alimin*). teacher

Mu'taqalat   concentration camps

mudir   administrator of a subdistrict or *nahiya*

mufti   scholar of outstanding knowledge in religious matters who gives formal legal opinion or fatwa to questions given to him by a judge

mujahid   (pl. *mujahidin*). fighter against infidels, see **jihad**

muqadm foreman, military officer, head of a religious lodge

murabit (pl. *murabtin*). saint, individual who has *baraka*, client tribesmen in Cyrenaica

mutasarrif provincial governor of a district or *mutasarrifiyya* in Ottoman Libya in the second half of the nineteenth century

Nassara 'Christians'

pasha governor-general of a province or *wilayat*; big landlord, high military or ministerial person in the Ottoman Empire. The governor of Ottoman Libya in Tripoli was called *pasha*. The rulers of the independent Qaramanli state retained the title of *pasha* from 1711 to 1835

qabila (pl. *qaba'il*). tribe

qasida poem

Quraish prophet Muhammad's tribe; one of the most powerful tribes in seventh century Arabia, which controlled the city of Mecca. Muslims have always accorded respect to the descendants of Quraish. Some Muslim jurists even required Quraishi kinship as a qualification for leadership of the Muslim community

Qur'an or Koran the written words of Allah as revealed through the prophet Muhammad: Muslim holy book

Rihlan deportees forced trail to the concentration camps

Sa'adi from Sa'da, the ancestress of the ten Sa'adi tribes of Barqa, Cyrenaica. These tribes were members of the Arab Hilali conquering tribes of North Africa in the eleventh century. Hence, they have owned most of the fertile land and water resources at the expense of early Arab and Berber Murabtin tribes in Cyrenaica. These ten tribes are 'Abid, 'Urufa, 'Awagir', Magharba, 'Abadydat, Hasa, 'Aylat, Faid, Drasa, and Bra'sa

saff (pl. *sufuf*). tribal alliances and confederations

saniya (pl. *swani*). well, farm in North Africa

Shar evil, starvation, death, depression in Italian colonial concentration camps

sharif (pl. *asfraf* or *shurufa*). noble; a person who is believed to descend from the prophet's family through his daughter Fatima

shari'a law, Islamic law; includes the Qur'an, the deeds and the statements of the prophet Muhammad, the consensus of the Muslim community, and the reasoning of the *'ulama*

shaykh or shaikh elder, dignitary, leader of prayers at a mosque, *'alim*, tribal chief

Shura parliament council

sidi or sayyid (pl. *sada* or *assyad*). colloquial from *sayyidi*, Sir; respected person of status from *sharif* or *murabitic* background in North Africa

sirib oral tales

shabardag barbed wire, concentration camps in eastern Libyan Arabic

suff (pl. *sufuf*). line, tribal confederation and alliance in southern Tunisia, Tripolitania, and Fezzan in Libya during the nineteenth century

Sufi mystic; a major trend in Islam that stresses the inner spiritual experience. In North Africa, Sufi Islam dominated popular culture from the fourteenth century

Sunna   the deeds and statements of the prophet Muhammad as accepted by a reliable chain of transmitters. Muslims who believe in the Sunna are called *Sunni*

tahrir   liberation

Tarabulus al-Gharb   the name of Ottoman Libya until 1911

tariqa   (pl. *turaq*). path, religious Sufi order

Tilian   'Italian'

'umma   Islamic community

'Urf   Arab social and cultural values and practices in diverse regions and communities. In Libyan society it refers to tribal and locally agreed values and traditions

'ushr   (pl. *'ashar*). tithe, 10% tax on agricultural produce known also as *zakat*, one of the five pillars of Islam

wadi   (pl. *'awdiya* or *widiyan*). valley

wald   (pl. *'awlad*). child, boy, descendant, e.g., Awlad Sulayman

wali   (pl. *wulat*). provincial governor of *wilayat* in the Ottoman Empire

walii   (pl. *'a'awliya*). saint, *murabit* who is believed to have *baraka* in North Africa. After the death of a *walii* his tomb or lodge becomes a shrine and a place of sanctity

waqf   religious endowment, see **habs**

watan   homeland

wilayat   in Turkish *iyala* and *vilayet*; province of the Ottoman Empire. A *wilayat* is made of a district, *mutasarrifiyya*, a subdistrict, *qaimmaqamiyya,* and a sub-subdistrict a *mudiriyy* or *nahiya*. This was the administrative system of the Ottoman Empire during the second half of the nineteenth century

zakat   alms, see **ushr**

zawiya   (pl. *zawayya*). lodge, mosque, hospice, and school complex of a religious Sufi order, e.g., the Sanusiyya

ABBREVIATIONS

ACS	Archivio Centrale dello Stato (Rome)
ANT	Archives Nationales de Tunisie (Tunis)
ASMAI	Archivio Storico Diplomatico del Ministero Africa Italiana, Ministero degli Affari Esteri (Rome)
DMT	Dar al-Mahfuzat al-Tarikhiyya, Libyan Archives (Tripoli)
MDJL	Markaz Dirasat jihad al-libiyin, Libyan Studies Center (Tripoli), *Oral History Archives* (Tripoli)
PRO	Public Record Office (London)
USNA	United States National Archives (Washington, DC)

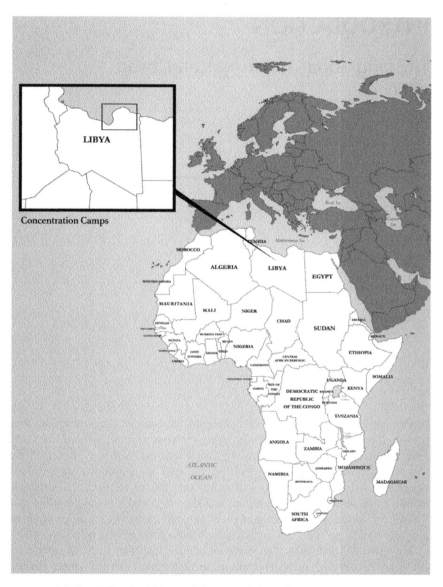

MAP 0.1 Modern Libya in Africa and the area of the Italian concentration camps

INTRODUCTION

Thinking about the forgotten Libyan genocide

Will answers be found
Like seeds
Planted among rows of songs?
Will mouths recognize
Hunger in their voices, all mouths in unison?
The ah in harmony, the way words
Of hope are more
The truth when whispered?

Khaled Mattawa, Libyan-American
poet, Tocqueville, 2010

In October 1911, Italy invaded and occupied the coast of the former Ottoman provinces on Tarabulus al-Gharb. Invoking the restoration of Roman rule, they renamed the province Libya, forming a new colony. With the advent of the fascist regime under Benito Mussolini in 1922 a new brutal policy was designed to conquer the colony and defeat the interior resistance. The people of Libya had resisted from the outset, and they mounted a major rebellion that the Italians would suppress only after 20 years of counterinsurgency culminating in genocidal policy. I am a grandson of those anti-colonial resistors.

Between 1929 and 1934, thousands of Libyans lost their lives, directly murdered and victim to Italian deportations and internments that, I argue, amount to genocide. It was the first genocide after the Armenian and Herero genocides during World War I. Libyans were forcibly removed from their homes, marched across vast tracks of deserts and mountains, and confined behind barbed wire in 16 concentration camps. This is a story that has escaped serious reckoning by the perpetrators and has been soft-pedaled at best in the West. The Italians, according to the commonly held myth, are not a people capable of genocide, certainly not when compared to their brutal German neighbors. Yet, it is a story that Libyans have recorded in their Arabic oral history and narratives, while remaining hidden and unexplored in systematic fashion, and never in the manner has that allowed us to comprehend and begin to understand the extent of their existence. That is what I set out to do in this book, through cross-cultural critical, anthropological, literary, theoretical, and comparative readings of genocide studies. Why call it genocide? I would argue that it fits the requirements defined by the father of modern genocide studies, the Polish legal scholar Raphael Lemkin, in 1948 at the UN Convention. He specifically identified two conditions. First, the intentionality of killing and, second, the policy of destroying physical, biological, and cultural patterns of life.

This book examines the hidden history of the Libyan genocide by the Italian colonial state that took place in eastern Libya between 1929 and 1934. The genocide resulted in a loss of 83,000 Libyan citizens as the population declined from 225,000 to 142,000 citizens. Some 110,000 civilians were forced to march from their homes to the harsh desert and then were interned in horrific concentration camps. Between 60,000 and 70,000 mostly rural people (including men, women, elderly, and children) and their 600,000 animals were starved and died of diseases. This mass killing and destruction of people and culture was the result of a 20-year anti-colonial resistance and represented, by all measures, genocide based on a racist colonial plan to crush local resistance and settle poor Italian peasants in the colony. The Italian state suppressed news about the genocide; evidence was destroyed, and the remaining files on the concentration camps were hard to find even after the end of fascism in Italy in 1943. After visiting Italy, in an attempt to locate files on the concentration camps, I came to the realization that it was not simply these sensitive files that were missing, but that there was a collective silence and amnesia which persisted. It is about time it is recognized that the archives are ideologically constructed and they privilege and exclude certain groups and voices and, in the case of Italian colonial fascism, they cover up atrocities and genocide.

The Italian public's refusal to recognize fascist colonial atrocities and Cold War politics compromised any attempt at war crimes trials for Italian Fascist leaders and generals. It is not surprising, then, that this case, until recently, was not even cited in books on comparative colonial and forgotten genocides. The invisibility of, and silence about, this story became a puzzle that needed to be solved. This awareness led me to pursue two strategies: to travel to eastern and southern Libya in order to find the survivors and listen to their stories about what had happened to them and their families, and to read and research the fields of modern genocide and Holocaust studies and comparative fascism to understand how we might resolve these studies. The book has evolved as a critique and a recovery of alternative examination of the politics of language, identity, and cultural history of survival and healing.

Long ago, Frantz Fanon argued against universalizing and applying Western Freudian psychoanalysis when he examined survivors of colonial trauma in Algeria and Tunisia in 1952. Instead, he advocated paying attention to local cultural and colonial specificity of trauma under colonialism. I found his critique helpful for understanding this hidden colonial history and questioning the American focus on psychoanalysis and cultural representations. Capturing the Libyan case required specialized knowledge of local culture, language, and collective non-Western views of suffering and healing. The survivors relied on their Muslim and Arab/African regional culture and values, but the colonial internment and the genocide created a new collective identity for them after 1934. My biggest challenge was in examining and understanding the ways that the survivors mediated and negotiated their early modern non-nationalist culture and values and the violence of settler colonial "modernity."

For the last two decades, I have been invited to give talks on this case at many leading American universities. The colleagues and graduate students who invited me were sympathetic and supportive of my new research. Yet, when I often asked the audience at the start of my talks whether they had heard about or knew the history of Italian colonial concentration camps in Libya, the reply was often "no." "Were there really concentration camps in Libya?" they would ask me. One has to remember that the name Libya was invented by Italian colonialism in 1911; the country, for centuries prior, was known as Tarabulus Gharb – Tripoli of the west – a province of the Ottoman Empire between 1551 and 1911.

This book challenges colonial and nationalist assumptions so as to understand the culture and the history of the people who were forced into the Mu'taqalat, or colonial concentration camps. The elites, such as the Sansui Monarchy (1951–1969) that dominated the postcolonial independent Libyan state after 1951, chose to ignore the history of the genocide and remain silent about the whole history of the resistance and internment. While Mu'ammar Qadhdhafi, leader of the military nationalist coup in 1969, used and spoke loudly about the Mu'taqalat, the reality of the archives told quite a different story. When I surveyed Libyan college knowledge of the history, I found that local academia had overlooked it as well. The exception was the research on oral history collected by the scholars of the Libyan Studies Center after 1977. Three central questions guided the initial research for this study: how the Italian state hid and covered the story of this genocide, how the recovery of the survivors of this genocide can break the silence, and, finally, what both collective amnesia and living history can tell us about Libya and Italy and inform us about the larger meaning of the post-genocide world today.

This book is the product of a long personal and academic journey of discovery that began nearly 20 years ago. However, making sense of the material and overcoming the obstacles required deep reflections and assessment of my early childhood and education in central and southern Libya, my college education in Egypt, and my graduate schooling in the United States. I had no idea what I was going to discover – this book evolved as a journey and a challenge to make sense of the discovery. In short, when I could not find the main files on the case in Rome and only some in Tripoli, I turned to oral history in eastern and central Libya.

I began to realize that this hidden history is not just about a sad colonial brutality, but it is about Libya, Italy, and, above all, the discovery of a dynamic creative oral culture. The discovery of living survivors' narratives and culture became my most significant contribution. Prior to this investigation, I had decided to critically examine my own nationalist public school education in independent Libya. This self-reexamination allowed me to discover and understand the regional culture of the people who were interned, and how they interpreted their experiences and reactions during and after the years of internment. It allowed me to investigate the silences and representations of colonial and nationalist historiographies, and to locate this hidden case within a larger comparative and transnational perspective, especially the merging links between colonial genocide and Holocaust scholarship. Above all, I had an opportunity to meet and listen to hundreds of ordinary Libyans and learn about their passions, views of colonial history, and humanity.

Libyan interior country culture is known for its love of poetry and oral traditions; storytelling and poetic recitation and memorization permeate everyday modes of communication. It is a different form of knowledge and learning, especially for the majority of the people interned in the concentration camps. Many of these people were illiterate; only a handful of the interned Libyans were educated. Consequently, the most significant and vivid records of the history of the genocide were poems and oral narrative crafted inside the camps. Orality and poetry are cultured modes of resisting colonialism and keep the memory of the concentration camps alive, and I relied on these sources to understand the views of the victims of the concentration camps and to comprehend the mass deaths in five of the 16 camps.

I grew up in an extended family with multigenerations living together. Orality, proverbs, and poetry were common means of communication. When I learned how to read and understand the local culture of my own mother and grandmother, as well as that of the interned people, I realized that they relied on their faith, poetry, and values to support each other, resist, and assert their own worldview in the face of genocide and death. They reacted to the ordeal of deportation and internment through reliance on the social and cultural Sanusi Muslim education and organization – in other words they were resisting members of the Sanusi social movement. My task then is to explain both the Sanusi movement and the anti-colonial resistance to make sense of and understand how the people reacted to internment in the concentration camps.

Part of the success of the anti-colonial resistance has to be attributed to the role of the leaders of the Sanusi Islamic social movement who made the choice to unify the people of Ottoman Tripoli, especially in the region of Barqa and Fezzen, by educational policies, institutions, and organized trans-Saharan trade during the second half of the nineteenth century. The investment in these choices and institutional and social capital unified the diverse ethnic, tribal, and peasant population of the province. Perhaps this unity is an even bigger achievement than the heroic, long resistance to the modern armies of Italian colonialism. I argue that this living culture and living history from below is the most significant discovery of the whole book. I seek to examine this culture not as premodern, traditional, or anti-modern, but as a starting point with a human and profound agency of its own. While it was not my original intention to bring my family and early childhood background into my research, I discovered its relevance and found that it could help me overcome the riddle of silence and allow me to understand the hidden culture of remembrance.

The first time I heard about the Italian colonial concentration camps was as a young child in southern Libya. I grew up in an extended family; my paternal grandmother lived with us, as was the way of life in rural Libya in the middle of the twentieth century. As a young child I would often hear my late mother and paternal grandmother recite the start of the poem "Mabi-Marad ghair dar-al-Agaila" ("I Am Not Ill except Agaila"). My mother in particular cited the poem whenever she was down or depressed. I was not sure what to make of the poem, but from an early age I realized that Agaila was a significant event. This poem, I later realized, became the most recited and memorized verse across the eastern and southern regions of Libya. It tells the horrors of the Agaila concentration camp, my mother explained, where thousands of Libyans suffered and died. When I was in sixth grade at Sabha Central Elementary School, my classmates and I read an assigned long poem by Libyan modern nationalist poet Ahmad Rafiq al-Mahdawi, "Little Ghaith." It tells the story of a young orphan child at the concentration camp called Slug. The teacher told us about the Italian concentration camps. We recited the poem and were excited to make it into a play. I connected this poem/play to the stories told by my mother and grandfather about the family struggle, exile, and longing to return to Libya. Still to this day, I remember the story, which made me sad and, like my family, caused me to dislike colonialism. The hinterland culture values honor, dignity, family, and autonomy: that is the refusal to be governed by the central state.

Those were my first encounters with the history of the Italian concentration camps. Both my mother and grandmother did not have the chance to go to school. My mother was born in exile because of her family's direct involvement in the anti-colonial resistance. Both of my grandfathers, Ali Muhammad al-Sanusi and Ahmida Abdullatif, fought in the resistance until 1930. They both refused to submit to the colonial state and so made two different choices: one went into exile in Chad, and the other took refuge among the Magharba and Warfalla people, who hid him inside central Libya for ten years. Upon his return, my paternal grandfather Ahmida taught the Qur'an to their children. The family in Waddan assumed he had died until he reappeared in 1943. I learned more background through my mother and paternal grandmother, who told me, along with my sisters, an oral history of the resistance, famine, and colonial atrocities. My maternal grandmother, Aisha Bumriz, died in exile in Chad when my mother was only five years old. It wasn't until five years ago that I learned that some of my grandmother's relatives were put in concentration camps. My paternal grandmother who lived with us told me that she had three brothers – two older and one younger than her. Her parents decided to let one son join the resistance, and the other one had to stay to take care of the women and the children. The one who joined the resistance fought until they were defeated in 1930 and left the country for exile in Chad, married there, and did not return until the end of the Italian colonialism in 1943.

There were no books or radio in central Libya until 1960. Oral storytelling was both entertainment and a way for my mother to educate me and my two sisters. My mother and paternal grandmother shared vivid stories with us, which paralleled my modern early school education in Waddan and Sabha. It was an oral culture in which people had a keen and fertile memory. When asked, both my mother and grandmother would recite a proverb or poem and tell the story of places and battles, exile, and the names of people who died during the colonial period. For my extended family, the Sahara was an open frontier and for generations they moved between Fezzen, Chad, and Niger. Countries are referred to as *barr*, or land, and *bilad*, or country). Until her death, my mother referred to Saudi Arabia as *barr al-haramin* (the land of the two holy places), and Chad as *Bilad al-Sudan* (the country of the blacks). The point here is that borders and the nation-state are recent constructions and other older fluid identities existed for a long time. After the Italian defeat in World War II in 1948, my mother returned with her father to Waddan – her culture, Arabic dialect, and her form of cooking now combined both Libyan and Chadian influences.

This social and cultural family background was like that of the survivors that I interviewed for this book. I was raised in the same culture and listened to the same oral anti-colonial histories of resistance suffering and exile. As a child, I memorized the names of the battles and the mujahidin, because my grandfather Ali told me many times about them. I was accepted by the survivors and we related to each other with ease and intimacy. Furthermore, these family experiences and values became essential for my research on the history of the Libyan genocide and reminded me that the nation-state is a recent construction, and that people for a long time had other cultural identities that were based on Ottoman, African, and Arab-Islamic interconnected cultures.

My education in Cairo, Egypt, and Seattle, USA, allowed me to learn about the larger world, but did not help me to understand the roots, the culture, and the history of the genocide of eastern Libya. Most of the social science courses I took in the 1980s focused on development and modernization theories of third world countries, including the country in which I was born and raised. The exception was Latin American Dependency Theory, which challenged the assumption of modernization theory and the idea of progress. Yet, even Dependency Theory overlooked agency, culture, and diverse social history. I began to pay more critical attention to the counter oral history of ordinary people, like my family. The research on the history of the Italian genocide became a journey of discovery and road-mapping, which took almost a decade. Through this journey, I realized that there are two intertwined histories: one of silence, and one that intentionally obscured truth.

The book, however, is not motivated by a quest for new archival empirical facts, nor is it confined to the modern area study boundaries of European, Middle Eastern, and sub-Saharan. The archives are based and organized on a racist utility and ideology, and to justify the colonial project. Modern area studies are problematic. As Mahmood Mamdani argued,

> The single most important failing of the area studies is that it has failed to frame the study of the "third world" in broad intellectual terms. If the "area" in the area studies was perceived through the narrow colonial and Cold War lenses, then the end of apartheid regionally and Cold War globally offers us an opportunity to liberate Africa from the shackles of area studies.[1]

According to the field of area studies, Italy would be a separate case within European studies. Libya is included in Middle Eastern North Africa and has no connection with African studies because the Sahara is assumed to be a divide and a barrier. This is a colonial myth that was uncritically accepted by even African and Middle Eastern elites. Instead of the misleading and confining epistemological boundaries of area studies, I propose four alternative assumptions.

First, I examine the history of genocide in both Libya and Italy as interrelated and interconnected. Above all, I approach this history from the point of view of the victims, the Arab-Muslim people of eastern Libya, and the larger African perspective. Second, I argue against the assumptions and the boundaries of modern Western social science studies – such as European, Middle Eastern, sub-Saharan, and North African studies – in addition to modern genocidal studies, which focus on the Holocaust as a unique European case. Third, I assume the equal agency of Muslim North African people who have living history and are capable of voicing their own views of the genocide from 1929–1934.

Finally, I realized I could not investigate this complex topic from a single disciplinary perspective, and instead needed to apply a critical multidisciplinary method, which represents the fourth assumption. The quest in researching and writing this book was challenging and difficult, especially with the task of learning hinterland oral language, poetry, cultural studies, and modes of communication. I started with a central question of how to think about genocide in the Italian Fascist Empire from 1922–1943. Specifically, I wanted to understand the history of genocide in Libya, Italy, and outside of Italy. Who were the ones behind the racial genocidal policy, who contributed to the acts, and who was responsible for the silence that followed? Why has Italian Fascism been viewed as a moderate or lesser evil than Nazi Germany?

This book is the outcome of an investigation of the history of the present not only in eastern Libya, but also in Italian society. Both are linked. Italian society, despite the end of the fascist regime in 1943, is a post-genocide society. The research was inspired by insights from multidisciplinary fields such as historical sociology and anthropology, genocide, and postcolonial studies. I aspire to bridge the gap between the two emerging fields of oral history and memory studies. Oral history is not just a technique of colleting knowledge, but an examination of the content and values of the orality itself. I approach memory as a fluid process mediated and contested regionally, nationally, and transnationally.

In 1922, the Italian Fascist state inherited from the "Liberal" government two colonies in East Africa and Libya. The fascist elite felt justified to inherit them in the name of Roman history and its empire. Italian Fascist counterinsurgency ideology was clearly racist and viewed native resistance as a threat to its plan to settle millions of poor Italians into the Libyan colony. It viewed Arab Muslims as subhuman, primitive, unruly, and anti-modern nomads. Italian colonial policies pursued three military strategies with a clear plan to exterminate native people. First, they pursued a brutal strategy to crush the well-organized anti-colonial resistance through the use of tanks, airplanes, and modern firearms. The second military strategy targeted the civilian population that supported the anti-colonial resistance by providing volunteers, food, and information to the fighting groups. This strategy was followed by a plan of deportation and internment of the whole population in concentration camps to isolate the resistance, even if it meant annihilation. The deportation of the civilian population took three months and led to their internment in 16 collective concentration camps. Five of them became death camps where thousands died from starvation and diseases. The third and final strategy was to cover up the crime from world media, make propaganda about modernization, and hide the files on mass deaths. The exception to this policy of covering up was the Italians' communication with German Nazi officials who were interested in the Italian model of colonial "success" and settlement after 1938.

The German Nazi state was an ally which, I discovered, looked at the Italian Fascist genocidal policies in Libya as a model for success. The cover-up continued after the collapse of the fascist regime in 1943. The Allies needed the help of fascist politicians and officers during the Cold War tension to fight communism in Europe. I discovered that fascist officers and officials continued to administer the Italian Archives. The archives on the concentration camps were manipulated, highly monitored, and many records either disappeared or were lost. When I began my research in Italy in the late 1980s, I learned that there was a pattern of hiding or destroying the incriminating files. The Italian officials provided misleading information about the records of the concentration camps, an obvious cover-up and silence about what happened. Consequently, I shifted my focus to oral history. However, locating the survivors and gaining their trust were not as easy as I'd assumed, and it took ten years of research. I analyze the methodological challenge and fieldwork politics in Chapter 1.

This book is based on their views of their history, the victims of the genocide. This rich oral history is diverse, complex, creative, and still cognizant of what happened in the camps. I argue for a shift in the genocidal research paradigm, which is still Eurocentric, colonial, and remains silent about a people without history in Anglo-American scholarship. Meanwhile Italian Fascism continues to be viewed as moderate in mainstream scholarship, media, and film. I hope to challenge this myth as well; Italian Fascism resulted in a brutal genocide in Libya, which became a model pursued in Ethiopia, the Balkans, Greece, and Albania. In fact, the use of gas to exterminate people was first applied in Libya in 1929 and then in Ethiopia in 1935. For example, General Graziani was in charge of the invasion in Ethiopia and ordered his troops to kill thousands of Ethiopian civilians. My biggest discovery to challenge the image of Italian Fascism as somehow benign came late in my research, and was the Nazi connection with Italian Fascist colonialism in Libya.

Three years ago, I was reading an Italian colonial-sponsored Arabic language magazine published in Benghazi called *Libya al-Musawara* (*Illustrated Libya*). In it was an article on the Nazi leader, Marshal Hermann Göring, and his official visit to Tripoli in April 1939.[2] He met with the Italian colonial governor Italo Balbo, the man who came after Marshall Pietro Badoglio. Badoglio was the architect behind the original plan to put people in concentration camps with extermination in mind. Göring was no marginal figure in the Nazi state. Rather, he was an old associate of Hitler and became a significant figure in the Nazi Party. Göring was close to Hitler and was appointed by him as head of the air force as well as other positions. I asked myself whether this was just an official public relations visit between two fascist states, or was there more to it than that. Also, what were the motives behind the visit? I realized that Marshal Göring visited Tripoli and joined in the public colonial occasion of the arrival of 20,000 Italian settlers who were given land that had been taken from the Libyans for future colonial settlement. In fact, this was not an isolated visit; instead, German Nazi officials looked at the Italian "success" in removing the native population and emptying eastern Libya as a model for their future plan in Europe. The Nazi state sent delegates to Rome and Tripoli, invited Italian Fascist officials to Germany, published books, and organized seminars on the Italian success in Libya and, later, in Ethiopia. This shouldn't be surprising, as the brutality of the Italian policy was clear through the crushing of the resistance, concentration camps, and the high death toll, all of which were very influential on Nazi Germany.[3]

Even Heinrich Himmler, the head of the SS, visited Libya in 1939. He was the organizer of the concentration camps and conceived the idea of the Final Solution: the Holocaust. It is not a coincidence that the two architects of genocide in Libya and Europe met and exchanged ideas about removing the "enemy" to pave the land for Italian and German settlers.[4] This new evidence provides a clear connection between colonial genocide and the Holocaust. Consequently, the Holocaust should be understood from a newly revised view as an application of the brutal Italian model of genocide, which included Libya. Before Auschwitz, there was Agaila, Slug, Braiga, and Magrun. I contend that a shift in genocide studies is essential and necessary. This connection proves not only the hidden genocidal nature of Italian Fascism, but its impact on the regimes that emerged later in Europe. My contention is that the entire constructed theory of genocide in Europe is myopic and false. The Italian Fascist regime is indistinguishable from that of the Nazis – both Italian and German genocidal histories are linked. The fact that there is no "Jewish question in Italy," and that many Italian Jews were members of the Italian Fascist party and regime before 1938, misled many scholars to conclude it as a lesser evil, and even moderate or "ordinary dictatorship." In some fundamental aspects, I seek to shift the paradigm of thinking about the African and European genocides by challenging both colonial and area studies.

This book is about both a critique of colonial ideology and the language used for covering up atrocities. It is an analysis of the process and institutions behind ideology and language, and the native subaltern oral history of the survivors. Four scholars provide insights on how to read this hidden history: Hannah Arendt, Mike Davis, Mahmood Mamdani, and James Scott. Here, I give homage to Hannah Arendt who, very early in 1950, made a connection between colonial genocide and the genocides that took place in Europe. She argued that it was during the age of imperialism between 1884 and 1914, described as the scramble for Africa, that: "Some fundamental aspects of this time appear so close to the totalitarian phenomena of the twentieth century that it may be justifiable to consider the whole period a preparatory stage for coming catastrophes."[5] In other words, she views the Holocaust as a colonial genocide. She does not state detailed evidence for this argument, except for the genocide in the Congo. Yet, her brilliant observation was overlooked for a long time and only recently was it revived. Was that because of the Cold War's ideological impact on mainstream scholarship? She had two blind spots: she erred in the case of fascist Italy, and she was silent on perhaps the first genocide in modern history, that of Native American Indians between the sixteenth and the nineteenth centuries. It is a huge oversight. I shall be engaging her thesis in depth throughout the following chapters of my book. This book elaborates on Arendt's insights and presents evidence and analysis. Like her, I argue for a transnational way of viewing modern genocide, inside and outside of Europe.

In addition to Arendt, I find equally useful the book *Late Victorian Holocausts* by American labor and environmental historian Mike Davis. He addresses history writing by critiquing imperial history and presents an alternative reading of genocide at the end of the nineteenth century. Davis argues that colonial famines in the late nineteenth century were not a matter of natural disaster, but the result of colonial policy. He states that colonial European policies and Japanese economic policies destroyed local systems of agriculture and contributed to death from famine for between 31 and 60 million people in India, China, and Brazil between 1870 and 1902. He targets, for example, British colonial policies of export and prices that caused famine and starvation. He called this colonial economic policy the secret history of famine under the dominant silence and narrative of traditions and lack of modernization in non-Western societies. Davis challenges historians to recognize genocide as an integral part of modern world history and face the silence about it today, which exacts a heavy price in the historiography.[6] This book is not just a critique but also an argument for the diversity of survival and other histories that are not part of the narrative of modernization or the nation-state; it is a discovery of a living dynamic and the ordinary people of the living culture that is modern but values its autonomy and transnational Islamic outlook. This is why one has to be clear about the name Libya and the modern nation-state.

Mahmood Mamdani is the leading scholar on genocide in Africa. His postcolonial methods have linked the past to the present through studying the impact of power, knowledge, and constructed colonial identities. He traced the historical roots of African identity and institutions constructed in the colonial period. Furthermore, he analyzed the specter of violence and genocide in two original books on modern genocide rooted in colonial instutions in Rwanda and Darfur which continued after independence.

I find James Scott's critical and multidisciplinary formulation of power, language, and the intersection of domination and resistance insightful. He distinguished between public and hidden transcripts, recognition of public interaction, and behind-the-scenes expression by the dominated people.[7]

My method is transnational, comparative, and multidisciplinary to the use of language, context, and the struggle over history-making, orality, and writing. For example, silence has a different meaning in everyday life, domination, and resistance. Marnia Lazreg argued that women's silence was a form of resistance against the French in colonial Algeria, while I examine silence as a tool for the dominant state, as well as a form of resistance.[8]

My hope is that this book will be read not just as a critique of Eurocentric and colonial theories of knowledge and history. The hegemony of colonial Eurocentrism normalizes the European experience and reduces the rest of world cultures to either following or deviating from this unique racialized model of modernity. Rather, the book is a critical and self-reflective conceptualization and discovery of a new narrative of a living culture and society based on non-nation-state views and institutions. The meaning of concepts such as Shar, the subtitle of the book, is a case in point in the time of internment. Its roots are moral and religious, but language is not static and is changing, and so Shar took new meaning in the concentration camps.

The word *Shar* means evil in the Qur'an and in Arabic culture. Evil is a religious, traditional moral concept in the Old and New Testaments and in the Qur'an. Here, it signifies a malaise of the heart, while modern views such as Arendt's understand it as a historical evil created by imperialism and the totalitarian, modern nation-state. Sartre argues modern evil is based on intentionality, bad faith. The subtitle of this book is derived from the oral history of the survivors who viewed the whole genocide as evil. To them, Shar meant death, depression, and starvation. Italian colonialism for them was Shar. In short, language is an arena contested by the dominant state actors to cover up atrocities, and contested by hidden and oral histories as a weapon of the weak by the dominated people. One cannot be studied without the other; we need both to capture the history of the present. What Scott overlooked is the content and the meaning of the dominated people, in this case the culture and values of the interned people of Barqa, the eastern region of the Tarabulus al-Gharb, the last province of the Ottoman Empire in Africa.

The use of the name "Libya" is a recent construction. It was used during earlier Pharaonic times – the people were referred to as the "Libyan tribes" who were making incursions into one of the kingdoms – and during the Greek and Roman periods, and was revived by the Italian colonialists in 1911. The first modern use of the name Libya appeared in 1903, and the official name was given to the colony in 1934 after the defeat of the anti-colonial resistance in 1932. This revival of the name was an integral part of the imperial policy to justify colonization by linking it to the Roman empirical rule of the Mediterranean Sea. The name Libya has a special and ideological justification for colonial conquest. Libya is also called *Quarta Sponda*, the fourth "Shore of Italy" and Libya was called the fourth sea of Italy when it was under the ancient Roman Empire, and the name now claims it is coming back to modern Rome, a fascist empire.[9,10]

Prior to 1911, between 1551 and until the Italian conquest, the country was a province of the Muslim early modern Ottoman Empire and the Ottomans designated the name Tarabulus al-Gharb (Tripoli of the West, in contrast with Tripoli of the Levant in Lebanon). The western part of the province is known as Tripolitania and the south Fezzen, but the region of Barqa is known in European languages as Cyrenaica, a Greek and Roman name. I shall use the Arabic name used since the eleventh century: Barqa. Ottoman rule of the province was limited to western cities and towns, and the population viewed itself as an essential component of the larger Islamic Maghrib, a region that connected Muslim inhabitants from Morocco to western Egypt economically, socially, and culturally up until the end of the nineteenth century.

The use of "Libya" and "Libyans" must be understood as referring to Tarabulus al-Gharb and the Mutasarifiyya of Benghazi. It shouldn't suggest, as many Libyan nationalists do, that a nation-state existed prior to the colonial period. This is not just the case with Libya. The nation-state is a recent invention, not only in the way of ex-colonies, but even in Europe itself. Like other Maghribian countries like Tunisia, Algeria, Morocco, and even Egypt, the nation-state was created in the colonial period due to outside meddling and the local reaction to its impact. This should not be viewed as a negation of political atrocities or weaken other concepts of political order and cultural identity, nor of Ottoman social history dynamics and institutions. The eighteenth and nineteenth century history of Tripoli under the Ottomans had its own dynamics and innovation. Ottoman and regional history experienced local attempts to organize such as the state of the Muhammad in Fezzen from 1551–1813, and the innovative and dynamic Sanusi movement between 1858 and 1932. These Ottoman and local institutions and organizations provide a context for understanding the manner and choices made by people in reaction to the coming of colonialism in 1911 and the genocidal fascist regime in 1922.

The native reactions to Italian colonialism varied due to social and regional economies and integration. In Triploitania the resistance was defeated in 1922, while in southern and eastern Libya it continued to 1931. Equally significant is the Italian state control over the population in the main coastal urban cities, which continued from 1912 and until 1943, while the interior rural country resisted and governed itself through local institutions and organization and Sanusi Islam. It should not be surprising that the Italian influence was strong in the coastal and urban areas especially the western region and the city of Tripoli, and many colonial soldiers and native officials who served in the camps came from the west. Most of the leaders of the resistance and the leaders of the Tripolitanian Republic (1918–1920) left the country and chose to live in exile in Arab and African countries such as Syria, Tunisia, Egypt, Palestine, Jordan, Oman, Niger, Nigeria, and Chad. In the eastern region of Barqa, the resistance was organized through the Sanusi movement. The rural population, which was forced into concentration camps, were members of the order and most of the leaders of the resistance were educated in Sanusi lodges and schools. In other words, the Sanusiyya, the resistance, and the internment of the population of eastern Libya are interconnected. Consequently, understanding the social organization of the Sanusiyyia is essential for the historical context of the Italian internment of the local population as a collective punishment of the resistance and as a prelude to bringing Italian settlers to the fertile agricultural land of northeastern Libya, the region of al-Jabal al-Akhdar, Green Mountain.

The organization of the book

The book is organized through multidisciplinary reading of the representations, narratives, and primary sources. Each chapter builds on the previous ones, and, as a whole, the book cross-examines the archival, oral, literary, and theoretical sources and debates inside Libya, Africa, and Europe.

Chapter 1 presents a critique and mapping of the politics of the colonial and Arabic language sources and archives. In addition, the chapter highlights the reflexive and ethical challenges that the author has encountered in finding and interacting with survivors and their families in eastern Libya. It narrates the process of pursing the survivors and their oral testimonies and history, and eventually confronts the question of power and ethics of fieldwork during his visits to the locations of five concentration camps.

Chapter 2 presents a critical review of the historiography of Italian Fascism, the question of genocide and silence, and the alternative scholarship in Anglo-American scholarship. It ends by introducing orality and poetry as a mode of cultural communication. In addition, it examines the remarkable epic poem that kept the memory of the genocide alive since the internment in 1929 and up until now.

Chapter 3 focuses on testimonies, oral narrative, and poetry of the survivors during their internment. It sheds new light on the forced deportation, the march, how people died in the camps, and to what extent age, gender, and class shaped their experiences and chances for survival. This new material recovers a complex social history of a living culture that has survived the state and elite control in eastern Libya during and after the end of colonialism.

Chapter 4 traces the aftermath and the process that took place after the end of the internment in 1934: what happened to the survivors, the history of the genocide after Libyan independence in 1951, and an analysis of university students' views of the genocide. The chapter also explains the process that produced the official and hidden history of the genocide in Italy, the UK, and the USA by examining the cases of the BBC film *Fascist Legacy* in 1998, and the media coverage by *The New York Times* and the *National Geographic* magazine.

Chapter 5 traces the politics of independence and the origins of the modern Libyan state from the monarchy in 1951, to the republic in 1969, the dictatorship from 1977 to 2011, and the uprising that followed and eventually collapsed the state. It advocates a new reading of the postcolonial Libyan state and its history after 1951, and the current crisis in Libya after the end of the Qadhdhafi Jamahiriyya in 2011.

The conclusion returns to the original critical questions of the book stated in the Introduction, focusing on a critique of Eurocentrism, the myth of moderate Italian Fascism and colonialism, and challenges the work of three main theorists of modern genocide: Foucault, Agamben, and Arendt. It ends with a new argument debunking the Holocaust as a unique European experience. Instead, the Holocaust is rooted and modeled in colonial genocides in Africa, especially the Libyan case. The Libyan genocide took place only ten years earlier, and this study brings in new evidence of direct Nazi interest in the fascist Italian genocide in Libya.

Notes

1 Mahmood Mamdani, *When Victims Become Killers*, (Princeton: Princeton University Press, 2011), XIII–XV. Also, his "The Politics of Naming: Genocide, Civil War, Insurgency," *London Review of Books*, 29:5 (March 8, 2007) 5–8.

2 "Marshal Goerhing in Tripoli," *Libia al-Musawra* [*Illustrated Libya*], 10 (Benghazi 1939) 19. There is also a YouTube video of the visit that took place in April and May 1939.

3 On German Nazi visits to Italian Libya see Patrick Bernhard, "Borrowing from Mussolini: Nazi Germany's Colonial Aspirations in the Shadow of Italian Expansionism," *Journal of Imperial and Commonwealth History*, 41:4 (2013), 617–643.

4 Patrick Bernhard, "Hitler's Africa in the East: Italian Colonialism as a Model for German Planning in Eastern Europe," *Journal of Contemporary History*, 51:1 (2016), 62–63.

5 Hannah Arendt, *The Origins of Totalitarianism*, (New York: Harcourt, Brace and Jovanovich, 1973), 123, 185, 206, 221. On the Native American genocide in North America see David Stannard, *American Holocaust*, (Oxford: Oxford University Press, 1992) and Tzvetan Todorov, *The Conquest of America, The Question of the Other*, (New York: Harper & Row, 1984), and Pekka Hamalainen, "The Future of Native American History in The United States" http://historians.org/perspectives/issues/2012.

6 Mike Davis, *Late Victorian Holocausts*, (New York: Verso, 2002), 7–8, 50, 139.

7 James Scott, *Domination and the Arts of Resistance*, (New Haven: Yale University Press, 1990), X–XI. Also Russell Jacoby, *Social Amnesia*, (Boston: Transaction Books, 1997) 1–18.

8 Marina Lazreg, *The Eloquence of Silence*, (New York: Routledge Press, 1994), 17–18, and Abdealmajid Hannoum, *Violent Modernity* (Cambridge: Harvard University Press, 2010).

9 On the Concept of "Bad Faith" see chapter 5 "What is Bad Faith" John Carney, *Rethinking Sartre*, (Latham: University Press of America, 2007), 53. And Sheldon Wolin, "Injustice and Collective Memory" in Sheldon Wolin, ed., *Presence of the Past*, (Baltimore: John Hopkins University Press, 1989) 32–46.

10 Marla Stone "A Flexible Rome: Fascism and the Cult of Romanita" in Catherine Edwards ed., *Roman Presences*, (Cambridge: Cambridge University Press, 1999) 205–220. Annie Esme Lewine, "Ancient Rome in Modern Italy: Mussolini's Manipulation of Roman History in the Mostra Augustea della Romanita," *Studies in Mediterranean Antiquity and Classics*, 2:1 (2008) 1–10.

1

WHERE ARE THE SURVIVORS?

The politics of missing archives and fieldwork

Thus, the files which have finally been made available to independent researchers in recent years have been skimmed of documents considered to be of major importance. Despite this gap the official Italian state version of history manufactured the publication of the volumes in the collection entitled L'Italia in Africa.

> *Italian historian Giorgio Rochat on the silence of Italian Archives on the concentration camps in Libya, in Santarelli et al., eds.* Omar al-Mukhtar *translated by John Gilbert (London: Darf Publishers, 1986) 39, 40*

Despairing, entrenched days and nights
Forced me to dream of sleep and its solace
Telling others about it would be gossip
Yet they make me cry
My mood swings back and forth
They leave impossible, tangled knots
Only God may open these doors of Salvation
Only God can overcome them

> *Poet Muhammad Zaidan al-Sharif, 1935*

We keep talking about what happened to us in the camps to stay alive; the stories keep us alive.

> *Haj Yusuf Said al-Bal'azi al-'Aquri, a survivor, Agaila concentration camp*

On September 11, 1931, the Italian army brought the captured 'Umar al-Mukhtar, the leader of the anti-colonial resistance, to the concentration camp of Slug, and forced over 20,000 interned people including the old, children, men, and women to attend the hanging of their old, beloved leader. After this public hanging spectacle, the soldiers took the corpse and buried him in a secret grave. The stories of the resistance and the interment of the rural people of eastern Libya are interconnected. Two factors are crucial to understand the making of the Italian genocide: the well-organized and mobilized anti-resistance, and the censorship, the manipulation of the evidence, and the propaganda to cover what happened during and after the internment. The struggle to overcome dead ends and to piece together the story of what happened was long, complex, and frustrating as data was hidden, and most survivors are dying and the evidence is on the verge of disappearing. The complex research journey and the hard task of piecing together the story of what happened became as significant as the history of the genocide. It reveals the impact of the power of knowledge and it helps to explain why this case disappeared from Western scholarship for a long time.

I argue that the internment of the civilian population of Barqa was linked to the resilience of the anti-colonial resistance, and the racist fascist ideology. The anti-colonial resistance was deeply rooted in local society and culture and an in innovative social movement, called the Sanusiyya, which unified and integrated society 50 years earlier during the second half of the nineteenth century, prior to the Italian invasion in 1911. Consequently, the settler colonialism, resistance, native culture and institutions, and the concentration camps as genocidal reaction are all interlinked and essential for interrogating the history of colonial policy and the native social and cultural reactions. The main sources for the study were the colonial archives, the survivors' oral history, and the poetry composed to record the facts and the emotional and human expressions of this tragic phase.

This chapter will map out four interrelated sources and topics of the book: the historical and social bases of the anti-colonial resistance of eastern Libya; a critical analysis of the public and private archives in various locations and countries; oral history and interviews; and, finally, my multiple fieldwork visits to the five concentration camps. Prior to this stage, I had a long period of searching for the files and the primary material on this period. I still remember my initial visit to the Italian Archives, decades ago in 1986.

In the fall of 1986, I traveled to Italy to investigate the National Archives at the Italian Foreign Ministry in Rome. I arrived with a strong recommendation from a respected Italian sociologist, Franco Ferrarotti, and friend of one of my professors, Dan Chirot, at the University of Washington. After spending one week at the National Achives, I was told by an apologetic employee that I could not continue my research. I asked her why, and she informed me that it was because I was of Libyan origin, and, as her boss claimed, because Libyan officials bar Italian scholars from doing research in Libya, no Libyan scholars are therefore allowed to conduct research in Italian Archives. This was after I had asked to check the files on the concentration camps. I tried to keep an open mind about this encounter in Rome. I traveled to Tripoli, Libya the next year and I asked Dr. Mohamed Jerary, the director of the Libyan Studies Center Jihad, about the Italian official's claims. He informed me the claim was false and introduced me to two Italian scholars who had full access to the

Center's primary sources. Later on, I faced other challenges when I tried to find the survivors and gain their trust and approval to talk to me.

In the early summer of 2000, I shared a proposal on my research project on the Italian Fascist concentration camps in Libya with my friend, the Ottoman historian Rifa'at Abou-El-Haj. My project was aimed at shedding light on the atrocities that occurred in Libya under the Italian Fascist regime by focusing on the survivors' testimonies and the lives it has affected since then. My seasoned senior friend proposed that I focused on the narratives of the survivors, their reactions, and culture. He added that this undertaking would take about ten years, and I am afraid he was right. Indeed, I have faced dead ends, limited access to Italian Archives, missing files, and, later on, a cover-up of the evidence. Also, I realized in researching this topic that it requires not only collaborative work and multidisciplinary knowledge in political science, but also within social history, theory, and comparative cross-cultural methods. Inevitably, the reader needs to understand the historical context of the genocide and the tough journey of discovery of finding out why there were dead ends and the hidden evidence kept in oral and poetic sources by the survivors and their families. The challenges were both empirical and ethical: how to find the archival evidence and how to read it, and, as insider/outsider native anthropologist and social historian, how to gain the trust of the survivors and reflect about power and social science and the purpose of scholarship.

The challenges I encountered included research that was in three languages and was fragmented. Additionally, some of the documents pertaining to the genocide have been either destroyed or removed. Furthermore, conducting fieldwork and oral interviews required trust, contacts, and the willingness of the survivors and their families to recount their stories. Such epistemological and historical research required time, patience, and rethinking of archival, anthropological, and oral history methods of conducting fieldwork and interviews. I realized that the modern Libyan elite after independence in 1951, the monarchy, and the nationalist military coup in 1969 did not preserve the sites of the concentration camps or repair them, and most of the survivors of the interment are dying from old age and health-related issues. My multidisciplinary background in comparative analysis, social history, and anthropology enabled me to deconstruct the complexity of the Libyan genocide and the politics of memory in Libya, Italy, and contemporary scholarship after World War II. Prior to narrating and navigating these historical and methodological challenges, a mapping of the historical roots of anti-colonial resistance in eastern Libya will introduce the context which led to the fascist interment and genocide of the whole civilian population of the eastern region, Barqa. The region went through social, educational, and economic transformation under a reformist socioreligious movement called the Sanusiyya during the second half of the nineteenth century. This indigenous social movement integrated the population and created powerful institutions that enabled people to fight European imperialism, specifically, the Italian occupation from 1911 to 1932. The region of Barqa was a Sanusi stronghold that refused to be governed by either Ottoman or Italian states. To understand the reactions of the interned civilian population one has to study both the Sanusiyya and the social bases of the anti-colonial resistance.

Historical context to the internment: anti-colonial resistance in eastern Libya 1911–1932

The Sanusiyya emerged as the most influential anti-colonial socioreligious movement rooted in Islamic traditions and institutions in eastern and southern Libya, and which then expanded to the central Sahara and western Egypt during the second half of the nineteenth century. It became one of many resistance movements that appeared in the Middle East and East, West, and North Africa during the eighteenth and nineteenth centuries. The other notable movements were the Mahdiyya in Sudan and the Maji Maji in Tanjanika (today Tanzania), among others. It was based in the Islamic and regional culture of Barqa, and the revivalist traditions of the Maghrib and the Sahara, and above all in the historical context of the late eighteenth and nineteenth centuries.

The rise of these revival and resistance movements came as a reaction to the decline of Oriental trade, as was the case of the Wahhabi movement in Arabia in the eighteenth century, while the Mahdiyya and the Sanusiyya emerged as a reaction to the weakening of the Muslim states (Ottoman and Egyptian) to counter the colonialist British in the Sudan and the French in North Africa. Just as Sufi movements had led the anti-Iberian attacks on Morocco in the sixteenth century, new Sufi reformist movements, such as the Sanusiyya, Mahdiyyia, and the Maji Maji resistance against German colonialism, took the initiative to organize local resistance against European imperialism in the late nineteenth century. This should not be surprising as people expressed themselves through their own culture, living North African and Saharan Islamic values and institutions linked to socioeconomic conditions. The Sanusi movement was a remarkable reformist movement based on new interpretations and new organizational choices which took root in the second half of the nineteenth century. These innovations, such as focusing on education and trade, were choices that allowed the movement to integrate several groups and communities in a new society that was Islamic but also rooted in local traditions. The Sanusi movement also provided new answers for the challenges of trade, disputes, and how to face the calamity of European imperialism.

The Sanusiyya movement was named after its founder, an urban Sharifian scholar from Algeria by the name of Muhammad b. Ali al-Sanusi (1787–1859), better known as "the Grand Sanusi." He was a scholar who had studied in Algeria, Morocco, Egypt, and in al-Hijaz in Arabia. His order, the Sanusiyya, stressed austerity, moral commitment, self-reliance, and anti-colonial resistance. The main goal of the Sanusi was to build a coherent, unified community through education, work, and self-reliance, based on local institutions and resources. The order was built on an Islamic model of state taxation, law, education, and mobilization for *jihad* – or the defense of the faith. The Sanusiyya relied on the North African Sufi institution of *zawiya*, or lodge, which began to emerge in the fourteenth century, as Sufi orders assumed the leadership of the resistance against the Iberian crusade in Spain and North Africa. The *zawiya* was a place for worship, a center for the followers of a given brotherhood, a sanctuary, and a shrine where the *murabit*, or founders of a brotherhood, were buried.

The Grand Sanusi adapted his reformist call to the needs of tribesmen and merchants. His call for simple Islamic practice appealed to many poor tribesmen, and his emphasis on *ijtihad*, meaning opening the gates for reasoning and individual morality, was attractive to the merchants of the Sahara. Therefore, many seminomadic and trading tribes became Sanusi followers, such as the Zintan, Rijban, and Awlad Busaif of the Gibla, the Awlad Sulayman of Sirte and Fezzen, and some of the Tibbu and Tuareg of Fezzen and Chad. Among the merchant tribes in the Sahara who became Sanusi were the Zuwayya, the Majabra, and the Ghadamsiyya.

By 1870, a Sanusi lodge was more than a place to worship. It was a mosque, a children's school, a residence of the *shaykh*, the head of the lodge and his family, a guesthouse for travelers, an accommodation for caravans and refugees, and a storehouse for supplies and caravan goods. The management of each lodge consisted of a head *ikhwan* (the brotherhood), a *shaykh* or *muqadm* (leader), a Sanusi administrator or *wakil*, and a third, aide, or *agha*. This staff educated people, led prayers, collected religious taxes from tribes and caravans, invested in the Sahara trade on behalf of the order, and acted as judges and arbitrators among tribesmen. The Sanusiyya, comprising a de facto state, provided an elaborate socioeconomic and legal organization for the tribes and the Sahara trade. It supplied the trade with a network of communication and administrative structures through its lodges and missionaries, equivalent in strength to the Ottoman state bureaucracy and town markets in Tripolitania.[1]

The order unified traders, religious scholars, and the tribal divisions of Barqa, as well as the dwellers of Jalu, Awjila, Siwa, and other Saharan oases. A general policy of its leaders was to avoid Ottoman strongholds along the coast. The three capitals of the order were all major stations of the trans-Sahara trade between Wadai and Barqa: Jaghbub (1856–1895); Kufra (1895–1898); and Quru, in today's northern Chad (1899–1902). The Sahara trade became a crucial source of revenue for the order after the 1870s, and a network for its missionaries in the Greater Sahara.

The Sanusiyya's success as the major religious social movement in late nineteenth-century North Africa and the Sahara resulted from the Sanusi's ability to transcend ethnic and local tribal identifications. The order provided a supratribal and ethnic institution for the Sahara trade. This unity became a key to anti-colonial resistance in Barqa, more so than in Tripolitania, where factionalism among the notables in the nineteenth century weakened the resistance and led to its defeat in 1922. In Barqa, the resistance continued till 1932.

The coming of European colonialism tipped the balance of power in the Sahara. First, French expansion into Bilad al-Sudan posed a threat to the Sanusi influence. The Sanusi fought the French army in what is today's Chad from 1897 to 1910. Second, the Italians invaded Libya in 1911. Third, the Sanusi fought with the Ottoman Turks against the British in western Egypt in 1916. The Sanusi leadership faced these new threats with two strategies. The first strategy was to invite the Ottomans to Sanusi territory in Barqa to benefit from the Ottoman Empire's legal, diplomatic, and military status. Therefore, when the Sanusi forces were defeated in Chad in 1902 at Bir'Alali, Sayyid Ahmad al-Sharif, the head of the order, asked the Ottoman authorities to send a governor to Kufra, the center of the order. This policy was effective as evidenced by the French army's inability to expand into Kufra.

The real threat to the Sanusi order came from the north, beginning with the Italian invasion of Libya in the October of 1911. When the Ottoman Empire signed a peace treaty with Italy in 1912, the threat became even greater. The Ottomans, after the Italian attack on Ottoman strongholds, were too weak to wage a full-scale war against Italy. They signed a peace treaty, left Libya, and, to avoid embarrassment, granted independence to the Libyans. Left alone, the Sanusi declared *jihad* the ideology of their independent state in 1913. This was part of the second strategy.[2]

Italy first began to prepare for the conquest of Tripolitania in the 1890s. Italian banks, schools, and newspapers began to flourish, especially in the city of Tripoli and powerful Jewish and Muslim merchants were contacted by Italian consuls in Tripoli as early as 1890. Some of them collaborated with the colonial elite to further their commercial interests. Finally, in 1907, the Bank of Rome became the vehicle for buying land, investing in trade, and employing key people to work for the Italian cause.

Italian colonial policy faced strong resistance, which led to colonial compromises, especially when Italy entered World War I in 1914. Between 1914 and 1922, autonomy and self-rule were granted to the Libyans because of their resistance. However, the policy was changed by the fascists in 1923. The Italian Fascist government pushed the colonial plan of the "liberals" to full scale, declaring that Libya was essential for settling Italian peasants and thus eliminating any compromise; only force would succeed in clearing the land for settlement. Fascist imperialism threatened all non-collaborating groups, especially autonomous states, tribal confederations, and peasants. The fascists' goal of conquering the hinterland was not as easy to accomplish as had been expected.[3]

The Italian conquest began in 1911, but only by 1932 did the Italian armies succeed in controlling the whole country. That period is divided into three phases of the conquest of Libya: 1911–1914, 1915–1922, and 1923–1932. The first phase began with the successful conquest of Tripolitania Jabal in 1913 and Fezzen in 1914. Yet, a rebellion began in November 1914 in Fezzen and

Jabal and spread throughout Tripolitania and had defeated the Italian army and pushed it to the east by 1915.

When the Ottoman Empire entered World War I, it mobilized many allies, including the Sanusi in North Africa, against the British forces in Egypt. The Sanusi forces were defeated by the better-equipped British army during the 1915–1916 war. This disastrous war split the Sanusi leadership and had far-reaching consequences for the resistance in Barqa and Tripolitania. Sayyid Ahmad al-Sharif, the third leader of the movement, was opposed by his cousin Sayyid Idris al-Mahdi al Sanusi who blamed him for the disastrous war against the British. The British had been aware of Idris' willingness to form an alliance with them since 1913, when they had contacted him in Cairo on his way to Arabia. Apparently, Sayyid Idris al-Sanusi wanted to preserve the order's influence, which had been weakened by military defeats against the French in Chad in 1902 and the British in 1916. Thus, the elimination of the militant pan-Islamic Ahmad al-Sharif paved the way for a Sanusi–British alliance through the pragmatic faction led by Sayyid Idris.

Between 1915 and 1922, Italian colonial policy, unable to crush the resistance, shifted its course to make peace with the Sanusi, who had strengthened as a result of their alliance with resistance fighters. The Sanusi, under the leadership of Sayyid Idris, signed three major agreements with the Italian government. In April 1916, a British-arranged meeting took place alongside the Italians and the British, and a Sanusi delegation signed the Agreement of al-Zuwaytina. This treaty was later ratified in another agreement made on April 17, 1917, at 'Akrama. According to these two documents, the Italians and the Sanusi agreed to cease hostilities, to recognize Italian sovereignty along the coast, Sanusi sovereignty in the hinterland, to allow free trade, to remove "troublemakers" from Cyrenaica (like Ahmad al-Sharif and the Ottoman officers), to exempt Sanusi land and *zawiya* from taxes, and to grant the Sanusi family and the senior *ikhwan* monthly salaries from the Italian government in exchange for a Sanusi agreement to disarm and disband their tribes. They also agreed to meet in the future to reevaluate the results of their compacts.

Sayyid Idris al-Sanusi could not convince the resisting tribes and middle-level commanders to give up their arms. The opposition to these agreements was led by a charismatic and brilliant military leader Sanusi Shaykh 'Umar al-Mukhtar. He was born in eastern Barqa to the Minifa tribe in 1862 and educated in Sanusi schools and seminaries. Like other Sanusi leaders of the generation he became a veteran of the anti-colonial wars with the French in Chad and the British in Egypt. Many of them believed he came from a humble Murabtin tribe and because of the educational egalitarian system of merit and excellence, they were appointed as leaders of lodges and bands of resistance. Mukhtar emerged as the face of the resistance first under Sayyid Ahmad al-Sharif's pan-Islamic anti-colonial ideology and later after the deportation of Sayyid Ahmad and the exile of Sayyid Idris in 1924. Idris was the most respected and effective leader of the struggle, but he was not alone. The other commanders, like 'Umar al-Mukhtar and his deputies Yusuf Bu-Rahil and al-Fadil Bu'umar, all from Murabtin tribal backgrounds, led the guerrilla war against the fascist army between 1923 and 1932.

By 1930, Barqa's tribesmen were well organized under the direction of 'Umar al-Mukhtar, as they continued guerrilla resistance from 1923 until 1932. To crush this resistance, Italian military leaders used tactics unmatched in brutality at any other time during the colonial wars in Africa. The tactics included sealing wells, confiscating herds, closing Libya's borders with Egypt, and dropping rebels from airplanes. The most devastating tactic included forcing 110,000 tribesmen and their families to leave their homes to be consigned to horrifying concentration camps in the desert of Sirte. As stated in the introduction, by 1934 only a third of them were still alive, the rest had left for exile in Egypt, Syria, and Chad. The colonialist goal was to separate the resistance from its social base. To this end, al-Mukhtar was eventually captured and hanged in September 11, 1931, and in January of 1932 four of his commanders were trapped along the Egyptian borders; one died, two were captured, and one escaped into Egypt.[4]

This historical context of the resistance is essential for understanding the factors behind the Italian policy to crush the Libyans, including designing a genocidal plan, as the archival evidence shows. It is worth going back again to what my friend, Rifa'at Abou-El-Haj, said earlier. He reminded me that this project is complex and challenging and requires patience and endurance. He was right; it took me over ten years of research. I decided to incorporate these challenges and dead ends in this chapter as it is an essential section of the story as is my struggle to overcome them and find answers to my original questions.

An issue of analyzing this particular genocide is that the advanced age of those who witnessed the genocide complicates our understanding. This project is complex and challenging and required patience and endurance over the ten years of the research. Next, I present a narrative of the obstacles and challenges I faced in discovering the archival and the oral evidence of this hidden genocide. This narrative is useful in analyzing the empirical, ethical, and theoretical challenges and how I was able to resolve them in a journey which I could not predict, simply because I did not know what I was going to discover. The survivors' testimonies and oral history led me to look critically and comparatively at the meaning of the genocide. This was a methodological challenge all of its own. The challenges of the research and the frustrating efforts to find the data and the files on the genocide will be presented next.

Missing colonial archival files and fieldwork research

My research on the history of the Italian concentration camps went through three stages: 1986–1994, 1995–2000, and 2000–2015. The first began in 1986 when

I examined colonial archives in Italy and Libya during the period of research for my PhD dissertation on the social origins and politics of the Libyan anti-colonial resistance, which I completed and defended in 1990. I assumed early on that the internment of over 110,000 Libyans, between 1929–1934, was a well-known topic in both Western and Arabic scholarship, especially since this genocide took place before the Holocaust and was the first genocide after World War I. I realized that the most significant files on deportation, the names of the interned, and the deaths in the camps were missing in the National Archives in Italy.

The second phase of my research started the year after I published my dissertation in 1994 and edited a book on various critiques of colonial and nationalist scholarship on North African studies. I began my research on the Italian concentration camps with specific attention to archival and visual primary sources and, above all, the oral and written sources in Arabic left by those interned inside Libya and those in exile. My experience in critical anthropology fieldwork methods, including ethnography, helped my examination of both written and oral sources.

The third stage of the research focused on the study of genocide and the material related to the Libyan case, including a plan to conduct interviews and fieldwork visits to the locations of the five punishment camps between 2000 and 2015. An early result of my examination of the Italian camps and genocide in Libya was published as a chapter in my book *Forgotten Voices: Power and Agency in Colonial and Postcolonial Libya* in 2005. I spent the last ten years continuing my examination of the topic, including locating primary sources and histories of both comparative genocide and fascism, and, above all, listening to the oral history and reviewing documents, poetry, and physical evidence left by the survivors, as well as the reactions to the genocide inside Libya since 1934. This included an analysis of the monarchy from 1951–1969, the republic from 1977–2011, the February 17th uprising in 2011, and the reaction of writers, artists, and a young generation of university students in seven Libyan universities.

How should we interpret the actions of the Italian official at the archives? I asked myself whether it was an anomaly, or if there was a pattern among other colonial states. In 2015, Caroline Elkins showed in her study of the Mao Mao repression in Kenya that the British destroyed the archives of this brutal phase and that it took her ten years to discover this cover-up. Her case and mine are not exceptional, and as archives of colonial atrocities were in England, Belgium, and France, this seems to be a common pattern.[5] In short, the colonial archives produce sites of "colonial knowledge" and construction of their own ideology. Now we can find the names of the tribes interned in the Italian Archives and the files of General Rodolfo Graziani who was in charge of the Italian military, including the internment in Barqa. However, the sensitive files on the camps and the mass deaths and the names of the victims are missing. Instead, he lied in his books and files about the real number of people interned and, worse, the whole internment is viewed as a case of disciplining and civilizing the "savage" nomads.[6]

In the fall of 2005, I contacted the two leading Italian historians who broke the official Italian and academic silence on the colonial internment, Giorgio Rochat and Angelo Del Boca. I asked for their help in regard to the Italian Archives on the camps. They confirmed my conclusion and informed me that, after decades of research, they had found that the Italian state archive files in the camps had been manipulated and some crucial files on the camps had been "misplaced," or taken out by what they described as the "colonial lobby," which referred to ex-colonial and fascist officials who dominated the administration of the Italian National Archives after the fall of the fascist regime in 1945. These ex-colonial and fascist administrators created obstacles and restricted access to sensitive and colonial crimes, especially the concentration camps, which were perhaps one of the worst genocidal crimes in the history of Italian colonial fascism and the history of colonialism in Africa and the Middle East, with the exception of the Congo, Namibia, and Algeria.[7]

This critical view of the removal of the evidence or silencing of the colonial archives was confirmed by the Italian-educated Libyan historian and diplomat, Wahbi al-Buri, whom I interviewed in Benghazi before his death in 2010. When I interviewed him in 2008, Dr. al-Buri informed me that he had rare access to the Italian Archives. He was an Italian-educated scholar and had served as a minister of foreign affairs of independent Libya in 1951. I assumed with these impeccable qualifications, he would be able to give me some guidance and answer my questions. When I asked him about the internment camp files, he said that those files were missing. We know there are records on the camps, and the location and names of the tribes of the interned, as the works of Gorgio Rochat, Angelo Del Boca, and Gustavo Ottolenghi have shown us. Furthermore, the books and the papers of General Graziani show similar material. There are no names or numbers of the interned, deaths, diseases, or deportations. Not only is the number of the interned and dead minimized, but the entire genocide in the camps is viewed by fascist generals as a positive effort in the modernization and settlement of "savage" nomads. We still may yet discover missing colonial documents inside and outside of Italy. The organization and the codification of the colonial archives are not neutral, based on empirical records of facts. Rather, what we find is an expression of a colonial system, a fascist ideology and racist policy that aimed to erase its sins. In short, this was a blatant attempt to eliminate the history of the genocide.

In the fall of 2012, I had a breakthrough in Italy when I was able to gain access to the papers and files of General Rodolfo Graziani at the Archivio Centrale dello Stato (ACS). The files are valuable on the official Italian policy of the period and the views of the military strategy, letters, diaries, and Arabic letters of Libyan resistance leaders, colonial soldiers, and collaborators. Graziani oversaw the Italian Fascist military during the internment and was subsequently responsible for the genocide of 60,000 people out of the 110,000 Libyans interned between 1929 and 1934. This discovery was significant for my research not because it reveals the truth about what happened, but as it justified and defended the whole mass killing. He is silent on the number and names of the interned who died. The papers are

FIGURE 1.1   Heads of captured anti-colonial fighters, circa 2015
Reproduced with permission by the Libyan Studies Center, Tripoli

crucial, yet apologetic and similar to his narrative published in his book *Cirenaica Pacificata* (1932). The narrative is defensive, the numbers of the interned minimized to only 80,000, and denys the crime of the policy of killing thousands of interned Libyans. Instead, the "Butcher of Libya" Graziani defended the internment of the whole population of Barqa as an act of "civilization" and "legal" punishment for an unruly and dangerous native, nomadic population. The files provide visuals, photos, and new, original Arabic and Italian documents and letters of Libyan colonial soldiers and collaborators. The files of general Graziani provide significant evidence of the Italian Fascist, military, racial, and colonial justification of the genocide.[8]

English and American archives

In 1998, thanks to the then new internet, computer archival files became attainable through the public record office in England and I was able to order materials on the Italian colonial policy during the period of internment in Libya. The files were useful on the larger, historical context, but not on the camps themselves. There might be more files that are still classified, but the most useful material and critical scholarship have been done by English anthropologists such as E.E. Evans-Pritchard, Emory Peters, and John Davis, and the insightful scholarship of the English historian of Italy, Dennis Mack Smith. Very early in his work, Smith recognized the brutal record and atrocities in the Italian colonies of Libya and Ethiopia. Yet, above all, the scholarship of British social anthropologist Evans-Pritchard is worth a second look and should be recognized as an early valuable record of the genocide in Libya.

Evans-Pritchard was a political officer working for the British colonial army in Sudan and Egypt. He was in Egypt during the mid-1930s and met many exiled Libyans in the early 1940s. He was a well-informed anthropologist who came to Barqa with the British forces and conducted fieldwork among the people in the countryside for two years. The fact that he was in eastern Libya and talked to people who were either interned or had family members who were interned, made his work credible and authoritative. I was initially too critical of his work during my research for my PhD dissertation because of his position as a political advisor to the British colonial army. However, after reading the oral history on the eastern region published by the Libyan Studies Center, and conducting my own interviews with the survivors, I reached the conclusion that his notes and analysis of the impact of the internment were correct. His work should be recognized and appreciated, regardless of his official colonial position.[9]

His student, anthropologist Emory Peters, followed him to Eastern Libya and left us detailed structural functionalist studies on the social and cultural values of pastoral nomads in rural Barqa in the 1950s. A third anthropologist, John Davis, came to Eastern Libya much later in the 1970s. He conducted fieldwork research in the eastern Libyan cities of Ajdabiyya and Kufra. Davis' scholarship on kinship and revolution does not cover the internment, but it is the most astute social and cultural analysis of Libyan politics under Qadhdhafi's regime. He had a deep knowledge of the intersection between local kinship and populist mobilization in eastern Libya, his being one of the few studies, up until the late 1980s, that took local culture and agency seriously.[10]

In the early summer of 2000, I flew to Baltimore, Maryland to investigate the American National Archives with some hope that it housed material on the Italian internment in Libya. I was hopeful, but also aware of the fact that the American army, after they occupied Italy, removed some of the major files and material from the Italian Archives. I did not find Italian documents on the internment, but instead found valuable diplomatic reports from the American Embassy in Rome with detailed information that shed new light on the internment, such as the names of the camps, the brutality of life within those camps, and Italian censorship of news. Most of the American files focused on the Ethiopian crisis after the Italian invasion in 1935. This is not surprising for two reasons, first, as the Italian Fascists did not allow foreign journalists to visit the concentration camps, with the exception of Nazi officials, and, second, when in 1928 Knud Holmboe, a Danish journalist and convert to Islam, visited the colony and wrote a book critical of the fascist policies, his book was banned in Italy in 1931. The Italian invasion of Ethiopia created an international crisis and led to the end of the League of Nations. Even today, Italian colonialization and atrocities in Ethiopia are better studied and more well known than the Libyan case.

Egyptian and Tunisian archives

I have conducted research and cultivated professional ties with local archivists and scholars since my early research for my PhD dissertation in 1988–1990 and have continued to communicate and visit both countries whenever I have visited my family in Libya. This collaboration and these scholarly ties helped me with my research on the camps. In the summer of 1997, I was awarded a social science research council grant for conducting research in Tunisia and Egypt for several months. Important to my research was that Tunisia and Egypt were places of refuge for thousands of Libyan exiles during the Italian colonial period between 1911 and 1943. I encountered openness and support of my research in both countries. In addition, I found that there was an active Arabic press and well-kept French and English colonial and Arabic archives, French in Tunisia and English in Egypt.[11]

The Tunisian National Archives in Tunis have both the French colonial state archives and the Arabic sources as well. The French material was well organized, and the staff was helpful in allowing access to all the files available on the topic of my research. After a month of research, I realized that there were only a few files on the internment, as it seems that the French colonial state was more concerned about their security in Tunisia, the challenge of refugees coming from Libya, and the threat of nationalist voices. Still, the most valuable material at the Tunisian archives was the critical Arabic language Tunisian press on the Libyan resistance and the coverage of the brutality of Italian colonialism. Also, the Tunisian archives had a rich collection of Libyan letters and petitions on their plight, the agony of walking across borders, and the quest for asylum and refuge in French colonial Tunisia.

In Egypt, I realized after several weeks at the National Archives, that there was little information on the camps in Libya. The late, distinguished Egyptian historian, Raouf Abbas Hamid, advised me to look at the papers of the late historian Muhammad Fu'ad Shukri and the library of the Arab League's Institute of Arab Higher Studies in Cairo. This was a valuable tip for my research. Muhammad Fu'ad Shukri was the Arab league-appointed advisor to the Libyan anti-colonial Nationalist organization Hay'at Tahrir Libya, the Nationalist Commission for the Liberation of Libya in 1946. Dr. Shukri published two major scholarly books on the creation of the Libyan state and the anti-colonial movements. The value of his work rests on the fact that he was an eyewitness and an insider to the exiled anti-colonial Libyan movement. He was a well-educated historian who documented the most significant formative period of Libyan state and nationalist formation. I was able to locate the Shukri papers at 'Ain Shams University after two weeks of research, and the quest paid off because I found letters, petitions, and stories about the political struggle and the impact the camps had on the Libyan struggle for national independence.[12]

My other significant discovery in Cairo was the collections at the library of the Arab League's Institute. There, I experienced the assistance of the Dean of the Institute, Dr. Ahmad Yusuf Ahmad, a respected political scientist at the College of Economics and Political Science at Cairo University. Dean Ahmad remembered me, as I was a former undergraduate student of his. He was very

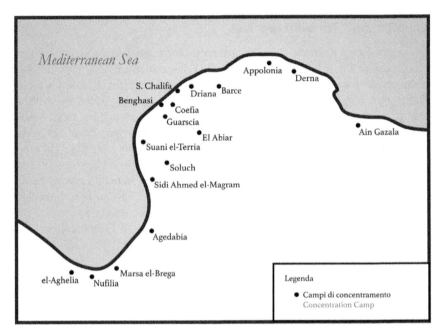

MAP 1.1 Italian concentration camps in Libya, 1929–1934
Author collection

gracious, and allowed me access to the library collection, that included rare books, manuscripts, and journals. The library also contained three unknown Arabic language books on colonial Libya with sections on the internment written during the early 1940s, based on archives in Egypt, primary Arab sources, and Libyan exiles' testimonies. I also located Libyan pamphlets and Arab League material on the Libyan struggle for independence that included the camps, as well as the most-cited arguments for freedom from Italian and colonial domination. Last, the collection also included newspapers in Arabic in support of the struggle for independence, as well as pro-Italian colonial press and propaganda in Egypt.

Archived and fieldwork research in Libya 2000–2015

> We no longer be content with writing on the history of the victorious elites, or with detailing the subjugation of dominated ethnic groups. Social historians and historical sociologists have shown that the common people were as much agents in the historical process as they were its victims and silent witnesses.
>
> *Eric Wolf,* Europe and the People without History, *1982*

The bulk of my fieldwork and research was conducted inside Libya where I discovered the most valuable, direct, original material on the interned Libyans in both national and private family archives, as well as my own 30 interviews with the survivors, and fieldwork visits to the former camps between the years 2000 and 2015. I also visited public Libyan institutions that housed original material. In addition, I spent much of my time studying collections on the camps, conducting interviews, and visiting the five main former concentration camps south of Benghazi. I chose these five camps because they were the most well known and were where the mass deaths took place.

The investigation of the historical oral and written records was challenging and, at times, frustrating. I did not know all the families and where they lived, who was still alive, and whether they and their families would trust me and talk to me about such a horrific and painful memory of internment and trauma. In addition, some families opposed the state under Qadhdhafi, so they were suspicious of the motives of scholars and researchers aimed at spreading the truth of their history. Through the support of Libyan scholars and survivors and their descendants, I was allowed to meet some of the survivors and listen to the original views of the victims, and what happened during the genocide between 1929 and 1934. Taking Libyan histories seriously was the key first step to understanding the context, finding the locations of survivors, and building on what Libyan historians had accomplished in studying the internment in the camps.

I began by reading their works and then started contacting them to ask for help on where to find the survivors and the primary historical sources on the internment, as well as what happened before and after the genocide. Among the best historians, folklorists, and literary critics of the genre of Libyan folklore, poetry, and culture during the colonial period and the internment, I recognize scholars such as Mohamed Jerary, Habib Wadaa El-Hisnawi, Aghil al-Barbar, Abdal-Mola al-Harir, Abdalla Ibrahim, Atiyya al-Fituri, Saʻid al-Hindiri, Mahmood al-Deek, Yusuf Salim al-Barghathi, Ali Burhana, Yusuf Fanush, Wahbi al-Buri, and Zainab Zuhry. I also recognize writers, nonacademic historians, and cultural critics such as Salim al-Kubti and ʻAbdalali Abu ʻAjailla al-ʻAwkali.

In Libya, three universities house valuable material on the internment and the culture of the victims. These universities are Benghazi University, the Libyan Studies Center in Tripoli, and the Center for Folklore and Popular Heritage at the University of Sabha in southern Libya. However, I discovered very early, after I spoke with Libyan historians, the existence of valuable private family archives as well. These are archives held by some families or writers that are related to the genocide, as well as oral and written histories of the internment. Among the valuable family archives are the collections and libraries of the Libyan writers Ali Mustafa al-Misurati, Salim al-Kiubti, Abdalla Milatan, the Irfad family, and the late Uthman al-Ghazali, to mention just a few. Keeping family archives is not unique to Libyan society, but I would stress in the Libyan context that it is very common to find such private collections all over the country. This guarding of local files and documents among Libyan families is a result of the bitter colonial experience, exile, and displacement of thousands of people up until 1951.

Consequently, social Libyan memory views the state as alien and hence the records of people's history are guarded in private family collections and passed from one generation to another. Since independence in 1951, Libyan state elites have spoken symbolically about the Mu'ataqalat, but done very little in reality to restore, build infrastructure, and study this traumatic phase of Italian colonialism. I did discover one town who took civil initiative by non-state actors to recover a collective history of repression under colonialism.

One of the most remarkable local Libyan collections is the work of Jam'iat Dhakirat al Madina, "The Association of the City Memory on Hun." Hun is a small town in the region of Jufra in central Libya and this Association was founded by the late poet and political activist Senusi Habib in 1992. One of its goals is to collect the oral history of the colonial period and the repression of the town by the Italian army in 1928. The Italian army accused the town of aiding the mujahidin resistance who attacked the Italian army at Bir Afiyya on October 31, 1928. The army exiled and imprisoned 14 mujahidin from Waddan in the western city of Zuwara, and then made a case out of the nearby town of Hun. The Italian army collectively punished the town by hanging 19 men and in January 15, 1929 it deported the whole town, consisting of 1,078 people, to the coast. The victims of the deportation were forced to walk for a whole month without food or medicine in the middle of the cold winter. On August 1, 2015, I interviewed the director of this association, Abdallah Zagub, who gave me the collected oral interviews and the history of this association. The Association was financed and supported by a civic initiative of this remarkable, small Libyan town. They provided me with some of the main oral interviews and documents of what happened to their town. It became clear from these documents that the interment in eastern Libya was not an isolated event but was linked to a colonial genocidal policy, which originated in the deportation of Libyans to Italy, and, ultimately, their execution and internment in Benghazi, the capital of eastern Libya and the second largest city in the country.

I was able to meet and interview some of the family members who owned valuable letters, photos, poems, and recordings of material from the prisoners of the camps. I also found poems and drawings of the camps by some of the survivors in Benghazi. I should add that such interactions with survivors and folks who had family archives were not simple, nor immediate. I was endorsed by colleagues, and I learned that I was checked out by the survivors who asked about me, my family, and the purpose of my research. Here, I was aware of the value of being honest and reflective about my research based on the long self-criticism that has taken place in the field of anthropology for the last four decades, and the fact that I was a bicultural scholar who is both an insider and outsider. An insider by being born and raised in Libya by a family that was deeply involved in the anti-colonial resistance and *jihad*, and was able to understand the language, suffering, and oral history. Like the survivors and their children, I remembered the names of the battles, dates, and poetry and the names of the fallen fighters against colonialism. I am also an outsider due to the fact I left Libya after high school and have been educated and lived in the USA for three decades. Despite a connection with the survivors and their families, I faced some challenges and ethical questions. I was aware as a grandson of two grandparent freedom fighters and I learned from the study of oral history, genocide, and testimony that one has to be aware of the complexity of witnessing. It includes being aware of the testimony of oneself and of others, and the whole orality of witnessing is a struggle and a process.

For example, when I started my research and asked to meet with some of the survivors of the genocide, I had to work via contacts, such as students at the university working with my colleagues in Benghazi, some of my high school and college classmates, and the Libyan writers' union whom I knew in the 1970s. Specifically, the contacts in Benghazi, Derna, and Toubruq, and my classmates at Cairo University who returned to eastern Libya, were generous and supportive of my research. Still, families who did not know me checked me out as well. I realized I was vetted. But I realized that I got a chance to learn, to learn so that I can write about their hidden history with depth. Once people began to trust me, I was supported and welcomed, and families of the victims sent me interviews and letters about the camps and internment as late as 2015. I have kept in touch with some of their children and grandchildren.

A story worth sharing concerns visual and material evidence of the internment. Each camp had poets and poetesses who recorded and communicated the interned experience. One of the most remarkable poets was a woman by the name of Um al-Khair 'Abd al-Dayim, of the Braiga concentration camp, which was one of the largest, with 30,000 people interned. I searched for her photos and collected poetry inside the camp for years. I became lucky when, in 2005 and 2010, I met two of her grandsons, Abu 'Ajailla and Abdal-Razaq. I met Abu'Ajailla in 2005 in Benghazi and he provided me with a copy of his grandmother's collected poems. In 2010, I met Dr. Abdal-Razaq al-Murtada at the Libyan Mission to the UN in New York. I asked him to locate a photo of his grandmother, and after three months he sent me a gift: a rare, unknown photo of the famous poetess. Later, he informed me that the family checked on me, my family, and my background before they decided to send me the photo – a common theme in my fieldwork. I was, in short, vetted, and only then was I accepted as an insider not an outsider. I was so excited I gave a high five to many of my colleagues.

Salim Al-Kubti was a key help for me to find and interview the families that I had not known in eastern Libya. Professors Abdalla Ibrahim and Atiyah al-Fituri of the Libyan Studies Center were helpful in connecting and introducing me to the survivors who they wanted to interview, and I took advantage and joined them. Both are well-known Libyan historians who teach in the Department of History at Benghazi University (formerly known as Garyounis University until 2011). One has to keep in mind that names of universities and streets in Libya have changed since independence in 1951, again in 1969, and more recently after the 2011 uprising which removed the Qadhdhafi regime from power.

The faculty of the Benghazi University's collection on Libyan folk poetry was of great significance to my research on the internment. Libyan national and rural culture is oral in nature, and one of its main forms of communicating is composing, memorizing, and reciting folk poetry. People memorized and recited these poems during and after the end of the interment in 1934. The majority of the interned in the camps were illiterate seminomads, and folk poetry was a main cultural method of communication inside and outside of the camps. For example, the memory of the camps has been kept alive because of an epic poem that was memorized all over the country and in exile, which is called "Mabi-Marad," ("I Am Not Ill, Except") by the poet Rajab Buhwaish al-Minifi. This poem was broadcast after Libyan independence on December 24, 1951 and Libyan radio aired it many times, to the point that generations of Libyans can recite it, despite the fact that the in-depth history of the internment was still not well known by younger generations after the 1980s. When I asked a Libyan intellectual about the camps, he replied "thank God we had this epic poem, which kept the memory alive." Al-Minifi broke the silence and cover-up of the history of the Libyan interment and the Italian genocide of Libyans.

In the early 1970s, Benghazi University faculty contributed major scholarly research on the recording, editing, and publication of two volumes of a major period of Libyan folk poetry, including the internment and genocide under Italian colonialism and fascism. The university organized a committee of scholars and faculty specializing in Libyan poetry, literature, and colonial history. This committee, under the leadership of the late scholar Ali al-Sahli, worked for years, and the fruit of its labor was two volumes published in 1977 and 1979. Also, Tripoli University (Al-Fatih University until 2011) published another volume in 1984, and two major books on the structure and outcome of Libyan folk poetry in 2006 and Italian occupation viewed through folk poetry in 2008. Finally, scholars of folk poetry, Yusuf Fanush and the late Al-Hamali Sh'aib al-Hudhairi, edited two major collections by Libyan poets Fadhil Hussain al-Shalmani (1877–1952), who was a prisoner on the Italian island Favignana, and Hussain Muhammad al-Ahlafi (1905–1974) in 2004. These poets kept the memory of the internment alive as they wrote about life inside the camps and communicated with other poets in exile. Al-Shalmani's poetry signifies the plight of Libyans deported to 21 Italian prisons between 1911 and 1940.[13] We know only 5,151 names, and we still have not recovered the names of the 10,000 others. The Italian policy of deporting and exiling people who are suspicious, or active in the anti-colonial resistance, originated as early as 1912 and continued until 1943. The colonial archives indicate that, for example, in the year 1912, 3,053 native people, including both men and women, were sent to prisons in the penal colony islands of Gaeta, Ponza, Tremiti, Ustica, and Favignana in southern Italy. The archives also included the number of the dead who were buried in Italy near the prisons. In short, Italian colonial policy of exiling, deporting, and imprisoning the natives originated afresh in 1912, 1915, and 1928. The massive scale of 1929 is a culmination of an old violent policy. The recent scholarship by Italian historian Francesca Di Passquale[14] on penal colonies is a welcome contribution on this significant topic and period.

The collected folk poetry inside and outside of the camps is the most significant source for the anger, humanity, and agony of the people interned, as well as those who witnessed the colonial fascist genocide. I discuss that this is not just past history, but a living one that was, and still is, cited, narrated, and communicated in Libyan society during and after the internment. It is a history of the present. Whenever I attended a talk or conducted interviews, I encountered this living poetic history.

The oral history project at the Libyan Studies Center in Tripoli was a major source of my research on the history of the genocide. The Center has collected one of the most remarkable oral history projects in the world, including oral interviews of people who were still alive between 1977 and 1985, as well as in 2005 and 2008. The Libyan Studies Center was founded by Libyan historian Mohamed Jerary in March of 1978. Dr. Jerary, who finished his PhD at the University of Wisconsin in Madison, brought his professor Jan Vancina, the father of the field of oral history in Africa, to Tripoli, Libya. It is here that he trained and organized the project of collecting Libyan anti-colonial oral history. Dr. Vancina came to Tripoli and trained 14 young Libyan historians between January 23 and April 23 in 1978. The Center continued this impressive project up until 2006. The Center's accomplishment included a collected 15,000 oral interviews that were transcribed and published under the series, *The Mawsu'at Riwayat al-Jihad, The Encyclopedia of Jihad Oral History*. So far, 42 volumes have been published, as well as two volumes of folk poetry. I read all of the published volumes and was given access to the ones on the internment that were kept on discs or cassettes. I focused on the volumes on the eastern region where there were valuable interviews on the camps.

I discovered 220 interviews of survivors of the internment in the published volumes, and I conducted another 30 interviews between 2005 and 2008. In addition, I had access to the unpublished concentration camps' oral history interviews, called *Arshif al- Riwayat al Shafhiyya, The Oral History Archives*, at the Libyan Studies Center. I found only one book on the internment. It is a master's thesis on history by one of the historians at the Center, Yusuf Salim al-Barghathi. He was born in eastern Libya and educated at Benghazi University. This thesis was published as a book, *Al-Mu'taqalat al-Fashistiyya bii Libia*, by the Center in 1999. This book is still the only major study of the interment in Arabic, from the point of view of the interned, and is still the best in any language.[15] Yet, it lacks archival sources, a larger comparative context of Italian Fascism, and a comparative awareness of the critical study of genocide. Yusuf Salim al-Barghathi was very helpful and shared with me 50 interviews with Libyan survivors of the genocide during the early 1980s, many of whom had passed away by 2000.

One must bear in mind that the Libyan population, which opposed the colonial state in eastern and southern Libya, had to either submit or escape to exile after the end of the resistance in 1932; the Italian policy was to execute many leaders and fighters even after surrender, unlike what had happened under the French in Algeria and Morocco. There, leaders such as Amir Abdalqader and Abdalkarim al-Khatabi, were exiled, while in Libya, 'Umar al-Mukhtar and other leaders were hanged. This brutal collective punishment pushed thousands of Libyans, especially the resisting tribes and towns, to escape by crossing the harsh Sahara and to walk for thousands of miles to Chad, Niger, Egypt, Algeria, and Tunisia. During this voyage to escape Italian imprisonment, armies, and airplanes, many children and elderly people were lost or died of thirst and hunger. The survivors of these tragic losses kept oral stories of what happened. Their oral history is a moving tale of tears and broken hearts when they remembered their loved ones who did not survive the unmerciful trek across the Sahara.[16]

In 2003, I interviewed the last survivor of the Libyan refugees from central and southern Libya, who had escaped Italian aerial bombing after the battle of Um al-Aranib and Wawu in 1928. Salim Mhimmad Saif al-Nasr was 13 years old at the time. I interviewed him in Sabha with my late father in January 13, 2003. He shed new light on the plight of the resistance and their families who crossed thousands of miles across the Sahara on foot and camels in an attempt to escape Italian armies and airplane bombing attacks. The three-month-long walk across the harsh Libyan Sahara was an effort to take refuge and asylum in Chad, Niger, Egypt, or Tunisia. This interview brought my attention to the forgotten suffering and death of many of these refugees, including stories of thirst, starvation, and loss.

As stated earlier, I was born and grew up in a family that participated directly in the anti-colonial resistance, and which shaped my early understanding of the personal and the emotional human side of the Libyan experience with colonialism. Both of my grandfathers were active fighters in the anti-colonial resistance. My maternal grandfather, Ali, fought until 1930 and was forced into exile after the end of the resistance. I think he told me his story over 20 times, perhaps so that I could remember it and tell it one day. When I asked him why he chose exile, he said that they would hang him, and that he did not want to live under their rule. My paternal grandfather, Ahmida, also fought in the resistance and, instead of leaving, he was protected by the Magharba and Warfalla tribes for ten years. My late father told me that in central Libya people knew about the camps and the internment through some men from Waddan, my family hometown. These men joined the resistance in eastern Libya under the leadership of 'Umar al-Mukhtar. One of them was Muhammad Abdulhadi Sal'um. In 2017 I contacted his grandson, a local judge in Waddan, who sent me his photo and told me that he had settled in Massa near al-Bayda and married a woman in eastern Libya. This fact was also confirmed later during my research when I found one of the main poets, Muhammad Zaidan al-Sharif of Waddan, who was exiled and imprisoned in Zuwara in 1928 because of his anti-colonial poems. He wrote a replying poem to Rajab Buhwaish al-Minifi, the famous poet interned in the Agaila camp, as well as the poem "Mabi-Marad." This epic/ poem is remarkable as it kept the history of the genocide alive and deserves translation and detailed analysis in Chapters 2 and 3. Poetry in Libyan culture was a cultural weapon for resistance and survival and, therefore, it was recited and valued by society.

Fieldwork and visits to the camps, 2007–2008

I was able to travel to Benghazi and then the camps after much preparation and consultation with my friends to find a time to visit and guides to the locations. I traveled to the five camps on May 2, 2007. The camps I visited are located south of Benghazi and as far as the desert of Sirte. I visited Benghazi to meet survivors who still live in the city, as well as in other towns including Rajma. In Benghazi, as stated earlier, I visited and interviewed the Libyan diplomat and historian Wahbi al-Buri. Dr. al-Buri was one of the founders of the Libyan state in 1951. Interviewing him was a valuable opportunity to understand an elite nationalist view of the colonial internment and genocide, as well as the larger context in Benghazi before, during, and after it took place. He confirmed my conclusion that the Italian state officials took or destroyed the sensitive files on the camps. While in Benghazi, I visited Haj Muhammad 'Usman al-Shami, son of the anti-colonial leader 'Usman al-Shami and a deputy of the charismatic 'Umar al-Mukhtar. He was interned with his mother at the Agaila camp as a strategy to punish his father. Haj Muhammad had an excellent memory and kept his ID card and a map he drew of the camp. The map is remarkable. It shows the fence, the towns, and the cemetery from memory.

His interview was most detailed and documented a survivor's perspective of this concentration camp. Before I interviewed him, he interviewed me. Once again I felt I was being vetted me despite the fact that I came to see him with people who know him. He asked me where I and my family is from and our tribal background. When I told him that I am a Sharif from Waddan and that both my grandparents fought in the anti-colonial resistance, he was happy and opened up to my questions. He, like many other survivors in the eastern region, was skeptical of people coming to study history of the genocide. One has to remember that the eastern region was the social base of the monarchy and viewed the regime after 1969 as hostile one. I knew Libyan social history and was able to prove that to him. Being a Sharif is significant in eastern and central Libya; Ashraf are the people who trace their genealogy to Prophet Muhammad in the seventh century. Waddan is the capital of Ashraf in Libya. The people are respected as dependents of the prophet and because they stay neutral among the tribes, and often are asked to mediate among them in time of conflict, war, and disputes over land and water. I asked him after my trip to the camps, including Agaila, about my shock to see so many graves and why so many people died. He replied: "we died because of Shar, evil, my son." He meant starvation and disease, which are named evil in this specific context. His answer still moves me and stayed in my head to the point that I wanted to call the book "we died because of Shar,

evil, my son." My editor and some of the referees objected and recommended that I should have a clear title. My view is to honor the survivors
and their language and narrative, and, in addition, I wanted to make the
word Shar like shoah, or the Holocaust, a common worldwide name as part
of historical justice and recognition of the horrors of racism and genocide
in Libya. Haj Muhammad asked me to send him the book when it was

FIGURE 1.2 A map drawn by Muhammad 'Usman al-Shami, survivor of Agaila concentration camp, 2007
Author collection

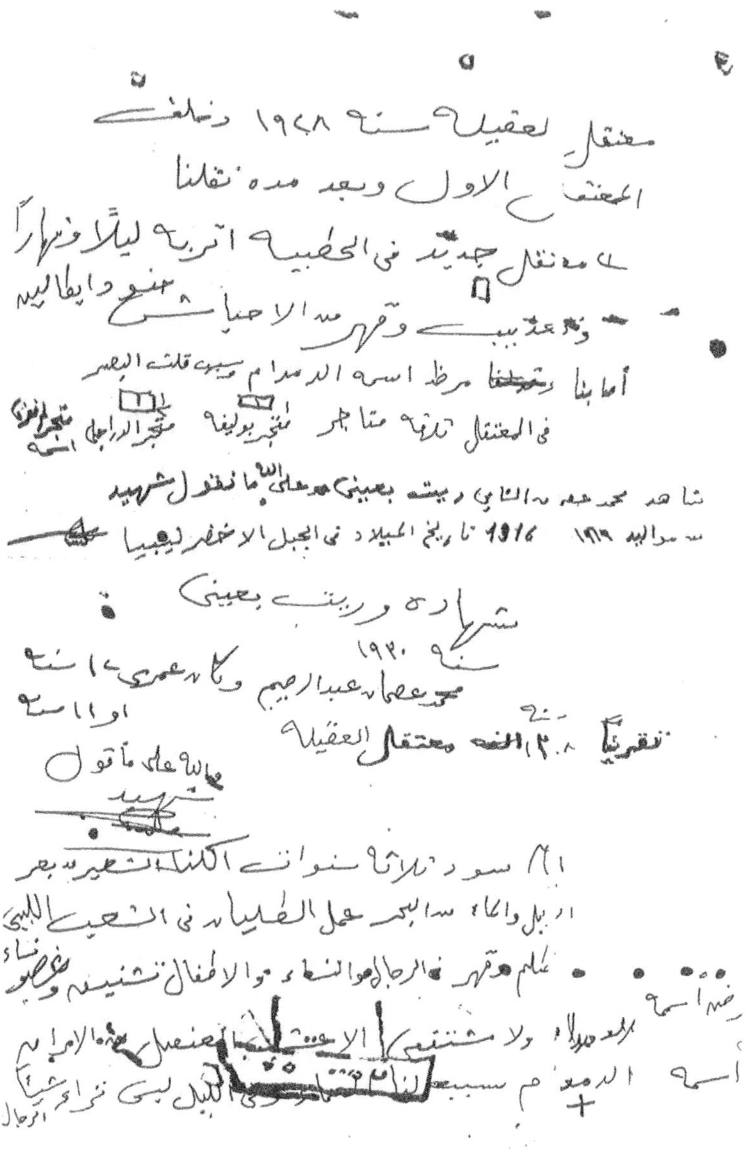

FIGURE 1.2   (Cont.)

finished, and I promised to mail him a copy. I kept my promise and interviewed him a second time to learn more and to see if the narrative had changed or not, and why. I was very sad to hear that he passed away in 2010. I plan to reach his family and give them a copy of the book one day, just as I promised to this kind and dignified survivor.

FIGURE 1.3 The author interviewing survivor Haj Jaballa Muhammad al-Minifi, at his house in Rajma, 2010

Author collection

Salim and I then traveled to the town of Rajma, a one-hour drive east of Benghazi, to meet and interview Haj Jaballa Muhammad al-Minifi. He was a funny old man, and his wife is the daughter of the brilliant poet Rajab Buh-waish al-Minifi. Finally, Salim drove me to meet an urban middle-class writer, Ramadau Jarbu', who took us to meet his sister, Haja Zuhra Jarbu'. She was interned as a child with her family in the Agaila camp. This interview was interesting because it was with a survivor who came from an urban middle-class family, not a rural, poor, and seminomadic one – as was the case with the majority of the victims of the concentration camps.

When people began to know me, they became more helpful to the point where they shared the interviews that they had conducted in the late 1970s and early 1980s, but they also took me to meet other survivors and their families. Dr. Abdalla Ibrahim drove me to meet more survivors for more interviews outside Benghazi on May 9, 2007. We left very early in the morning and visited the towns of al-Abyar, Jara, and al-Nawaqiyya. His home is located at al-Abyar, near the local mosque. I interviewed Haj Nuh Aawadallah Dighaim al-Fisi, who was waiting for us with his son. Haj Nuh Aawadallah Dighaim al-Fisi was interned with his family at the al-Abyar camp. Following the interview, he asked where I was from. I informed him that I'm a professor teaching in the United States but that I am a Libyan. He was displeased with my answer, so

I asked him to explain. He asked what I plan to do with our history and I promised to send the book after it's finished and translated into Arabic. This exchange is legitimate, as power and research has been debated in anthropology and the use of research to legitimize colonialism. I told my hosts that I seek to confront colonial claims, break the silence on the hidden history of the concentration camps, and bring justice for the victims through writing their history.

We then drove to the town of Jara to interview Haj Abdulhamid Abdrabah Younis al-'qubi. When we arrived, we were told that there was a death in the family and that he was receiving people who were giving respect and condolences to the family, as Libyan Muslim traditions required. Haj Abdulhamid felt sorry for me when I told him I had come from America to interview him and others. He agreed to be interviewed and I did my best not to burden him under such sad, unexpected circumstances. Finally, we drove to the town of al-Nawaqiyyia in the beautiful green plains of the rich country. We had lunch and then we drove to the house of another survivor, Haj Naji Ibrahim Abdalla al-Badri, who was interned at the al-Abyar concentration camp with his family. Haj Naji was an impatient old man but had vivid stories about the internment and the draft by the colonial army for Libyans to fight in Ethiopia. This pattern was so common for many young men, especially the orphans in the concentration camps. They were indoctrinated in fascist colonial schools and drafted as cheap labor soldiers to fight for the colonial empire when Italy invaded Ethiopia in 1935. It would be worthwhile to research whether some of these young men were also sent to the Spanish Civil War when Mussolini sided with his fellow fascists led by General Franco.

I had two main observations regarding the fieldwork and the interviews. First, the interviews were not just one-on-one, but were family and community affairs. Adults, children and grandchildren, and extended family members sat around and listened carefully and often reminded their father or mother about some details that they knew or wanted to hear again. This transgenerational collective family interest suggests the history of the camps is still a living reality of the community and not a forgotten, private, and painful struggle for the survivors. Second, I was moved by the warm reception, the generosity, and the humanity of the families who insisted that I stay for dinner or lunch and were happy to talk to me after they realized where I was from and that I knew the history, culture, and some of the tribes, cities, and towns where they lived. The interviews were more like conversations, in which I, too, was asked many questions. They asked about the purpose of my research, who was sponsoring it, and if I was going to talk truly and justly, and challenge the Italian view of what happened to them and their families.

I must be reflective about my fieldwork comparative experience in multiple locations and how I was received by the survivors and their families and the questions regarding the ethics and the purpose of my research. I expected to be vetted before they would talk to me. First, one has to be aware that the eastern region was the social base of the monarchy, and consequently it viewed with suspicion Qadhdhafi's regime and questioned its anti-colonial rhetoric. Second, due to the fact of being a Libyan-American scholar, I expected pressure to prove myself not just as an outsider, but as a native ethnographer and intellectual. The fact that I had friends and colleagues from the region validated my introduction to the people, and one person told me "we vetted you and we learned that your first book in Arabic was banned by the regime." Third, I was helped because my grandmother came from the eastern region and my family is of Ashraf background, people who descended from Prophet Muhammad's family. I felt at home with them before I gave them some of my family background that was directly tied to the anti-colonial culture. My fluency of their dialect of Arabic, history of resistance, and social and tribal background made people open their homes and agree to talk to me. I have kept in touch with many of them and their children and promised to send them a copy of the book when it is finished and translated into Arabic.[17] Next, I planned to visit the location of the five camps where the majority of the population, perhaps 70%, was interned. The Italian army interned the population in 13 camps. Future research should shed more light on the others.

Visiting the location of the camps: July 12–14, 2007

By the end of June 2007, I knew that it was time to visit the locations of the camps. I decided to visit the camps and see where the genocide took place and to determine what physical evidence still existed in the five locations between Benghazi and Agaila. The visits to the camps were significant; they provided an opportunity to assess the empirical evidence of the remains of the original camps, especially the design, the barbed wires, the watchtowers, and, above all, the graves and cemeteries. In addition, the current status of the camps shows the lack of interest, neglect, and even the erasing of what happened after Libyan independence in 1951. I was shocked during the visits when I found that the camps had almost disappeared – aside from a few buildings and cemeteries – with the exception of Agaila camp. There is no escape from a damning conclusion that the post-colonial Libyan state decided to ignore the history of the genocide, not only under the Sanusi Monarchy in 1951, but also under the populist republican regime after 1969, despite its anti-colonial slogans and populism.

The trip required long preparation and planning. My colleague Dr. Ali al-Rishii, a Libyan-American professor of philosophy, arranged with a friend in Benghazi to find a guide and a driver to take me to the camps. Another colleague, Professor 'Atiyya al-Fituri, a historian at Benghazi University, agreed to be my guide at the camps. Dr. Mohamed Jerary and Salim al-Kubti arranged for some survivors to meet with us all at the Agaila camp. With my recorder and camera in hand, the driver and Professor al-Fituri, picked me up from the hotel very early so we could make a stop at all five camps and at the shrine of 'Umar al-Mukhtar in Slug.

We left Benghazi on July 12, 2007 at around 6:00 in the morning. We stopped to visit the first camp south of Benghazi, Swani al-Tariya, the smallest of all the five camps. The name of the camp came from one of the 'Urfa subtribes. The camp is half an hour drive south of Benghazi. The oral history of the survivors reveals that it was built in late 1928, while the Italian sources state 1930. It is 3 kilometers long, has two gates, a prison, an old airstrip, and a small school for orphans. When we arrived, I discovered that the remains included the camp officer's offices, the flagpole at the center of the camp, a cemetery with thousands of graves, and a recent monument to a Libyan mujahid, or freedom fighter, 'Isa al-Wakwak al-'Urufi, built in 1985. The Libyan Arabic written and oral sources state that there were 500 families interned and the majority were from 'Urufa, Dressa, Fuwakhir, and Bra'sa tribes. As for 'Isa al-Wakwak al-'Urufi, I found out that he was a skillful and daring fighter in the anti-colonial movement, marked by some stories of legendary tricks and disguises, before he and only a few other fighters attacked Italian enemies, until he was captured and hung at the gate of the concentration camp. I found only a modest sign at the terrible camp of Agaila. The plaque contradicts the official policy of commemorating anti-colonial battles and struggles by Qadhdhafi's regime. In addition, the simple unmarked graves at the cemetery stuck with me as the most acute symbol of the genocide. Encountering the graves was hard and depressing, as if the victims of the genocide are confronting this crime against humanity through their graves and deaths! At that moment I realized what the survivors were talking about and the absurdity of denying the genocide and the mass killing. The individual and mass graves are the most horrific reminder of the genocide. It is enough evidence.

We know that some people inside the camps were allowed to leave every once in a while, but they had to come back and show their permits. One has to realize that the camps were in the middle of nowhere, and if they were to escape and be captured they were severely punished, even executed. Also, this camp is the only one where I discovered the existence of the names of the people interned. I knew the record existed, as all the survivors told me it did, but it seemed that these records from other camps were destroyed or removed from Rome's archives and most sources were silent about the names. The record we discovered on the interned people in the Swani al-Tariya camp was 70 pages long. It was discovered by a Libyan who is a specialist on the history of this camp. I would argue that as we found the names at Swani al-Tariya camp, then one day we might discover the names of the other thousands of interned individuals, and once we discover them, the full silence of the genocide will be broken.

After leaving Swani al-Tariya, we drove to the Braiga concentration camp, which held 30,000 interned individuals. Of the 30,000, a mere 13,000 came out alive in 1934, according to Libyan Arabic sources. Most of the interned came from the 'Abaidat and Magharba tribes. Unfortunately, I did not find many remains of the old camp. Instead, I found constructions, roads, and infrastructure for the oil-exporting port. Once again, the cemetery though is still visible, containing thousands of graves. I felt very sad that the camp had almost gone and realized that the Qaddafi regime had done little to protect and restore one of Italian fascist colonialism's worst crimes in Africa. The only monument built was a small one for the battle of Braiga between the anti-colonial Libyan resistance and the Italian army, but not for the terrible concentration camp. There is no choice but to conclude that the modern Libyan state failed to preserve and maintain the sites of the camps and contributed to the marginalization of the history.

Next, we arrived at the Agaila camp – the most infamous camp of the five. This notorious camp was used to punish the relatives and supporters of the resistance movement led by 'Umar al-Mukhtar. It was the most complete and preserved camp. I found the fence, the remains of officers' buildings, the pole for the flag and the hanging and whipping of the interned, and a large cemetery with thousands of graves and tombs buried according to Libyan Maliki Islamic practices. I remembered the old cemeteries in Waddan, and Sidi Sahal and Sidi Hamid Sabha, where there were no names and no stones, just simple and humble graves. I asked my father, who was a religious scholar, about the significance of burial and graves in Libya and about why it is different from the traditions in Egypt where I attended college in Cairo. My father replied it is because of our Malki/ Sunni Maghribian traditions which instruct people to be simple and humble, as when we die we should be equal in the eyes of god. He also reminded me that Prophet Muhammad said we should accept difference and diversity among the faithful, it is mercy for all.

The most shocking and disturbing part was the sight of the beautiful beach along the Mediterranean Sea. The beautiful blue, clean, and shining Mediterranean

FIGURE 1.4 The ruins of the Italian officers' station at Agaila concentration camp, 2010

Author collection

contrasted with the site of death and destruction in the long, eerie cemetery to make a striking impression, as if the dead are still refusing to disappear. I admit the long lines of graves at Agaila shocked me as I came face-to-face with Libyan genocide. Here exist the fields of death and mass killing. The victims at the cemetery need no testimony. Their silence and modest graves are powerful enough, an eloquent silence. The powerful sight reminded me of a short story by the Libyan eminent novelist Ibrahim al-Koni called "When the Martyr Speaks," published in 1986. He imagined that in places in Libya where people were killed the spirit of the martyrs lives and hunts and unless one is respecting of the dead they could haunt you. He referred specifically to a Libyan colonial soldier called Muhammad Salih, who shot his white Italian officer because he insulted him near the town of Darj in western Libya. Salih and three of his associates fled to Algeria, but the French colonial state imprisoned him and turned him over to the Italian military in Libya, where he was executed and many of his people were forced into the Agaila concentration camp in the late 1930s. At that time, the Agaila camp had people from central and southern Libya there and continued to be used even after the end of the massive internment of the eastern people of Libya. Figure 1.4 is a photo of the officers' headquarter at the Agaila camp.

At the camp, we met Dr. Jerary, Salim al-Kubti, some local people of the town of Agaila, and five survivors who were driven to the camp and agreed to be interviewed in the very camp they were imprisoned in alongside their families, some of whom died of starvation and disease. The five survivors were Muhammad 'Usman al-Shami, Jibril Muhammad al-'Umrani, Jaballa Muhammad al-Minifi, Abdalrahman Muhammad al-Zwawai, and Muhammad Sulayman al-Zwawi.

FIGURE 1.5   An aerial photo of the al-Abiar [Abyar] concentration camp, 1930
Reproduced with permission by the Libyan Studies Center, Tripoli

These survivors were young teenagers between the ages of 13 and 17 years old when they were interned with their families in 1930. At the Agaila camp, I noticed an old building, perhaps for camp officers. It was half damaged, as if it had been bombed. When I asked the Libyan historian with us about what had happened to this building and why it was not restored, he said with a smile that the official state policy is one thing, and the reality on the ground another. I asked him to elaborate and he said that the regime bombed this building in 1984, fearing an attack by the Front for the Salvation of Libya, which opposed the Qadhdhafi regime. Perversely, it was destroyed to prevent the opposition from using it as a hiding place. The five survivors confirmed the fact that most of the prisoners came from northeast Libya, the region that supplies the resistance with fighters, food, guns, and intelligence. They came from various tribes and townsfolk, but most belonged to 'Awaqir, Mnifa, Masamir, Qut'an, and Abadlla tribes. Arabic sources state the total number of the interned was 20,000, and only one-third of them survived the ordeal by 1934. Figure 1.5 is an aerial view of one the camps.

After we left Agaila, we drove to the Sidi Ahmad Magrun concentration camp. The name came from a local Sufi Muslim Saint, Sidi Ahmad al-Magrun al-Fakhari. In rural Libya, like the majority of the north and Saharan Africa, Sufi saints and social movements have been the most influential local Islamic presence since the fourteenth century. Here, respect for saints, as well as asking for their blessings, is a common cultural practice, similar to Roman Catholicism's respect and worshipping of saints. At the camp we met with Haj Ibrahim al-Qadhdhafi al-'Urabi. He took us around the location where I found a few remains of the police station, the fascist Balila school for the orphans of the camp, and, once again, the cemetery. Here, I discovered two cemeteries linked to the concentration camp.

The Magrun camp was 6 kilometers long and it interned 18,000 from the Bra'sa, Dressa, and 'Urufa tribes. According to Libyan Arabic sources, only half of those imprisoned remained alive by 1934. I interviewed Haj Idris Hamad Muhammad Shyat al-Shilmani, who was 13 years old when he was interned with his family in 1930. His father was a fighter in the anti-colonial resistance. He told me that the people interned at Magrun were from nearby towns and many were forced to walk hundreds of miles from Toubruq to Susa and then to Magrun. He reminded me that some had died, especially the elderly and the children, and that most of the animals and herds were taken or lost. This loss of herds had severe consequences, as it led to starvation and high death rates at the camps, due largely to the Italian colonial military provision of only limited food and no medicine for the interned population between 1929 and 1934. Haj Idris told me that he lost two brothers and a cousin due to starvation inside the Magrun concentration camp.

The last camp we visited was Slug, located 6 kilometers south of Benghazi. The camp was 8 kilometers long and the cemetery at Sidi Bukhash was quite large. Like the other ones, the camp had almost disappeared due to urban development. However, a significant part of the camp, including the shrine of the modern father of Libya, 'Umar al-Mukhtar, has been preserved. 'Umar al-Mukhtar was hanged in front of the 20,000 interned Libyans at Slug camp on September 11, 1931. His remains have a significant symbolic history. They reflect the politics of colonial and post-colonial Libya from 1931 until today. The Italian army took the body of al-Mukhtar and buried it in a secret location in the cemetery of Sidi 'Abaida in Benghazi in the aftermath of Libyan independence on December 24, 1951. As stated before, his grave was discovered in a remarkable way due to the knowledge of a Libyan man who was a witness to the Italian secret burial. The monarchy built an impressive shrine in Benghazi in August 7, 1960. This shrine became a place for Libyans to visit and to pay respect. In addition, students and the critical movement against the pro-Western Sanusi Monarchy (1951–1969) often gathered around the shrine, which became a symbol of oppression and protest. Such traditions and rituals continued after the military coup on September 1, 1969, which brought junior Libyan military officers, led by Colonel Mu'ammar al-Qadhdhafi, to power. Once again, the strong independent Libyan student union movement continued to protect its independence and oppose the military by continuing the rituals of starting their protest by gathering around 'Umar al-Mukhtar's shrine, the father of modern Libyan nationalism. On September 16, 1980, the Qadhdhafi regime, facing growing opposition, moved the body of 'Umar al-Mukhtar to the town of Slug at the location of the old concentration camp. Such an action was justified by claiming he was hanged in Slug and it was more logical to bury his body there. However, the truth is that the regime wanted to stop the ritual of protests gathering around the old shrine of the symbol of Libyan nationalism, 'Umar al-Mukhtar, inside the rebellious city of Benghazi, which contains Libya's first and main university and is the cultural capital of the country. Whatsmore, the regime wanted to take away from the opposition the fact that al-Mukhtar was a Sanusi leader.

In other words, the history and the collective memory of the genocide is contextualized inside Libya as well. It is a living history. The challenge is to investigate the genealogy and the history of both colonial silence and the struggle over the history of the interment. It should not be surprising that all versions of the Libyan state, including the monarchy, the republic (1969–1977), Jamahriyya (1977–2011), and the February 17, 2011 uprising, linked their legitimacy to the anti-colonial resistance and 'Umar al-Mukhtar. The leaders of these various states knew that they had to support the role of resistance, the principal example of which was the colonial policy to defeat the resistance.

In short, I was shaken and overwhelmed by the end of the interviews and field visits to the five concentration camps, especially the graves and the cemeteries. I returned to Benghazi shaken and horrified. It is one thing to study mass murder and genocide but very hard to see thousands of graves and mass graves face-to-face. I decided to call them death camps. It was a violent and terrible genocide based in fascist bad faith and racism. If one has to accept the humanity and the agency of the native people as equals and members of a living culture, then you have to be morally outraged. I realized why the survivors are still haunted by the horrors of what happened in the camps, and how absurd it is to deny or debate whether what happened was an ethnic cleansing or a casualty of war. Here, the cultural trauma is still alive but also the process of collective recovery and healing through poetry, oral narrative, and interconnectedness with the new generations of children and grandchildren. Also, I realized the hypocrisy of the Qadhdhafi regime in talking about the crimes of Italian colonialism but doing so little to even repair or preserve the sites of the worse crimes of Italian colonialism and Fascism. The next chapter will examine Italian and Western historiography and the factors behind the silence on this case of genocide, in contrast with Arabic language historiography and the remarkable epic/poem which kept the memory alive inside Libya.

Notes

1 On the "Rise of the Sanusiyya and the Political Economy of Barqa," see my book *The Making of Modern Libya: State Formation, Colonialization and Resistance* second edition, (New York: State University of New York Press, 2009) ch. 4. On the region's anti-colonial historical background see Julia Clancy-Smith, "Saints, Mahdis, and Arms: Religion and Resistance in Mid-Nineteenth Century North Africa" in Edmund Burke III and Ira Lapids eds, *Islam, Politics, and Social Movements*, (Berkeley: University of California Press,1990), and on the Maji Maji movement see John Iliffe, "The Social Organization of the Maji Maji Rebellion," *Journal of African History*, 8:3 (1967) 495–512.
2 Ahmida, *The Making of Modern Libya*, 87.
3 On the "Social Bases of Libyan Anti-Colonial Resistance," see Ahmida, *The Making of Modern Libya*, ch. 5.
4 There are several biographies of 'Umar al Mukhtar in Arabic and one in Italian. In Arabic, see Ahmad Tahir al-Zawi, *'Umar al-Mukhtar*, (Tripoli: Dar al-Fijani, 1970) and Aghil al-Barbar, ed., *'Umar al-Mukhtar, Nashatuhu Wa Jihaduh, 1862–1931 ['Umar al-Mukhtar, His Upbringing and Jihad]*, (Tripoli: Libyan Studies, 1983). Also, see the critical studies in the book *Omar al-Mukhtar* by four critical Italian historians Enzo Santarelli, Giorgio Rochat, Romano Rainero, and Luigi Goglia, translated by John Gilbert (London: Darf Publishers, 1986).
5 On the colonial construction and manipulation of the archives see Caroline Elkins, "Looking beyond Mau Mau: Archiving Violence in the Era of Decolonization," *American Historical Review*, (June 2015) 852–868, and her original critical book, *Imperial Reckoning*, (New York: Henry Holt and Company, 2005) xi–xvi, and Tom Lawson, *The Last Man*, (New York: I.B. Tauris, 2014).
6 For Graziani's racist views and language see David Atkinson "Embodied Resistance, Italian Anxieties, and the Place of the Nomad in Colonial Cyrenaica" in Charlotte. Ross and Loredana Polezzi, eds, *In Carpore: Bodies in Post-Unification Italy* (Farleigh: Dickinson University Press), 56–79, Angelo Del Boca, "The Myths, Suppressions, Denials and Defaults of Italian Colonialism" in Patrizia Palumbo, ed., *A Place under the Sun* (Berkeley: University of California Press, 2003) 17–36, and Nicola Labanca, "The Embarrassment of Libya, History, Memory, and Politics in Contemporary Italy," *California Italian Studies*, 1:1 (2010), 1–19.
7 Communication with Angelo Del Boca in 2006. See his chapter "The Obligation of Italy toward Libya" in Ruth Ben-Ghiat and Mia Fuller, eds, *Italian Colonialism* (New York: Palgrave Press, 2005) 195–202.
8 I had access to General Graziani's papers in 2012. I am grateful for the two Italian archivists that helped me research these significant files. However, the papers are silent about the mass deaths and the atrocities in the five concentration camps.
9 There is no biography of Evans-Pritchard except for his own notes and fieldwork in Egypt and Barqa. We know that he met Libyan refugees and exiles in Cairo in

1932, and that he conducted fieldwork as a colonial officer between 1942 and 1944 in Barqa. I discovered that he had a Libyan translator called Salih Bu 'Abdalsalam. See his chapter "Tribes and Their Divisions" in *Handbook of Cyrenaica*. (Cairo: British Military Administration, 1947). See also David Pocock, "Sir Edward Evans-Pritchard 1902–1973, an Appreciation" www.Cambridge.org/com.

10 Peter's main research on Barqa was collected and published by Jack Goody and Emanuel Marx eds, *The Bedouin of Cyrenaica*, (Cambridge: Cambridge University Press, 1990). John Davis' main research in 1970 among the Zawiya tribe in Ajdabiyya and Kufra was published in his book *Libyan Politics: Tribe and Revolution*, (Berkeley: University of California Press, 1991).

11 On Egyptian press coverage of Libyan anti-colonial resistance see Muhammad Sayyid Kilani, "Al- Ghazu al Itali 'ala Libia wa al Maqalat al lati kutibat fi a Suhuf al- Masriyya, 1911–1917" ["The Italian Invasion of Libya and the articles that were written on the Egyptian Press"] (Tripoli: Dar al-Fijani, 1996).

12 Muhammad Fu'ad Shukri's papers are placed at the History Department 'Ain Shams University in Cairo. His main book on the Sanwsiyya is *Al-Sanusiyya Din Wa Dawla [The Sanusiyya: Religion and State]*, (Cairo: Dar al-Fikr al-'Arabi, 1948).

13 Yusuf Fanush and Al-Hamali Sh'aib al-Hudhayri eds, *Diwan al-Sh'ir Fadhil Hussain al-Shilmani* (Benghazi: Manshurat Majlis al-Iba'a al-Thawafi, 2004), and a second collections of poems by the poet Hussain Muhammad al-Ahlafi was also published, (*Hussain Muhammad al-Ahlafi*, Benghazi: Mansharat Majlis al-Ibda'a al-Thawafi, 2004).

14 The Libyan Studies Center has published documents, names, and letters of the Libyan's exiled to southern Italy. See Al-Zawawi, Ali et al., "Deportees and Exiled Libyans to Southern Italy" *Mawusu'at Riwayat al Jihad*, Special Issue 7 (1991).

For an overview of Italian scholarship see Francesca Di Pasquale, "The 'Other' at Home: Deportation and Transportation of Libyans to Italy during the Colonial Era (1911–1943)," *International Review of Social History*, 63:26 (August 2018), 211–231.

15 Al-Barghathi's book is *Al-Mu'taqalat al-Fashistiyya bi Libia [Italian Fasccist Concentration Camps in Libya]*, (Tripoli: Libyan Studies Center, 1993).

16 See Muhammad Sa'id al-Gashat, *Marahil al-'Atash fi Libia [The Trials of Thirst in Libya]*, (Beirut: Al-Dar al-'Arabiyya Lil Mawsu'at, 2008).

17 There is now a large critical literature on the ethics, power, and history of fieldwork in anthropology that calls for decolonizing fieldwork – see George Marcus, *Ethnography through Thick and Thin*, (Princeton: Princeton University Press, 1998) 5, 39, and the collection edited by Sorya Altorki and Camila Fawzi El-Solh, *Arab Women in the Field*, (Syracuse: Syracuse University Press, 1988) 7–9, a39, 46–47,139-140, and John Borneman and Abdellah Hammoudi, eds, *Being There: The Fieldwork Encounter and the Making of Truth*, (Berkeley: University of California Press, 2009) 259–292. On the politics of interview see Aballahi Ibrahim "The Birth of Interview" in Luise White, Stephan Miescher, and David William Cohen, eds, *African Words, African Voices: Critical Practices in Oral History*, (Bloomington: Indian University Press, 2001) 103–124, and Dori Laub "Truth and Testimony: The Progress and Struggle" in Shoshana Feldman and Dori Laub, eds, *Testimony* (New York: Routledge, 1992) 61–73. See the debate over sociologist's Alice Goffman's book *On the Run*, (Chicago: Chicago University Press, 2014) and for an overview see Gideon Lewis-Kraus, "The Trial of Alice Goffman," *New York Times Magazine*, (March 17, 2018).

2

EUROCENTRISM, SILENCE, AND MEMORY OF GENOCIDE

This chapter examines and challenges Italian colonial and Eurocentric his-toriographical views of the "benign" nature of Italian Fascism by exploring the genocide in Libya between 1929 and 1934. It looks at the ways in which this experience has generally been silenced or elided up to the 1980s from historical accounts of fascism that look only at Europe. This silence and underrepresentation of the Libyan genocidal internment is contrasted by the rise, in 1973, of a small but strong body of critical scholarship both outside and inside Italy. In addition to detailing the brutality of the regime's treat-ment of the Libyan population, this scholarship also draws on oral history and folk poetry as a means of establishing the ongoing bitter legacy of Italy's presence in Libya.

The genocide's history is divided; there exists a silence in Italy, but a living memory in Libya, especially in the eastern and southern parts of the country. I call this unawareness the "politics of memories." First, it is essential to iden-tify the schools of thought and review the assumptions and categories of the silences. Second, is the need to illuminate the examples and discourses in both academic and mass culture. We must never forget the evil deeds of the fascists in Europe, Libya, and Ethiopia. The notion of a reformed fascism, coinciding with the re-emergence of Italy's former neofascist party, is a dangerous new myth that no one should tolerate. A critical new study of Italian Fascism must overcome the Eurocentric view of Italian Fascism by looking at genocide in the colonies beyond Europe and insisting on the moral and political responsi-bility of the Italian state to open the archives so that we can find out how many skeletons are in its closet and provide a voice to those that have been unjustly forgotten.

With the exception of a few courageous anti-fascist scholars, the genocide of Libyan nationals between 1929 and 1933 remained virtually unknown to most people, with the exception of Libyans, until the 1970s. The silence regarding this atrocity was from the most respected Italian and Western scholars of comparative fascism. These scholars contributed to a notion that has persisted over time that Italian Fascism was somehow moderate, or "benign." Some were not aware, nor educated, while others accepted the colonial claims of people without history.

This chapter challenges the dominant historiographical view, which is based on the myth that Italian Fascism did not encompass acts of genocide and mass murder. This entirely false claim reinforced the notion that Italian Fascism was a lesser evil than fascism practiced under the German Nazi regime. Second, it argues against the use of the nation-state and the region as units of analysis. It is far more revealing, I believe, to use a comparative analysis that includes the European colonies in a global capitalist world system, especially after the eighteenth century. I argue that one could not write the history of Italy without studying the history of its colonies, especially Libya. Similarly, one cannot write the history of Libya without studying the history of Italy, and this method could be applied to: Algeria, Haiti, Vietnam, Cambodia, and France; Egypt, India, and England; the Congo, Rwanda, and Belgium; South West Africa, "Namibia," and Germany; and Japan and Korea. This transnational and comparative postcolonial method is a key to understanding the genealogy of the present. Both Italian and Libyan colonial and nationalist historiographies are limited, if not distorted, if the nation-state alone constitutes the unit of scholarly analysis. This chapter seeks to address three questions:

1. Why does the dominant image of Italian Fascism as benign persist in the public media, films, and scholarly Italian and Western studies when compared with Nazi Germany's model of fascism up to the 1980s?
2. What are some of the moral and scholarly flaws in this silence and in the myth of Italian Fascism?
3. How does recovered evidence of genocides of Arabs between 1929 and 1934, along with oral narratives of some of the 100,000 to 110,000 victims of Italy's concentration camps in Libya, undermine common misconceptions concerning the nature of Italy's brand of fascism?

While none of these questions may be answered definitively here, the material analyzed in this chapter sheds light on the actual record of Italian Fascism, and thus has the potential to reorient current historiographic views. It is my main argument that Italian Fascist brutality was not just a byproduct of war, but rather of calculated genocide experienced by real human beings who are capable of telling us, in their own songs, words, and poems, what they went through. This genocide continues to have a profound impact on contemporary Libyan society. The argument I make includes examples of public perceptions and scholarship; the context and causes for such views; alternative critical scholarship; the history of fascist genocide in Libya based on the agency and narrative of a Libyan who survived the concentration camps between 1929 and 1934; and suggestions for a new research agenda based on a critical model of

Italian Fascism. I identify five schools in the scholarship on the Libyan internment and genocide:

1. A school that is Eurocentric and reproduces colonial knowledge and Ital-
    ian Fascism as authoritarian yet civilizing the natives in Libya. It focuses
    mainly on Italian Western sources. Fascism is a model even in post-World
    War II politics. It accepts the archives as facts and does not challenge fas-
    cist assumption and propaganda.
2. A school that is silent about the genocide in Libya and advocates the con-
    cept "brava gente" choosing to see all Italians as good people. It assumes
    that the Italian national character is moderate and would not commit
    brutal atrocities and genocide as the anti-Semitic genocidal German Nazi
    regime did. Scholars of this school do not know Arabic and they focus on
    Italy and Italians in Africa, the reactions or the impact of this policy, and
    perceptions such as modernism, nationalism, and architecture and tourism.
3. A school that accepts fascism as an effective model for development and
    modernization without even mentioning the genocide human cost.
4. A school that recognizes that genocide was committed in Libya yet is
    silent and oblivious about its impact and consequences in Libya and Italy.
    Even today, one finds books and references to the concentration camps
    and mass death that assume that it was a sad part of history but that then
    move on to talk about Libya and Italy as if there have been no conse-
    quences that impacted society and the modern state of fascism and post-
    genocide society.
5. A school of contemporary comparative genocide studies, including forgot-
    ten ones that still exclude the Libya case.

Italian colonial and Eurocentric scholarship

Cultural stereotypes, as well as colonial and Eurocentric historiography, have
contributed to the myth that Italian Fascism was benign. Eurocentric scholarship ignores fascist policies in the colonies, while colonial scholarship views
fascism as one component of the modernizing phase of history. Turning
a blind eye to the nature of Italian Fascism is bolstered not only by the official
refusal to open the Italian National Archives to scholars – especially the files
on the concentration camps – but also by the decision not to hold war crimes
trials for individuals who carried out government policies as colonial officers.
In addition, the Italian former neofascist party has been waging a strong public
relations campaign in defense of fascism since its reemergence in the body
politic in early 1990.[1]

In 1972, Princeton University historian John Diggins published
a comprehensive book titled *Mussolini and Fascism: The View from America*,
on the official and popular images of Italian Fascism in the United States. He
argued that in the nineteenth century, Americans considered Italy to be, on the
one hand, a positive, romantic ideal and, on the other, a negative nativist

country. Travelers and expatriate writers who viewed Italy as a classical source of cultural values shaped the romantic image and, in turn, shaped the perceptions of scholars focusing on national character and political culture. One must ponder the cultural differences among the dead. German Nazis killed Europeans, creating outrage among other Europeans, but Italian Fascists killed North African Muslims, playing into Orientalist fantasies and racist and modernist colonial ideologies, about the dehumanized, backward natives, and the price of modernity to justify the need to "exterminate all the brutes." These perspectives created the context in which Italian Fascism was seen as gentle – perhaps an aberration – while the German character, commonly viewed as militaristic, naturally resulted in the horrors of the Nazis.[2]

At the turn of the twentieth century, in the United States, the nativist image emanated from a fear of Italian working-class immigrants, who were seen as ignorant, poor, Catholic, and oppressed. Even with the rise of fascism in 1922, American official and public responses to Italy were mostly positive, focusing mainly on Mussolini who, according to Diggins, represented a much-needed solution to a country lacking both discipline and work ethic, and corrupted by a fractured elite. In the popular view, Mussolini had multiple virtues; he was considered an accomplished writer, a violinist, a strong statesman, and a modernizer who "made the trains run on time." This image of Mussolini and his brand of fascism was popularized by the American films and documentaries of the 1930s.[3] In addition, many public American figures such as Henry Ford, Charles Lindbergh, and poet Ezra Pound expressed an open support for Italian Fascism and Mussolini.

One must also keep in mind the larger historical context between 1922 and 1939; Italian Fascism not only did not pose a threat to American interests, but the United States welcomed the anti-communist ideology of a country that had the largest communist party in Western Europe. Even critics of Mussolini portrayed him merely as a buffoon or ordinary dictator.[4] This theme has persisted both in mainstream scholarship and in modern Western films from the 1930s until today. Indeed, this representation may be found even in the works of critically acclaimed neo-realist Italian masters of the cinema such as Federico Fellini, Pier Paolo Pasolini, Franco Zeffirelli, Vittorio De Sica, Roberto Rossellini, Luciano Visconti, Michelangelo Antonioni, and Bernardo Bertolucci. The works of these brilliant filmmakers, while critical of fascism inside Italy, were silent about the colonial atrocities in Libya, Ethiopia, and the Balkans.

Indeed, movies played a major role in Mussolini's popularity. In 1931, the Columbia Studio Company produced *Mussolini Speaks*, a film based on the dictator's tenth anniversary speech in Naples. It presents a positive view of *Il Duce*. In the 1920s, the Italian government opened its doors to the American film industry and tried to use films as a public relations tool.[5] These images of a romantic Italy and moderate Italian Fascism are still present in popular culture, as demonstrated by Zeffirelli's 1999 film *Tea with Mussolini*, which claims to provide a more realistic view of its principal subject than previous works. This biographical film by the veteran filmmaker dramatizes two aspects of Italy's colonialist era: British and American romantic images and the rise of anti-Semitism. The film emphasized these themes through the lives of four expatriates and an Italian teenager (Zeffirelli as a young boy) in Florence in the late 1930s.

More of Shakespeare's plays take place in Italy than in any country except England. But possibly it was the Brownings, Robert and Elizabeth, who set the still-prevailing affinity for Italy. When Elizabeth died in Florence in 1861, the municipality placed a tablet on her house with some lines by an Italian poet: "here wrote and died Elizabeth Barrett Browning [...] who made of her verse a golden ring linking Italy and England." Since that day a steady line of English residents in Florence has kept that ring polished. It is at Elizabeth's grave that *Tea with Mussolini* begins. Stanley Kauffmann astutely captured the significance of the film when he wrote: "Italy has long figured in the English imagination, especially that of writers."[6] The movie is silent about the colonial fascist atrocities in Libya and Ethiopia despite the fact that these atrocities happened earlier, between 1929 and 1935. This romantic film genre reproduces the colonial notion of moderate fascism and "brava genti" as in the 2001 case of another film by Louis de Bernières, on the Italian invasion of Greece, titled *Captain Corelli's Mandolin*. Italian soldiers are depicted as humane and more as lovers than the brutal German occupiers who came to finish the occupation. A whole genre of Hollywood film popularized the myth of moderate Italian Fascism, while the Nazi-type is depicted as the prototype of the evil and genocidal state.

While European filmmakers romanticize Italy, two critical movies depicting the genocide in Libya, Ethiopia, and the Balkans were censored in Italy. The first of these movies is Mustafa Akkad's 1981 film *Lion of the Desert*, which dramatizes the history of anti-colonial Libyan resistance led by 'Umar al-Mukhtar, using real footage of the deportation and internment for the first time. The movie was banned in Italy. When it was released after Colonel Qadhdhafi's visit to Italy to sign a new treaty regarding colonial oppression in 2008, the movie was briefly shown in limited theaters. The second film is *A Fascist Legacy*, a 1989 BBC documentary on the Italian Fascist atrocities in Libya, Ethiopia, and Yugoslavia. It was based on the work of the American historian Michael Palumbo, who discovered classified files showing a post-World War II cover-up of war crimes committed by Italian Fascist generals and officials of the Allies. The Italian government protested the film, then bought the rights and shelved it. I tried to find a copy of the film for ten years and discovered only six libraries worldwide that owned it. When I requested it through my university's inter-library loan office, I was told it could not be provided to me due to legal arrangements. It is clear that censorship played a major role in silencing history of the genocide. It was only in 2017 that I was able to obtain a copy of the film from an Australian university. The two-hour-long film documents a record of the horrors and atrocities of the Italian Fascists and the Allies' cover-up, based on classified files at the British Archives which were discovered accidently by American historian Michael

Palumbo. In a January 2018 communication with the film producer Ken Kirby he informed me that the film script was based on Palumbo's memo and the evidence of cover-up. Palumbo discovered by accident at the British PRO (Public Record Office) classified files that prove a cover-up by the Allies to not push for war crimes against Italian Fascists. The files were removed immediately after he revealed them in the film.

Today, there are still scholars who advance the notion of moderate Italian Fascism and praise Mussolini's regime as an accepted legitimate state instead of a genocidal one. The contemporary rise of the former neofascist party in Italy, the Alleanza Nazionale (AN), lends force to the theory that Italian Fascism helped modernize Italy, especially after it captured 14% of the vote, or 100 of the 630 seats, in the Italian lower house, and joined the government as a legitimate party in 1994. In 2001, Gianfranco Fini, the head of the party, became deputy prime minister in Silvio Berlusconi's government and, on November 20, 2004, he became the new Italian foreign minister. *The New York Times* described him as a reformed leader who denounced anti-Semitism and visited Israel twice.[7] Denouncing anti-Semitism directed against Jews is a positive development, but what about the other Semites, namely, the Libyan Muslims who experienced fascist atrocities? As a new political party, it put one of its most charming members, Mussolini's granddaughter Alessandra Mussolini, on display for the American public. Her pictures in *People* magazine are revealing. In one, she raises her arm in the fascist salute, just as her grandfather Benito did on a balcony in the eastern Libyan city of Benghazi. The article in *People* identified the place, but misspelled Benghazi as "Bangali," and did not identify it as part of Italy's colonial holdings.[8]

Alessandra Mussolini originally represented the far-right Movimento Sociale Italiano (MSI), but having subsequently represented AN, has since formed a new breakaway group. She presents herself as an industrious modern woman who promises to show people what a Mussolini can do. Her grandfather's followers founded the MSI in 1946, but it was a marginal force until the mid1990s, when it became a partner in Berlusconi's coalition government. Fascism is becoming respectable again, not because it is less evil, but because we have forgotten what it means. It is troubling to know that President Donald Trump's former chief advisor Steve Bannon is fond of Julius Evola, one of the major Italian philosophers of fascism.

Advocates of the myth that Italian Fascism was moderate in comparison to Germany's, base their case on two arguments: (1) that the Italian approach to anti-Semitism was milder, and (2) that there were no mass killings or ethnic genocide such as that carried out by Nazi Germany. Here, the scholarship on fascism tends to focus on the regime's treatment of the European Jewish minorities. This thesis is supported with information such as the fact that the Fascist Party was open to Jews, and that more than 20 Jews joined the Fascist Party's March on Rome in 1922. Further, high-ranking officials in the Italian Fascist state included Italian Jews such as Aldo Finzi, a member of the first

Fascist Council, Guido Jung, Minister of Finance from 1932 to 1935, and Maurizio Rava, governor of Italian Somaliland and general in the Italian Fascist militia. Philosopher Hannah Arendt, author of the influential 1973 book *The Origins of Totalitarianism* on the origins of totalitarian regimes in the last century, erred in arguing that there was no Jewish question in Italy, and that only after pressure from the German Nazi state did Italy turn in 7,000 Italian Jews to the German concentration camps. She seemed to be unaware of what happened in Libya due to the closing of the colony and the censorship of any media access between 1929 and 1943. Consequently, for her, Italian Fascism became just an ordinary dictatorship, and because of her wide influence on postwar scholarship on genocide, her Eurocentric approach to Italian Fascism has contributed to the persistent myth that Italian Fascism was a lesser evil and even moderate.[9] This is a major error as we know now that the Nazi elite looked to the Italian brutal experience of settlers in Libya as a model to follow and the journalistic, scholarly, and official study of the Italian success was published in Germany.

Italian American historian Victoria de Grazia, on the other hand, points out that "racial laws of 1938, modeled on Germany's 1935 Nuremberg Laws, forbade interracial marriages between Italians and Jews, banned 'Aryan' servants from working in Jewish houses, removed Jews from influential positions in government, and education, and banking."[10] A scholar of comparative fascism, de Grazia focuses her attention on Europe, therefore concluding that the Holocaust was unique in its mass killing of Jewish and other ethnic minorities. Her perspective, while critical of the prevailing scholarship in some respects, is nevertheless shaped by exactly the same Eurocentric bias. Had she examined the other external cases of colonial genocide, the view of European cases would have had a new context and meaning, one of which is roots and interconnection, not anomaly and exception.

Alternative critical scholarship

During the second half of the twentieth century, two groups of critics challenged the assumptions and arguments of colonial knowledge: critics of Eurocentrism, and then critics of Italian Fascism and colonial atrocities. Among those who have challenged Eurocentric interpretations of history are Italian socialist philosopher Antonio Gramsci, and postcolonial intellectuals such as Aimé Césaire, Frantz Fanon, C.L.R. James, Eric Wolf, Edward Said, Noam Chomsky, Marnia Lazreg, Peter Gran, Rifa'at Abou-El-Haj, Samir Amin, Antonio Gramsci, and Mahmood Mamdani. Lisa Anderson, the dean of American scholars on Libya, did not say much about the Libyan genocide but was very clear about the Italian atrocities and brutality in Libya. These scholars have argued that colonialism, and the history of colonized peoples, requires acknowledgment.[11] Gramsci was aware of, and critical of, the brutal fascist colonial wars, despite the fact that he was locked up in a fascist prison for most of his adult life.[12] In his famous book *The Wretched of the Earth*, first published in 1961, Fanon contended, "Nazism turned the whole of Europe into a veritable colony."[13] The Africanist scholar Mahmood Mamdani, meanwhile, eloquently contextualized the debate about fascism, colonialism, and genocide, writing,

> The Holocaust was born at the meeting point of two traditions that marked modern Western Civilization: the anti-Semitic tradition and the tradition of genocide of colonized people. The difference in the fate of the Jewish people was that they were to be exterminated as a whole. In that, they were unique – but only in Europe.[14]

Only in Europe. If one believes as a moral principle that all people, regardless of origin, have the same intrinsic worth, then all acts of genocide must be recognized, and all victims counted.

Twenty-three years ago, when I wrote my book *The Making of Modern Libya*, I discovered that most scholars of fascism and totalitarianism viewed Italian Fascism as a lesser evil. My studies based on archival research and oral interviews with the elderly Libyans who fought Italian colonialism confirmed fascism's outrage, resulting in my discouragement and disillusionment of the appalling case of historical amnesia.[15] Sixteen years ago, I began to research primary material on fascist concentration camps in Libya, recognizing that there were indeed some scholars, and two journalists, who were pioneers in the study of the history of genocide in Libya: English anthropologist E. E. Evans-Pritchard, Italian anti-fascist historians Giorgio Rochat, Angelo Del Boca, and Nicola Labanca, journalists Eric Salerno and Gustavo Ottolenghi, American historian Michael Palumbo, and American historian of Italian Fascist cinema Ruth Ben-Ghiat and Libyan historian Yusuf Salim al-Barghathi.[16] Despite differences in age, background, method, and field of expertise, this group shares a focus on Italian Fascist atrocities in Libya, especially concerning the concentration camps that existed between 1929 and 1934. Labanca is correct in stating that Italian historians were silent about the Libyan colonial internment up to the 1970s.

Yet, even after the publication of the few critical works of this colonial historiography, scholars working on Italian colonial studies such as film, politics, architecture, literature, and tourism, have continued to mention the internment and, at times, the genocide without looking at their significance and resulting consequences, committing by omission a major failure in their representation of colonialism and contemporary Libya. One must bear in mind that there was no major anti-colonial movement inside Italy, and even the communist party was ambivalent about the colonies. The Italian neorealist cinema, celebrated for its critical examination of fascist ideology and culture inside Italy, is silent on colonial genocide, and postcolonial studies emerged only in the late 1980s. Most of the anti-fascist critiques were devoted to the internment conditions inside Italy – as if there were neither trail nor history of the atrocities and genocide. The absence of anti-colonial movement inside Italy contributed to the persistence of the myth even until today that Italian fascism was moderate, modernizing, and benign.

In 2005, Salerno republished and updated his pioneering book on the genocide in Libya, updating an original edition that had been published in 1979. Historians writing about the genocide include Giorgio Rochat, Angelo Del Boca, Nicola Labanca, Yusuf Salim al-Barghathi, and Ruth Ben-Ghiat. Rochat, the main Italian historian to courageously challenge official views, has been examining the colonial records on genocide in the concentration camps since the early 1970s. He published a seminal article in 1973, and called what happened in Libya a genocide, and a more elaborated revision in 1981. Del Boca, in 2005, updated his major critique in two volumes on the history of Italian colonialism in Libya. Both Rochat and Del Boca spent many years investigating the Italian Archives and became vocal critics of Italian scholarship. In 2002, Labanca contributed a new book on a significant topic[17]: the memoirs and letters of Italian soldiers who fought and served in the colonies of Libya and Ethiopia. He stated that the silence of Italian historians contributed to the Italian public's amnesia regarding the colonial period and its atrocities.

Al-Barghathi, should be recognized as the leading Libyan historian on the topic of internment. He published his master's thesis based on oral interviews with Libyan survivors. Ben-Ghiat, an American historian of Italian Fascist cinema, recently published an engaging and critical theoretical study of the notion of Italian Fascism as a lesser evil. These scholars offer a comparative perspective that brings the Libyan experience into the larger study of Italian Fascism and have begun to debunk the myth that Italian Fascism was moderate. Yet, the myth still pervades Western popular consciousness despite these critical studies and others. In the English language, a pro-fascist historian Renzo De Felice had tremendous impact on propagating the idea that Italian Fascism is moderate and different through the *Journal of Contemporary History*. Two journals – the *Journal of Modern Italian Studies* and *Italian Studies* – have only in the past ten years published more critical articles that investigated the impact and consequences of Italian colonialism on the genocide inside and outside of Libya. What is fashionable is to study the Italian policy and views overseas based on an uncritical use of Italian Archives and perceptions.[18]

The Libyan anti-colonial resistance and the internment

The Italian colonial policy of removal, deportation, internment, and killing the people active in or supportive of the resistance was not a fascist monopoly, but started early in 1911. When, in 1922, the Italian Fascist Party assumed power in Rome, it rejected the colonial practice (followed since 1911) of collaborating with local Libyan elites, terming it a failure. The fascists advocated military force aimed at "pacifying" the natives of Italy's colonies and continued to deport and exile Libyans in Italian prisons and exploit them as a source of cheap labor in Italy and as cheap fighters in the war in Ethiopia and in World

War up until 1943. Much like the German colonial genocide of the Herero and the Nama between 1904 and 1908 in South West Africa, the apartheid regime in South Africa, and Aryan supremacy in Nazi Germany, the Italian Fascist policy was based on an ideology of racial supremacy and the myth of reviving the Roman Empire to colonize Libya. The fascists viewed themselves as the heirs of the Roman Empire and the entirety of the Mediterranean Sea as The Roman Sea. Mussolini, after the invasion of Ethiopia in 1936, declared the birth of the New Roman Empire. Fascist racial policy stressed hierarchy, holding that, as a perceived superior race, Italians had a duty to colonize inferior races, which included, in their view, Africans. It was Mussolini's plan to settle between ten and 15 million Italians in Eritrea, Somalia, and Libya in order to populate what he heralded as the "New Roman Empire."

Fascist colonial policy meant the forced subjugation of Libyans. Rights accepted before 1922 by the previous government were dismissed. Educational policies, likewise, were changed in accordance with racial supremacist views. While previous colonial officials had moved to "Italianize" Libyans by broadening their access to education, the fascists barred natives from Italian culture, replaced the Italian language with Arabic in the classroom, and banned education to Libyans after the sixth grade. Beyond the sixth grade, Libyans could work only as laborers.

In 1928, Mussolini gave the task of the pacification of Libya to two of his top generals: Marshall Pietro Badoglio, the chief of staff who was appointed as the governor of Libya, and the brutal General Rodolfo Graziani, the architect of the reoccupation of Tripolitania and the western and southern regions of Fezzan. While he had been successful elsewhere, Graziani discovered that Barqa, the eastern region of Libya, posed the toughest challenge to the Italian conquest of Libya. The general faced a cohesive force of Barqa's tribesmen and merchants, forged from 70 years of education and mobilization by the Sanusiyya religious and social movement. Through their efforts, the Sanusiyya had brought together numerous tribes in an economically viable and culturally unified state. Under the Sanusiyya, taxes were levied on grain and animals, and on the trans-Sahara trade, that is on all caravans crossing Barqa, Cyrenaica to trade with Egypt. Importantly, the people of the eastern region shared an anti-colonial, pan-Islamic ideology. These economic and cultural forces cemented a unity in the eastern region that allowed Barqa's tribesmen to successfully resist Italian colonialism until 1932.

The volunteer-based native resistance movement that confronted General Graziani was led by a legendary, charismatic, 69 year old named 'Umar al-Mukhtar. The resistance's well-mobilized population included networks of spies, even inside Italian-controlled towns. Graziani estimated that the native guerrillas numbered approximately 3,000, and the number of guns, owned by Barqa's tribesmen, to be about 20,000. Unlike the Italian invaders, the Cyrenaicans were familiar with the geography of the Green Mountain valleys, caves, and trails; in 1931 alone, the guerrillas engaged in 250 attacks and ambushes on the Italian army. Italian colonial officials attempted first to bribe 'Umar al-Mukhtar, offering him a good salary and retirement. When he rejected the overture, Graziani moved to crush the resistance. The general's armies adopted a scorched-earth policy. This was compounded by cutting off the guerrillas' supplies with the construction of a 300 kilometer fence along the Libyan–Egyptian border, and then organizing a campaign to occupy Kufra, capital of the Sanusi order, deep in the desert. Graziani's army, including 20 airplanes and 5,000 camels, encountered fierce resistance by the Zuwayya tribe, but he succeeded in occupying Kufra on February 20, 1931.[19]

The success of the eastern Libyans in withstanding General Graziani's assaults forms the context for understanding why Mussolini ordered Badoglio, the colonial governor of Libya, and General Graziani to quell the resistance by any means necessary. The archival records show that the fascist state's strategy was clear concerning the destruction of the resistance, even if it meant killing its civilian social base. The fascists top three, Graziani, De Bono, and Badoglio responded by forcefully rounding up two-thirds of the civilian population of eastern Libya – an estimated 110,000 men, women, and children – and deporting them, by sea and on foot, to camps during the harsh winter of 1929. The deportation of the population emptied rural Barqa, and effectively cut off the resistance from its social base. Isolated on all sides and lacking supplies, the rebels gave up, especially after the capture and hanging of their leader, 'Umar al-Mukhtar, on September 12, 1931. He was 73 years old. Following the death of 'Umar al-Mukhtar, a majority of his aides were either arrested or put to death on September 24, 1932.[20]

The concentration camps

The policies of the Italian Fascist government were unprecedented in the history of African colonialism, but it is only recently that Western scholarship has acknowledged the forceful deportation of the rural population of Barqa, and the Libyans' confinement in concentration camps between 1929 and 1934. Historian Giorgio Rochat uncovered evidence, in a letter written from Governor Badoglio to General Graziani, dated June 20, 1930, that stated that the Italians were prepared for large-scale civilian deaths. Marshall Pietro Badoglio wrote,

> We must, above all, create a large and well-defined territorial gap between the rebels and the subject population. I do not conceal from myself the significance and the gravity of this action which may well spell the ruin of the so-called subject population.[21]

Until we find new evidence, Badoglio is the architect of the policy of "emptying" Barqa of its native population and the subsequent execution of the genocide by General Graziani.

The colonial state spent 13 million Italian liras on the construction of the camps. Double barbed wire fences surrounded them, food was rationed, and the pastureland was reduced and patrolled. Sixteen encircled camps

(Shabardag, the barbed wire) were constructed, varying in size and degree of brutality, outside towns such as Ain al-Ghazala, Diriyyana, Susa, al-Marj, al-Abyar, Benghazi, Sidi Khalifa, Suwani al-Tariya, al-Nufiliyya, Kuafiyya, and Ajdabiyya, as well as the largest and harshest camps of Agaila, Slug, Sidi Ahmad Magrun, and the Braiga. The terrible punishment camp, Agaila, was especially constructed for relatives of the rebel mujahidin.[22] In the five big camps, no prisoner was allowed outside except by restricted permit. Forced labor was common, and no serious medical aid was provided. Outside the camps, Graziani ordered the confiscation of all livestock, the main economic source for survival and livelihood. Most of the deaths occurred in the five concentration camps which I refer to as the "death camps."

For an independent seminomadic population, these conditions were devastating. As usual, the sick, elderly, and children were the most vulnerable victims of these conditions, especially because the death of most of the herds ensured the people's death by slow starvation. Evans-Pritchard, an expert on the tribes of Cyrenaica (Barqa), wrote,

> In this bleak country, in the summer of 1930, 80,000 men, women, and children, and 600,000 beasts were herded into the smallest camps possible. Hunger, disease, and broken hearts took a heavy toll of the imprisoned population. Bedouins died in a cage. Loss of livestock was also great, for the beasts had insufficient grazing near the camps on which to support life, and the herds, already decimated in the fighting are almost wiped out by the camps.[23]

With colonial archives still restricted and/or removed, there is little documentation of daily life inside the camps except for the oral history of the few Libyans who survived. Most scholars, including Evans-Pritchard, Rochat, Del Boca, and Labanca, agree that the camps decimated the population. Rochat summed up his research of Italian sources, writing,

> The fall of the [Barqa] population must be in small part attributed to war operations and, to a greater extent, to the conditions created by the Italian repression (hunger, poverty, and epidemics) and to the deportation of the people (transfer marches, death through malnutrition in the camps, epidemics, and inability to adapt to terrible new conditions).[24]

Estimates of the total deaths during the deportation process and interment in the camps range from 40,000 to 70,000. For now, I think the number is at least 60,000 based on the fact that the interned total number was not 80,000 but 110,000, and on the fact that many died during the deportation from the east to the desert of Sirte. All agree that people died in the camps due to shootings, hangings, disease, or starvation, but Libyan historian al-Barghathi places the death toll higher – at between 50 and 70,000. His estimate is based on Libyan Archives, and on oral interviews.[25] Yet, Del Boca notes a fact ignored by most historians: large numbers of elderly adults and children died during the deportation from the Marmarica and the Butnan in the Green Mountain region in eastern Libya to Sirte, in a grueling forced walk of 657 miles. The total death toll was made worse with the decimation of the herds. Rochat estimates that 90 to 95% of the sheep, goats, and horses, and possibly 80% of the cattle and camels, died by 1934. The destruction of the herds was intentional as a method to punish the people through targeting their social and cultural way of life. This annihilation of the animals contributed to famine and death among the seminomadic population.[26] I shall examine this mass killing next chapter.

This was not the first time that Italy had deported Libyans since taking over the country as a colony in 1911. Between 1911 and 1928, as many as 1,500 Libyans sympathetic to the anti-colonial resistance were exiled to Italian islands. People who led the Saif al-Nasr clan, as well as 14 men from Waddan, were exiled into the coastal town of Zuwara as prisoners in 1913 and 1928. Others who supported the resistance, such as the town of Hun, were collectively punished, perhaps to send a message to the rest of the population. The entire population of the oasis Hun in central Libya was deported to the coastal towns of Misurata and Khums in the aftermath of the battle of 'Afiyya on October 31, 1928. This was just a rehearsal for the massive deportation of the eastern region's population. The massive deportation of the majority of Cyrenaica's population was unprecedented. The agony suffered in the camps, along with the enduring loss of dignity and autonomy, has left deep psychological scars on Libya's national consciousness.[27]

The Libyans' colonial experience is unmatched, except perhaps by that in German South West Africa, Algeria, and in the Belgian Congo. Observers should note that the Libyan people's first major encounter with the West was as a colony under an Italian Fascist government. The facts that their experience, which includes exposure to genocide, has not been well studied or acknowledged, and that no military or civilian colonial officials were brought to trial, have not helped to heal the wounds of history.[28] I shall elaborate on this topic in the next chapter through both oral history and poetry.

In 1998, the Italian government made a joint public statement with the Libyan government acknowledging some responsibility for the Italian atrocities in Libya during the colonial period between 1911 and 1943.[29] While such an announcement was welcome, this vague and general statement fell short of facing the unresolved brutal history of genocide in colonial Libya. Italian Fascism committed crimes inside and outside Italy. Libya is the first and most brutal case, but people from Yugoslavia, Ethiopia, and Greece also experienced fascist oppression and internment. The study of Italian Fascist atrocities in Ethiopia and Yugoslavia are well known, but the Libyan case is still obscure. Full disclosure of the fascist archives must follow the 1998 admission of some Italian responsibility for what happened in Libya. Only then, can one talk of historical truth and reconciliation.

Recovering the oral history of the genocide: the legacy of folk poetry

The statistical records of the genocide are horrifying, and what is more significant, but missing from current scholarship, is the way that millions of Libyans have interpreted the memory of this genocide. During the last 15 years, I have searched for records of the people who experienced deportation or spent time in the concentration camps. Had they left diaries? Written memoirs? Did survivors of the deportation and camps remain alive, and, if so, how could I find them? I realized only a few were educat such as the poets Buhwaish and al-Ahlafi in the Sanusi lodges, schools and the High Institute at al-Jaghbub. As for written documentation, I found only a few published memoirs, but thanks to the Libyan Studies Center in Tripoli, many survivors of the camps were interviewed for a published collection called *The Oral History of the Jihad*. Since most Libyans during the colonial period were illiterate and relied on memory as a counter to the official state history, it is no exaggeration to state that some elders are walking libraries.[30] The main source of historical views and Libyan culture has been folk poetry. This should not be a surprise; widespread illiteracy dictates that oral traditions and poetry are highly valued in Libyan rural culture.[31] More importantly, in this rural culture, people express themselves through oral stories, proverbs, and the recitation and singing of poems and songs. For example, these modes of communication will be expressed during everyday life such as at weddings, the birth of a new child, burials, and collective mourning. My late mother would not answer a questions directly, but instead she would recite a poem or proverb and that was the way she was raised and communicated. Yet, one has to keep in mind that this cultural interaction is based on the values and philosophy of life that continued during colonialism and the modern nation-state, and that each generation reinterprets these values.

I was aware of the significance of poetry to moral and cultural beliefs, but it was only after reading the collected books of Libyan folk poetry written during the colonial period, that I realized that they offered the richest and the most illustrative source of Libyan colonial history, in particular pertaining to the camp internment years of 1929 through 1934. Among the most notable are published memoirs by Ibrahim al-Arabi al-Ghmari al-Maimmuni, who writes about his life in the Agaila (the most notorious concentration camp) and Saad Muhammad Abu Sha'ala, who also writes about life inside the camps.[32] These provide powerful testimony, along with works by the most outstanding poet of the period, Rajab Hamad Buhwaish al-Minifi, who was interned in the Agaila camp, and wrote the famous epic poem "Mabi-Marad" (I Have No Illness except Agaila Concentration Camp). Known by most Libyans, the poem is a brilliant and damning reaction to the horrors of the camp and the impact of killing and suffering on freedom-loving seminomads. To my delight, I also discovered women poets, such as Fatima 'Uthamn from Hun, who composed the poem "Kharabin Ya Watan" ("OurHomeland Ruined Twice"), and Um al-Khair Muhammad Abdaldiym, who was interned in the Braiga camp. These poets offer powerful testimonies concerning the views of the men and women who experienced uprooting, exile, and displacement. They suggest that the Libyans faced nothing less than a religious discrimination and

FIGURE 2.1 Photos of Libyan poets. From left to right: Um al-Khair, Fatima 'Uthamn, and Ahmad Rafiq al-Mahdawi
Author collection

war against their culture and way of life. Figure 2.1 shows photos of the three Libyan anti-colonial poets Um al-Khair Muhammad Abdaldiym, Fatima 'Uthamn, and Ahmad Rafiq al-Mahdawi.

The following summary is a new and original reconstruction of the history of the deportation and the concentration camps through the eyes of the Libyan people who experienced these events firsthand. The narratives focus on themes of the deportation experience and the daily life in the camps in relation to food, clothes, forced labor, hunger, disease, punishment, depression, death, mourning, and the struggle for survival. The Italian army counterinsurgency was based on collective punishment including destroying the material and social organization of the rebellious population and eventually being party to their annihilation by executing a genocide policy, as proven by the letters of the generals Badoglio and Graziani who were in charge of the colony.

The deportations and the Rihlan of tears

The forced walk, or shipping of people and their herds, from rural Cyrenaica, extended from Derna in the east to camps in the desolate desert of Sirte in northern central Libya. Tahir al-Zawi, a Libyan historian of that period, described the deportation of the people of Cyrenaica as the Day of Judgment described in the Qur'an: when people were resurrected from their graves in rags, skeletons to face God. As if those who were interned looked like the Qura'nic script of the Day of Judgment.[33] Al-Ghmari al-Maimmuni writes,

> We were forced on a ship in Benghazi without much food, and our women and children were crying and wailing. It was very cold winter and many of the children and women passed out. When we arrived at the Agaila, the wind was so strong that we could not get off and we had to sail to an island nearby. The following day we landed; the ship was so filthy due to seasickness.[34]

Salim Muftah Burwag al-Shilwi was only 13 years old when his family was deported from Darna by ship to Benghazi, and then to Zuwaitina. He wrote,

> As we arrived in Zuwaitina, the guards began to shove us to the shore. The hated military commander Col. Barilla of the Agaila camp gave a speech addressing the deportees: "You Abaidat tribe will be interned in the camps of Agaila and al-Braiga where you will die so we will have a stable Italian rule in Libya." Then he walked toward a young Libyan woman and touched her cheek, and said: "Your cheek is white right now but very soon it will be as black as a black servant's."[35]

These autobiographical documents and tidbits of oral history indicate that the aim of the fascist policy was the destruction of the culture and not just of individuals. It was a genocidal policy aiming to destroy the native people, institutions, language, culture, and property, with the goal of repopulating the region with a fascist culture and colonial settlers. Consequently, according to the Ottoman census of 1910, Tarabulus al-Gharb (the Ottoman name of Libya before 1911) had a population of 1.5 million. By 1951, Libya was one of the poorest countries in the world and its population had fallen to 1 million. Furthermore, by the midpoint of the twentieth century, the country's population included only 16 university graduates as the educated elite had been killed or forced to take refuge in exile. The forced march and deportation of the Libyan population of the eastern region is bigger, and yet similar to, the removal of 17,000 Cherokee Indians in January 17, 1839 by President Andrew Jackson, known as the Trail of Tears. (See Figure 2.2, a map of the deportation drawn by Yusuf Salim al-Barghathi). The Cherokee people were removed at gunpoint from their homeland in Tennessee and were forced to walk 1,200 miles. While there was an apology to the Japanese Americans who were interned after the Japanese attack on the American naval base at Pearl Harbor, there is no official recognition of the Indian genocide where many died mainly due to lack of immunity to new diseases between the sixteenth and the nineteenth centuries in North and South America. In addition, over 30 million buffalos were slaughtered by settlers and the army, and this contributed to the high death rate among Native American people.

Policing and daily life in the camps

The camp guards were Italian colonial soldiers from Eritrea and Libya. But, here it is also the time to recognize the fact that some Libyans collaborated and worked in the Italian army and the camps. I found the names of the capos (middle-level native police heads) in the camps. This topic is still taboo in postcolonial Libyan culture and nationalist historiography. Eritrean *Ascari (Askari)* were Italian soldiers, subjects who were recruited to serve as cheap military labor in Libya beginning with the conquest in 1911. Also, by 1929, the Italian colonial state had found some Libyan collaborators who worked as guides, guards, spies, advisors, and soldiers.[36] The Italian army was made of Italian officers and Eritrean and Libyan colonial soldiers. They restricted the daily life of their civilian prisoners to cleaning, loading and unloading

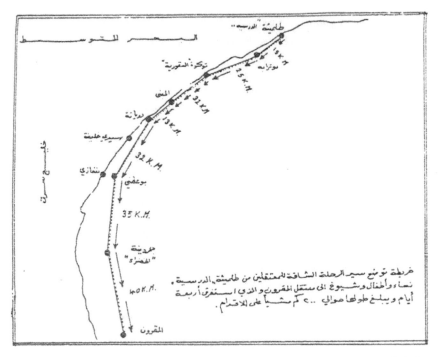

FIGURE 2.2 A map of the forced deportation drawn by Historian Yusuf Salim al-Barghathi, 1983

Reproduced with permission by the Libyan Studies Center, Tripoli

goods, collecting wood, forced labor on major projects, taking care of the ill, and burying the dead. All of the interned had to salute the Italian flag and witness the execution of those accused of collaborating in any way with the anti-colonial resistance. Any hint of disapproval or failure to salute the commander or the Italian flag meant verbal abuse and physical punishment by whipping and confinement. The poet Um al-Khair described the guards as "kinsmen of the devil."[37] Salim al-Shilwi recounts a time in the Agaila camp when a man who failed to salute the commander was whipped 100 times. Then, when he refused to say, "Long live the king of Italy," he was whipped 700 more times.[38]

Food and clothes

Food was scarce; survivors recount that they occasionally received rice, but mainly subsisted on a pound of poor-quality barley doled out each week. With the confiscation or death of their herds, the interned suffered malnutrition and death. Salim al-Shilwi remembered: "Many of us in the Agaila camp ate grass, mice, and insects; others searched for grain in animal dung to stay alive."[39] Ali Muhammad Sa'ad al-'Ibidi noted: "At one time we counted about one hundred and fifty deaths (mostly the elderly and children) and the cemetery shows

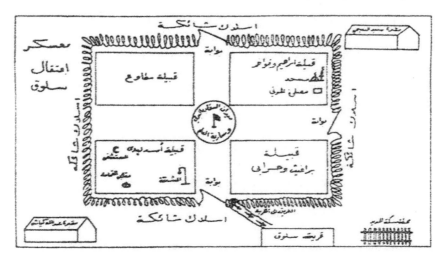

FIGURE 2.3 Slug concentration camp as imagined by a survivor Mahmud al-Ta'ib
Reproduced with permission by the Libyan Studies Center, Tripoli

the evidence."[40] Muhammad Muftah 'Uthman said the tribe of 'Abadlla alone
lost 500 people to starvation.[41]

Without the means to buy clothes, many of the interned were forced to wear
the same clothes they had worn for three years. Their garments became rags,
serving as a further humiliation to rural women who value their modesty in
dress.[42] Poet Muhammad Yasin Dawi al-Maghribi captured this loss of dignity
in his poem "I Saw a Shaykh," in which he described the status of a well-
dressed and respected elderly chief, who ended up in the camp with dirty, torn
clothes, and how his degradation was reflected in his face and body
language.[43] One survivor of the camps said that in the few cases where men
and women got married, the dowry was a quarter of a pound of sugar.[44]

Once again, the poem that kept the memory of the internment alive for
many is "Mabi-Marad" by poet Rajab Buhawish al-Minifi. During and after
the period of internment, his epic poem was memorized and recited all over
the country by generations of Libyans and, after independence in 1951, it was
aired by the new Libyan radio; even today it is recited and posted on the internet. The poem captures the humiliation of and the harshness toward women,
who courageous *badawi* (nomadic) men were supposed to protect. It seems he
witnessed rape but felt shame saying it openly due to traditions. The poem is
viewed by the people as a record and as speaking truth to the power and alternative history. Also, it is eloquent and recited as a mourning ceremony and
hence it provides a countervoice and cultural recovery and healing:

> I have nothing except the dangers of the roadwork
> My bare existence,
> Returning home without a morsel to move down a gullet.

Whips lash us before our women's eyes,
Rendering us useless, degraded,
Not even a matchstick among us to light a wick,

Nothing ails me except the beating of women,
Their skins bared,
No hour leaves them undisturbed,

Not a day without slander heaped on our noble women,
Calling them sluts,
And other foulness that spoils a well-bred ear.

I have no illness except the hearing of abuse,
Denial of pleas,
And the loss of those who were once eminent,

And women laid down naked, stripped
For the least of causes,
Trampled and ravished, acts that no words deign describe.

I have no illness except about the saying of "Beat them,"
No pardon,
And "With the sword extract their labor,"

The company of people unfamiliar to us,
A low life indeed
Except for God's help, my hands are stripped of their cunning.

I have no illness except the suppression of hardship and disease,
Worry over horses ...
And work for meager wages as the whips cry out lashing.

What a wretched life,
And when they're done with men, they turn on the women.[45]

Forced labor

Forced labor was another aspect of concentration camp life. The interned Libyans were compelled to work on the construction of a fence between Libya and Egypt, and on paving a new coastal highway between Sirte and Benghazi. Punishment, hunger, the lack of good hygiene, and minimal medical assistance combined to spread disease, and eventually led to high death rates. Some people went mad, and others fell into depression.[46] The poet Um al-Khair asked God to end this suffering for the Muslims and either let them die or help them defeat the Italian colonialists. While most prisoners eventually died in the camps from hunger and disease, those who survived carried with them mourning, sorrow, and the loss of human dignity and autonomy.[47]

Poet Rajab Hamad Buhwaish al-Minifi, who, as mentioned earlier, survived the Agaila concentration camp, expressed this loss of dignity and autonomy, probably more eloquently than any other poet in colonial Libya. His epic poem "Dar al-Agaila" ("Under Such Conditions") deserves translation and special attention. He belonged to the same tribe as the leader of the resistance, 'Umar al-Mukhtar, and to understand his poem, his background must be considered. He belonged to a tribe that was autonomous, prior to the Italian conquest in 1911. He did not talk about individualism and personal salvation, but reacted as a member of a collective kinship community that values chivalry, freedom, generosity, dignity, and the open space of nomadic life. Al-Minifi belonged to a culture that developed a system in opposition to collaboration that thrived under the Sanusiyya social movement for a long time prior to, and after, the colonial conquest of Libya. He was also an educated man, a religious teacher who was educated in the Sanusi Zawayya and the Higher Institute at Jaghbub.[48] He started his poem by stating that he was not ill, except for the illness of living in Agaila and its impact, especially the loss of beloved kinsmen and women:

I have no illness except this endless aging,
Loss of sense and dignity,
And the loss of good people, who were my treasure,

Yunes who rivals al-Hilali,
Throne of the tribe,
Mihimmad and 'Abdulkarim al-Ezaila,
And Buhssain, his sweet countenance and open hand,
And al-Oud and the likes of him,
Lost now without farewell to burden our day.

I have no illness except the loss of young men,
Masters of tribes,
Picked out like date fruit in daylight,

Who stood firm-chested against scoundrels,
The blossoms of our households,
Whose honor will shine despite what the ill-tongued say?

I have no illness except the absence of my thought,
My scandalized pride,
And the loss of Khiyua Mattari's sons,

Moussa and Jibril, sweet companions of night dirges,
Masters of horses, tamers of wild camels,
Unharmed by rumors calling them cowardly, meek.

I have no illness except . . .
Being imprisoned by scoundrels,
And the lack of a cohort to complain to when wronged,

The lack of those who rule with fairness,
Evenness nonexistent,
Evil leaning hard on good, dominant.

I have no illness except my daughters that serve in despicable labour,
The lack of peace
Loss of friends' death has taken.

The capture of Al-Atati, Azir al Nussi,
Aiyez as well,
Who soothes the heart in forlorn desiccated hours.

I have not illness except the loss of my herds,
And I'm not counting,
Even while the taker has no remorse, no pangs of guilt

They bring nothing except rule by torture
And the long. . . .
And the tongue rived and sharpened with pounding abuse.

I have not illness except the lack of defenders,
The softness of my words
The humiliation of the noble-named,

The loss of my gazelle-like unbridled,
Swift-limbed,
Fine-featured one like a minted coin of gold.

No strength, will, or effort to lift these burdens.
Of our lives we're ready
To absolve ourselves lest death's agent come.

Nothing ails me except the bad turn of my stars,
The theft of my property,
The tightness and misery of where I lie down to rest.

The fearsome horseman who on days of fray
Shielded his women folk
Now begs, straggling after a tailless monkey.

Every day I rise complaining of subjugation,
My spirit disgraced,
And like a woman I can't break my chains.

I have no illness except the bent shape of my life,
My limpid, wilted tongue.
I would not tolerate shame and now shame has overtaken me.

At the end of the poem, the poet asks God for solace:

Only God is eternal. The guardian of Mjamam is gone.
The oppressor's light
Has befallen us, stubborn, unrelenting

If not for the danger, I would say what I feel,
Raise him noble,
Expound my praise of him, sound the gratitude we owe.[49]

This epic poem highlights most prominently a theme we also find in many poems on the topic: the trials of internment and displacement are illness and enduring suffering. This poem strikes the reader as a significant alternative to death – a spirit of resistance, anguish, and recovery. The only rival to al-Minifi's brilliant poem is Fatima 'Uthamn's poem "Kharabin Ya Watan" ("Our Homeland Ruined Twice"), which she composed at the young age of 20 years old after she saw 19 men hanged by the Italian army in her hometown, Hun, as punishment for supporting the anti-colonial resistance in 1929. The rest of the people in her town were deported to the northern coastal towns of Misurata and Khums. Since the 1930s, many younger Libyans – especially in the central and eastern regions – have passed on their family's collective memory orally, from one generation to the next. Owing to the resilience of this oral tradition, Libyans have developed a deep distrust of colonialism, the central state, and Western policies in general.[50]

Critics of Italian neofascism focus on the Italian Fascist regime's anti-Semitic laws, but many commentators note that anti-Semitism developed late under the Italian Fascists, and then only under pressure from Nazi Germany in 1938. It is this fact that produces the myth that Italian Fascism was a more moderate form of fascism, ignoring the atrocities perpetuated in Libya and Ethiopia. Another 100,000 to 200,000 Libyans were forced into exile in Egypt, Chad, Tunisia, Turkey, Palestine, Syria, and Algeria. In 1935, the fascist colonial state drafted 20,000 young Libyans, including some young men who were interned with their parents in the concentration camps, to fight as a cheap labor force in the conquest of Ethiopia. This was hardly a new policy; earlier, in 1911, the colonial state drafted over 20,000 Eritreans as soldiers to invade Libya. The next chapter will present and analyze in-depth the survivors' narrative and their culture before and during the internment.

Notes

1 For a critical review of the field see Ruth Ben-Ghiat "A Lesser Evil? Italian Fascism in and the Totalitarian Equation" in Helmut Dubiel and Gabriel Motzkin eds, *The Lesser Evil: Moral Approaches to Genocide*, (New York: Routledge, 2004) pp 137–153; Adrian Lyttelton, "What is Fascism," *The New York Review of Books*,

(October 21, 2004) 33–36; and Robert Bosworth, *Italian Dictatorship*, (London: Arnold, 1998) 3–4.

2 John P. Diggins, *Mussolini and Fascism: The View from America*, (Princeton: Princeton University Press, 1972), 6.

3 Ibid., 241.

4 Gregory Dale Black, *The United States and Italy*, (Lawrence: University of Kansas Press, 1974) 13–14.

5 On Italian historiography see Peter Gran, *Beyond Eurocentrism: A New World View of Modern History*, (Syracuse: Syracuse University Press, 1996), 88–121. Also on Italian Orientalism see Anna Baldinetti, *Orieutalismo E Colonialismo La ricerca di cousenso in Egitto Per L'impesadi Libia*, (Roma: Insititutio Per L'Oriente "C.A. Nallino," 1997).See also, Patrick Bernhard, "Renarrating Italian Fascism: New Directions in the Historiography of European Dictatorship," *Conemporary European History*, 23 (2014), 151–163.

6 Diggins, *Mussolini and Fascism*, 243, Stanley Kauffmann "Under Florentine Skies," *New Republic* 2 220:23, June 7, 1999, .30.

7 Alan Cowell, "The Ghost of Mussolini Keeps Rattling His Chains" *The New York Times*, (June 1, 1994) A3, James O. Jackson, "Fascism Lives," *Time*, (June 6, 1994), and Ian Fisher, "New Italian Minister Sheds Far-Right Image," *The New York Times*, (November 19, 2004. For a sympathetic view of fascism see Renzo De Felice, *Interpretations of Fascism*, (Cambridge: Harvard University Press, 1977), on the historiography of Nazism see Ian Kershaw, *The Nazi Dictatorship*, (London: Edward Arnold, 1993).

8 "Duce with the Laughing Face," *People Magazine*, (April 27, 1992) 70.

9 Hannah Arendt, *Eichmann in Jerusalem*, (London: Penguin Books, 1994 [1963]) 178–180, and her other book *The Origins of Totalitarianism*, (New York: Harcourt, Brace and Jovanovich, 1973) 2, 5, 7, 8.

10 Victoria de Grazia, "Will IL Duce's Successors Make the Facts Run on Time?" *The New York Times*, (May 14, 1994) 21.

11 For a critique of eurocentrism see Samir Amin, *Eurocentrism*, (New York: Monthly Review Press, 1980); and Carl Levy's comprehensive review of the comparative analysis of fascist movements but which is still centered on Europe, "Fascism, National Socialism and Conservatives in Europe, 1914–1945," *Contemporary European History*, 8:1 (1999), 97–126. The Libyan case was overlooked in even recent and revisionist books on forgotten genocide, René Lemarchand, ed., *Forgotten Genocides*, (Philadelphia: University of Pennsylvania Press, 2011), Brian McLaren, *Architecture and Tourism in Italian Colonial Libya*, (Seattle: University of Washington Press, 2000), and Israel Gershoni, ed., *Arab Reponses to Fascism*, (Austin: Texas University Press, 2014).

12 See David Forgacs ed., *The Antonio Gramsci Reader*, (New York: University of New York Press, 2000), 112–113, 149.

13 Frantz Fanon, *The Wretched of the Earth*, (London: Penguin, 1967 (first published 1961)), 75, and Aimé Césaire, *Discourses on Colonialism*, (New York: Pantheon, 1988) 12.

14 Mahmood Mamdani, *Good Muslim, Bad Muslim*, (New York: Pantheon Books, 2004), 7.

15 See my book *The Making of Modern Libya: State Formation, Colonialization and Resistance* second edition, (New York: State University of New York Press, 2009), 135.

16 An early analytical analysis of the brutal fascist policies in Cyrenaica is made by E.E. Evans-Pritchard who was writing intelligence reports for the British army in 1945. See his book *The Sanusi of Cyrenaica*, (Oxford: Oxford University Press, 1949), 160–89. For an overview of the critical Italian scholarships on fascism see Nicola Labanca, "Internamento Coloniale Italino" in Colstantino Di Sante, ed., *I campi di Concentratamento in Italia*, (Milan: Franco Angeli, 2001), 40–67.

17 Nicola Labanca, *L'Oltremare: Storica dell'espansione coloniale italiana*, (Bologna: Societa editrice il Mulino, 2002).

18 For a recent study of modern genocide see Robert Gellately and Ben Kiernin, eds, *The Specter of Genocide: Mass Murder in Historical Perspective*,(Cambridge: Cambridge University Press, 2003). For the earliest analysis of genocide in Italian scholarship in Libya see Giorgio Rochat, *Il Colonialismo Italiano*, (Turin: Loescher, 1973), Angelo Del Boca, *Gli Italiani in Libia: Dal Fascismo a Gheddafi*, (Roma-Barie: Laterza, 1988), Eric Salerno, *Genocido in Libia*, (Milan: Sugarco edizioni, 1979), Gustavo Ottolenghi, *Gli Italiani E il Colonialiso I campi di detenzione italiani in Africa*, (Milano: Sugarco edizioni, 1997) 149–182, Michael Palumbo, ed., *Human Rights: Meaning of History*, (Lane/Malabar, Florida: Robert E. Krieger, 1982) 71–75, and Federico Cresti, *Non Desiderara la terra d'altri*, (Roma: Carlucci editore, 2011) 83–122.

19 I dealt with this question ten years ago in chapter 5 of my book *The Making of Modern Libya*, 103–140. For a detailed record of the atrocities of Italian colonialism in Libya see the book of the exiled Libyan Anti-Fascist Committee, *Ha'iyat Tahrir Libia, Al-Fadi' al-Sud al-Humr: Min Safahat al-'Isti'imar al-Itali fi Libia* [*The Red Black Horrors: Pages of Italian Colonialism in Libya*], (Cairo: Matba'at al-karnak, 1933, second edition, 1948).

20 See the collection of essays on the repression of the Libyan resistance and the concentration camps of 1929–1939 by Enzo Santarelli, Giorgio Rochat, Romano Rainero, and Luigi Goglia, *Omar al-Mukhtar* translated by John Gilbert (London: Darf Publishers, 1986).

21 See Rochat's seminal study,"The Repression of Resistance in Cyrenaica (1927–1931)" in Santarelli et al. eds, Ibid., 73.

22 See Santarelli, "The Ideology of The Libyan Reconquest," Ibid., 11–34, and Rochat, "The Repression," Ibid., 72–79.

23 Evans-Pritchard, *The Sanusi*, 189.

24 Rochat, "The Repression," 96–77 and his earlier article "IL genocide Cirenaico," *Belfagor*, 35:4 (1980), 449–454.

25 Yusuf Salim al-Barghathi, "Al-Mu'taqalat Wa al-Adrar al- Najma 'An al-Ghazwual-Itali" ("The Concentration Camps and their Impact on Libya") in Aghil al-Barbar ed., *'Umar al-Mukhtar*, (Tripoli: Center for Libyan Studies, 1983), 146–147.

26 Del Boca, *Gli Italiani in Libia II*, (Roma-Barie: Laterza, 1988), 175–232.

27 For a biography and full text of the poet Fatima 'Uthman see 'Abdallah A. Zagub, "Shahadat al-Mar'a Fi Zamin al-Harb," ["A Woman as an Eyewitness to War"] *Al-Thaqafa-al-'Arabiyya*, (1980), 85–117.

28 Ben-Ghait, "A Lesser Evil," 140.

29 I am grateful to Dr. Mohamed Jerary who informed me about the Italian government's official statement acknowledging some responsibility for colonial crimes in 1998. The statement was general and one brief page. See "Italy–Libya statement," BBC News (July 10, 1998).

30 The Libyan Studies Center has collected oral histories of the colonial period and was advised in 1977 by historian Jan Vansina of the University of Wisconsin, Madison. I was lucky to have access to this collected oral history at the Center's "Oral History Archives" in Tripoli, Libya.

31 For an introduction to the method of oral traditions and history see Jan Vansina, *Oral Traditions: A Study in Historical Methodology*, (Chicago: Aldine Publishing Company, 1956), and *Oral Traditions and History*, (Madison: University of Wisconsin Press, 1985).

32 Al-Maimuni, *Dhiqrayyat Mu'taqalat al-Agaila* [*Memoirs of the Agaila Concentration Camp*], (Tripoli: Libyan Studies Centre, 1995, and Saad Muhammad Abu Sha'ala, *Min Dakhil al-Mu'taqalat* [*From inside the Concentration Camps*], (Tripolli: Al-Munshaa al-'Aamma Lilnshar, 1984).

33 Tahir al-Zawi, *'Umar al-Mukhtar*, (Tripoli: Maktabt al-Firjani, 1970) 166.

34 Al-Maimuni, *Dhiqrayyat*, 68.

35 Salim Muftah al-Shilwi, interviewed by Yusuf Salim al-Barghathi, *Oral History Archives*, (Tripoli: Libyan Studies Center, June 25, 1981).

36 Ibid.

37 Abdali Abu 'Ajailla, *Um al-Khair: The Poet of the Braiga Concentration Camp*, (Benghazi: Al-Maktaba al-Wataniyya, no date) 73.

38 Salim al-Shilwi, interview, 1981.

39 Salim al-Shilwi, interview, 1981.

40 Al-Barghathi "Al-Mu'taqalat," 146, al-Maimuni, *Dhiqrayyat*, 71, See also al-Shilwi, Ibid.

41 'Uthman 'Abdulsalam al-'Abar, Rabab Adham, ed., *Oral History,* vol 29, (Tripoli: Libyan Studies Center, 1991) 228, and Muhammad 'Abdalqadir al-'Abdalli in Abu-Sha'ala, *Min Dakhil*, 43.

42 Shilwi, interview, 1981.

43 Al-Hindiri, Sa'id 'Abdrahman and Al-Kubti, Salim, eds, *Qusa'id al-Jihad Vol. I [Poems of the Jihad]*, (Tripoli: Libyan Studies Centre, 1984) 180–1811. On the study of oral folk poetry in Africa and the Middle East see the pioneering studies Said S. Samatar, *Oral History and Somali Nationalism*, (Cambridge: Cambridge University Press, 1982) and Steven C. Caton, *Peak of Yemen I Summon*, (Berkeley: University of California Press, 1999).

44 Khalifa Jadallah, interviewed by Yusuf Salim al-Barghathi, *Oral History Archives*, (Tripoli: Libyan Studies Center, June 24, 1981).

45 See Hussain Nasib al-Maliki, *Sha'ir Mu'taqal al- Agaila [The Poet of the Agaila Concentration Camp]*, (Benghazi: no date).

46 Muhammad 'Abdalqadir al-'Abdalli in Abu-Sha'alla, *Min Dahkil*, 48.

47 See Abu 'Ajailla Um al-Khair, *The Poet*, 26–27.

48 For a biography of poet Rajab al-Mnifi see al-Maliki, *Sha'ir Mu'taqal*, 4, 10, 41–51.

49 For a full text of the poem/epic see al-Maliki, *Sha'ir Mu'taqal*, 41–51.

50 One positive development after the Italian statement acknowledging some responsibility for the impact of the colonization of Libya in 1998, is the new collaboration between Italian and Libyan scholars. This collaboration had been between the Libyan Studies Center in Tripoli and the Instituto Italiano per L'Africa E L'Oriente. The result of this collaboration are three academic conferences of which two were published recently. See Francesco Sulpizi and Salaheddin Hasan Sury, eds., *Primo Convegno su gli esiliate Libici nel periodo Coloniale* 28-29 Otobre 2000, Roma, 2002, and Anna Baladinetti, ed., *Modern and Contemporary Libya: Sources and Historiographies*, (Roma: Institito Italiano per L'Africa E L'Oriente, 2003). The Italian government promised to help Libya with the maps of the land mines and the fate of many unknown exiled Libyans in Italy between 1911 and 1943. The fall of the regime in 2011and the election of a conservative coalition in Italy last year encouraged the new government to intervene in the Libyan civil war using the problem of illegal immigrants as a rationale.

3

"WE DIED BECAUSE OF SHAR, EVIL MY SON"

Survivors' stories of death and trauma in the camps

For Libyan nomads the camel is sacred animal and most valued friend. When he dies they morn his passing as if he was human.

Ibrahim al-Koni, a Libyan novelist, 2018

Ruined twice, our home land.
All have left you, some fled in exile
and others hung or murdered.
Poet Fatima 'Uthamn, 1929

A survivor told me a moving story of a woman with two children who was punished by whipping and then tied to the center pole at Agaila camp for the whole day. She asked a man to help her at night. He came closer to her and found the two children with her, a toddler clinging to her body and a baby whom she held despite the fact she was tied to the pole. She asked the man to press her breast, so the baby could drink, and he did. In a different situation, an old man was lying in the shadow of a tent, but a line of ants was on his arm. When a passing boy tried to remove the ants, the old man said not to. Only later did the boy realize the old man wanted to keep the ants because they were carrying grain from the camp supply store. These are not funny tales but the stories of people facing death.

The survivors of the camps talked about other events, which contributed to their explanations of why so many died in the four big camps. The Italian army did not provide the interned with medicine and clothes. Thousands of people had only one pair of clothes, no shoes, and did not bathe for three years to the point that fleas and infections became a widespread condition among the interned and made them susceptible to diseases such as smallpox, typhus, and blindness. Muhammad 'Usman al-Shami was 11 years old when he was interned with his mother at the notorious Agaila camp. He had one shirt for three years and no shoes. He recounted that because people had no soap for baths for that period, their clothes became infected with lice and bed-bugs to the point that his mother decided to take his rag of a shirt and boil it in water to kill the lice and the bugs.

Haj Muhammad Idris al-Shilmani (Magrun camp) said, "What happened to us did not happen to anybody, my dear." Harun Abd al-'Aziz Mustafa (Abyar camp) said, "The Italians took our property and animals, and made us desti-tute." 'Atiyya Mima al-Lafi (Agaila camp) recalled, "We died because of Shar/evil, and marad/illness. They wanted us dead. Many people died because of sadness and depression." Haja Bahiya Hamad al-Abaidi (Braiga camp) said, "They wanted to wipe us out, exterminate us. We the 'Abaidat were decimated in the war and the Braiga concentration camp." She added, "[B]ecause of our suffering, we wished death" and if she found the Italian camp officer Barilla in front of her again, she would beat him with a stick. She then simply added, "Thank God Libya returned anew." By this she meant, thank God our country Libya became free from colonialism and we are independent.[1] This vivid living communal history is what I discovered after I started my fieldwork, trav-eled around the country, and interviewed many of the survivors. It is as if the hidden voices challenge and talk back face-to-face with the official Italian colonial and the postcolonial Libyan states after 1951.

The policies set forth under Italian Fascists were aimed at targeting the resistance of eastern Libya, including the people who supported it with food andarms, and fighters who protected it and spied on the army. This colonial policy was designed by two generals who stated their intention to intern the civil population. They were the governor of Libya, General Marshall Pietro Badoglio, who was Mussolini's chief of staff, and the ruthless General Rodolfo Graziani. In 1928, El Duce ordered them to carry out the task of defeating the resistance using strategies including genocide and mass murder. Yet, the fas-cists were not the first colonists to use brutal policies of exiling, executing, and imprisoning the people of Libya. The so-called "liberal" Italian colonial-ists, who invaded the country in October 1911, committed massacres and exiled and imprisoned thousands of Libyans inside Libya and the southern Ital-ian islands in 1911, 1915, and 1930.

In short, the policy of internment is just one aspect of a more comprehensive strategy to crush the resistance by targeting its social base, along with brutal policies such as executing, confiscating land, poisoning and burning harvests, destroying livestock, and building a barbed wire fence along the Egyptian border to make eastern Libya a de facto prison, or camp. Thus, Benito Musso-lini, Marshall Pietro Badoglio, Emilio De Bono, and Rodolfo Graziani were the main architects of the internment and genocide. These fascist leaders were clear and blunt about their genocidal intention to crush the resistance and its social base by using any means, even if it meant the destruction of the whole population of Barqa. The genocide was designed to crush the resistance in order to accomplish the major fascist goal of taking the land for Italian settlers. Consequently, after the removal of the native population their land was giving to Italian settlers' with a first wave of 20,000 who arrived in the fall of 1938. This was the larger demographic plan. Fascist settler colonialism in Libya became linked to genocidal policy.

This chapter will examine the following topics: the deportation plan and the trail of tears, named Rihlan, as remembered by the interned; the destruction of 600,000 head of livestock; the reactions of the interned based on their social class, gender, age, and regional background; narratives selected from the five camps of the culture, poetry of trauma, and grieving in the camps; and finally what happened after the defeat of the resistance and the closing of the camps in late 1933 and early 1934.

The two central features of the culture are orality and poetic communication. I would argue that, from their childhood, rural Libyans learned to absorb oral traditions and poetry. They found it necessary to remember to continue to spread their history of oppression, so that it would not be forgotten. I remember that my own mother and grandmother cited oral poetry all the time. We were presented with poetry through schools, radio, and news. Poetry was introduced and taught in Libyan society, as it was deeply embedded in our culture. Children play a game called "mutarahat," like a poetic debate, reciting poetry by using the end of the last poem to start another. In short, poetry is valued both at home and in public, evidenced in schools, in wedding celebrations, and local gatherings. Consequently, the survivors were asked to recite entire poems – including the details of people who were interned, their names, ages, and personalities. The ones who fell along the way to the camps, were exiled, or starved to death, were all remembered by the survivors, their children, and their grandchildren.

Forced deportation and the trails of Rihlan

The Italian archival record is silent on this subject of deportation, as we found only one report about the deportation of the 'Awaqir tribe to the camp of Slug.[2] The oral history of the interned and the survivors, however, provides us with a detailed and specific narrative of this horrific uprooting from as far as the Egyptian borders and the region of Marmarica (known in Arabic as the Batnan) in the east and the Green Mountain to the harsh desert of Sirte (where the desert and sea meet). Sirte is characterized by its minimal trees, water, and natural shelter. The distance was not a straight road but had many turns and stops. Roughly, it was 1,100 kilometers from Saloum to the camps of Agaila and Braiga. The deported population refers to this time as "al-Rihlan." The majority of those affected by the deportation and internment policy were the seminomads and nomad tribesmen who were organized through the Sanusi order and the leadership of 'Umar al-Mukhtar in an integrated socioeconomic and cultural system. Only a small part of the urban population of the cities and the populations of the coastal towns of Barqa were targeted by the Italian policy. Consequently, the vast majority of the resisting population was interned in the four punishment camps, while the remaining nine camps were not as harsh as the infamous camps of Agaila, Braiga, Al-Magrun, and Slug. Consequently, the most horrific deaths occurred in these four punishment camps, where 65% of the deported were interned. It is not that surprising that relatives of the resistance fighters or mujahidin were interned in Agaila and Braiga camps. And when al-Mukhtar was captured, there was a collective mourning and depression in the camps, as he was hanged at Slug camp in front of 20,000 interned civilians to send a terrifying message to the native people.

Colonial soldiers and the policing of the camps

The Italian army, which executed the deportation plan in 1929 and 1930, consisted of Italian officers and soldiers, as well as Askari colonial soldiers, mostly from Eretria, and Libyan soldiers called Banda. In Libya, people called Italian colonial soldiers from Eretria the "Massuā" in reference to the port Massawa. Askari, or in Italian *ascari,* is a name that originated in Arabic and means a soldier, but in colonial Africa this word has a specific meaning: a native who became a colonial soldier. All colonial states, including Germany, France, Britain, and Spain, had their own colonial soldiers who were issued not only in Africa but also in Europe and thousands of them died during the two great wars.

In the Italian army the majority of the colonial soldiers came from Eritrea, the first Italian colony in Africa, while some Libyans serving in the Italian colonial army were even called Banda in Arabic, an Italian word meaning a military band. The Italian army used colonial native soldiers for various reasons, such as the fact that it is cheaper to pay them than Italian white soldiers, that the army can avoid a public opinion backlash inside Italy when soldiers die in battles, and that native colonial soldiers are adaptable to the ecology and the geography of the colony. Libyan native colonial soldiers, Banda, collaborated with the Italian colonial state for a variety of complex factors. Not aware of the whole concept of collaboration, they joined the Italian army because of economic needs, or an interest to get even with their rival either under the Ottoman state before 1911 or during the time of conflict over land and power. The Massuā colonial soldiers came from the first Italian colony in East Africa in 1869; this colony became a source of cheap labor in the Italian colonial army in Libya after 1911. The Italians recruited thousands of Eritrean, Somali, and Yemini in the colonial army. This was not surprising, as German, French, and British colonial armies recruited colonial soldiers to fight with them in Africa, Asia, and Europe during World Wars I and II. The vast majority of the Askari in the Italian army was Christian and was mobilized to fight Muslims in Libya. The first Italian colony of Eretria provided between 60,000 and 150,000 colonial soldiers who served in the Italian colonial conquest and occupation of Libya and Ethiopia between 1911 and 1943.[3] This colonial policy continued in the 1930s when colonial soldiers policed and guarded the camps, and the orphaned children of the interned were recruited into the army and used later in the invasion of Ethiopia in 1936. The Libyan colonial soldiers were led by Akif Msayk, an officer from the western town of Ghiryan, and before him the Amazigh notable Yusuf Khirbish.

The critical phase of forced deportation, while silenced in the Italian colonial sources, has been kept alive and remembered in detail by the people who survived the internment and by young children, who memorized some of the folk poetry from the camps. These factors are crucial in clarifying the history of the rounding up of civilians for deportation, understanding why they were deported, characterizing the deportees' encounters with the Italian colonial army, and, finally, understanding what happened to the deported during the long trail of tears and fear that brought them from as far as the Egyptian borders, as was the case of the Marmarica tribes and the 'Abaidat of the Green Mountain who walked for 1,100 kilometers, and others from the rest of the region who traveled either by foot, camel, or old ships, to the harsh desert of Sirte.

The available Italian archival sources indicate that Mussolini pressed for a defeat of the eastern resistance in Libya, but, according to Angelo Del Boca, it was Libyan colonial governor Marshall Pietro Badoglio who came up with the actual genocidal plan for the "Cyrenaica problem." The task of executing this final solution of crushing the resistance using all violent tools was given to the most ruthless Italian general, Rodolfo Graziani, the vice colonial governor of Cyrenaica. Italian historian Rochet argued that the fate of the Libyan civilians was sealed the minute Graziani was appointed as executor of this genocidal plan.[4] Marshall Pietro Badoglio (1871–1956) was Mussolini's chief of staff between 1925 and 1940 and became the governor of Libya between 1928 and 1933. He and his deputy, General Graziani, were in charge of the mass killing in Barqa. One has to add the name of a third general Emilio de Bono, Minister of Colonies, as well. Mussolini instructed Governor Badoglio to crush the resistance at any price. Badoglio came up with the idea of concentration camps, as his significant letter ordering his deputy Graziani, the governor of Cyrenaica, shows very clearly on June 20, 1930. The letter about the extermination plan reads very clearly "now the cause has been set, and one must carry it out to the end, even if the entire population of Cyrenaica must perish."[5] General Graziani (1882–1955) is another top colonial military officer who served in all Italian colonies including Libya. He had earlier gained notoriety in Libya in his repression of the resistance in Fezzen, and was named the "butcher of Fezzen" when he used airplanes, mobile tanks, and even poisoned gas to defeat the resistance. Libyan historians of the period call him "Safaah Libya," the assassin of Libya. He was appointed as governor of Barqa in 1929. He executed the deportation and the mass killing in the concentration camps.

After Libya he was tasked to be the viceroy of Ethiopia where he continued the brutal policy against civilians that he had mastered in Libya, including the use of poison gas, collective punishment killing, and concentration camps. Both generals continued to be top military leaders of the fascist state until its end. Badoglio collaborated with the Allies and became prime minster in 1944. He never faced war crime charges. Graziani was faithful to fascism and even became a minister of defense in the German puppet Italian Social Republic in Salo. He was not prosecuted by the UN War Crimes Commission, but. in 1948, Graziani was convicted by an Italian court, and was sent to prison for 19 years for collaboration with the Nazis – but not for his role in the genocide in Libya and the other massacres in Ethiopia after 1935. However, he was released after four months. He defended his actions and the fascist atrocities in three of his books and supported the neofascist party until his death in 1955. The oral history presents some interesting notions about who came up with the idea of Mu'taqalat. Here rests the main problem of the scholarship on "moderate" Italian Fascism: the uncritical acceptance of colonial archives. If one reads the archives as facts, as the widely influential Italian historian and biographer of Mussolini Renzo De Felice did, then you would accept the assumptions and claims of the fascism and colonialism as a positive and modernizing stage of history.

The oral history collected on that period in Arabic reveals some new information. Bearing in mind that fascist authorities sealed the operation from Western media and instead made a huge propaganda campaign about disciplining the wild nomads and seminomads, eastern Libyan tribesmen, the fanatical resistance, and outlaws. Some survivors indicated that they were punished because one Libyan collaborator, al-Sharif al-Ghariani, who was an advisor to the Italian state in Libya, recommended to them that the only way to defeat the mujahidin was to "cut the roots and the tree will fall." Here, the tree symbolizes the anti-colonial resistance known as the mujahidin. The roots refer to the civilians providing the social base. I found no evidence to support the claim that al-Sharif al-Ghariani was the one behind the idea for internment. One may interpret such a notion as an expression of anger or the reaction of a resisting population against collaborators with the Italian military, especially when listening to the narrative oral history of the survivors' strong and organic unity with the anti-colonial resistance.[6]

Muftah al Shilmani, a survivor of the Magrun concentration camp, said we were arrested and interned because "we were the suppliers, our people fed and armed the resistance led by 'Umar al-Mukhtar." Yusuf Sa'id al-Bal'azi, a survivor of the Slug concentration camp said, "we supplied the Mujahidin with food, sugar, shoes, clothes, and ate from our donation." Ali Majidal-Aquri of the Slug concentration camp said "[t]he tribal camps were the ones that fed our lord 'Umar al-Mukhtar and his men."[7]

The population also provided fighters and intelligence to the resistance. This organic unity between the armed resistance and the civilian population was based on free and volunteer resistance, as Italy was the only fascist regime with colonies in Europe. Here we have a combination of fascism and colonialism, imposing a double dose of racism on Libya. The larger fascist objective was the demographic settlement of Italians in Libya, which proceeded after the genocide in 1934 under a new colonial governor, Italo Balbo, who brought 20,000 settlers to Libya in 1938 and planned to bring 500,000 by 1950.[8]

The initial deportation plan began with the arrest and forced move of Libyans to the coastal camps. The second stage was designed to force the deportation of the civilian population by foot, camels, and ships to the desert of Sirte, while the Slug, Magrun, Braiga, and Agaila camps held 65% to 70% of all the interned. The tribal heads were imprisoned in Binina near Benghazi, and others were exiled in prisons on the islands of southern Italy, especially the prison on the island Ustica.

The first phase began with a decree warning the population to surrender and stop its support for the mujahidin, then three days later the army, with its colonial Askari soldiers and Libyan Banda, arrived and rounded up the population and its livestock. The archival evidence indicates the first date of arrest as June 25, 1930, but most of the oral history of the interned agrees that it started earlier in the fall of 1929. Haj Abdalnabi Abdalshafi al-Rifadi said the Italian army came and

> told our elder shayhks, you have two options: either you fight with us against the mujahidin and the state will arm you, or you refuse and then you will be deported to internment camps. The elders asked for time to deliberate and talk to their people and then they told the Italian army we cannot fight the mujahidin. Thus, we were sent to Binina then the army came and deported us to the camps.[9]

The 'Abaidat tribe was marched in the winter season for a long distance of 1,100 kilometers to the concentration camp of Braiga in the Sirte desert region. The Italian army was given orders to shoot any person or animal who did not hurry and follow the orders to march toward the camps. The survivors tell stories of brutal punishment by the colonial Askari soldiers who, during the long trail of Rihlan, that took weeks for many, whipped and shot people and animals who stopped or fell unconscious due to old age or exhaustion. In the case of the 'Abaidat and Marmarica tribes, the journey took months. In summary, the Italian army's forced deportation combined two policies: the forced walk all the way to the desert of Sirte and the walk followed by transport by ship from Susa and Benghazi to the final location 400 miles south in the desert prisons in the middle of nowhere.

Ibrahim al-Arabi al-Ghmari al-Maimmuni of the Agaila concentration camp, with the worst punishment designed for relatives of the mujahidin, told his story of deportation by foot and then ship:

> We were deported from the camp of Diryana to Benghazi without food and water. The following day, they put us in a small boat and were ordered to sit in the back and the lower level of the boat. The boat was dirty, and we were exhausted, and the children were crying under the hot sun and the cold nights. When we arrived at the Agaila camp, the wind was strong, and the boat could not dock. It was a horrible day.[10]

Muhammad 'Usman al-Shami was interned at Agaila camp. He is the son of one of 'Umar al-Mukhtar's deputies and an officer who graduated from the Istanbul military academy under the Ottoman Empire. Muhammad was arrested with his mother and his grandfather. Muhammad was 11 years old at the time of his arrest. The army asked the grandfather to identify his daughter and grandson. When he refused, they whipped him 50 times and then put him in a well and sealed it. The old man relented and said she was his daughter and, consequently, he and his mother were ordered to march with the others toward the concentration camp. His grandfather, Ma'uf Sa'id al-Drisi, was imprisoned at Binina, and then exiled on the island of Ustica. He was with 40 people and after three years only 16 remained alive; the rest died on the island due to disease, ruthless treatment, and depression.

Muhammad and his mother, Maktuba, were ordered to march to Talmetha for 15 days. His father came at night and told them they were taking him to Agaila and asked if they wanted to come with him. His mother refused. They were then put on a ship for three days. Some people died on the ship, and the Italians dropped the bodies into the sea. At Agaila, Muhammad recalled,

> they treated us like animals, boxing us in nets and using a cargo arm to lift us then dropping us at the shore. At the Agaila camp, we were assigned in various Arba, sections and lines we called Saff, ours was number 11, tent number 19. Yet because my father was a leader under al-Mukhtar, the Italian army exiled us to Palermo, Italy, and when they wanted to separate me from my mother, she jumped into the water and threatened to kill herself. The Italian army official changed the order and after six months, we were returned to the Agaila concentration camp where we were imprisoned for three years.[11]

Haj Muhammad Idris al-Shilmani of the Magrun concentration camp told the story of his family's deportation:

> They deported us without telling us where they were taking us. The Askari guarding me, my mother, and brothers and sisters first from al-Tariya to Talmetha and then to Agaila and Braiga concentration camps. The distance from our home to camp took nine days by foot and camels. The soldiers burned and shot the camels that stopped and many people died in the stampede at Wadi al-kuf. The winter was cold and rainy, and we were thirsty and hungry. They did not feed us.[12]

Haja Bahiya Hamad al-Abaidi confirms the narration. She was interned at the Braiga camp, which was chosen for the 30,000 members of the 'Abaidat tribe:

> First, they deported us to the Ain al-Ghazala camp on camels or walking. We were kept for four days at Bengis without food, and we stayed alive

only because my mother had some Zimita (a grain that is roasted and then grinded and mixed with water or dates), and dates, at night. My father used his Aba, camel wool cloak to cover us. The army whipped any person who slowed down and any person or animal [who died] was left behind. There, they put us in a ship, which was very crowded and when a person died they would throw him to the sea. At Braiga camp, the desert was so difficult for us who [were] used to the lush and breezy green mountain climate. The desert of Sirte at Braiga [was] harsh with no trees nor fresh water, and for the three years under internment, there was no rain at all.[13]

Muhammad Abdalqadir al-'Abdali of the Abadalla al-Bid tribe tells of a specific case of collective punishment and the reasons behind interning people in the harsh camp of Agaila. He said:

five members of the tribe joined the Mujahidin. General Graziani retaliated through collective punishment and ordered the deportation of the whole tribe, 1,000 people, to the Agaila camp and in three years only 83 came out alive of the internment.[14]

Mtawal 'Atiyya al-'Abaidi was 13 years old when he was deported with his family to the Slug concentration camp. He remembered:

We, the 'Biid tribe, were deported from our home at Jardis al'Abiid, forced to march to al-Marj for a month, and then we were ordered to move to Tukarah with our herds and then again, we were forced to the camp of Selouq, where we were interned for three years. We were guarded by the army, Askari soldiers, and Libyan Zuptie and Banda. The march took 15 days. A woman had labor and a baby during the march, and my mother cut a section of my uniform to cover the baby in the traditional Libyan custom of Taqmit.[15]

Sa'ad Salim al-'Amruni, born in 1924, recalled:

We were ordered to march from the Oasis of Jalu for seven days without water and food, and they treated us like animals until we were interned at al-Abyar camp. Like others, the deported were harshly treated and anybody who [slowed] down was whipped or shot. Many elders and some young children died during the deportation. The army took our animals and out of the 70 camels we were allowed to keep only five. It is clear that the Italian army marched some to the ports of Derna, Toukra, Susa, and Benghazi, then shipped [them] by sea to Braiga and Agaila, while others were forced to march on foot or ride camels to the camps.[16]

The survivors' oral history confirms the facts of brutality, harsh treatment, no food or water, or medical treatment in a trail of Rihlan, as it is called, which caused the death of many people and terrorized the ones who stayed alive. We still do not have a precise number for the total deaths. The colonial military repressed records of the horrors of the Rihlan trail of tears and terror. This clearly would have exposed the fascist regime. Therefore, the silence of the Italian colonial state archives on the subject should be understood as a cover-up of this genocidal plan to collectively punish the civilian resisting population of eastern Libya. The vast majority of the Rihlan deportees were forced from the eastern regions to the Sirte desert; only a few thousand were deported from the southern oases of the interior and the western Barqa known as Barqa al-Bayda such as the Magharba, and Zuwayya, Fawakhir, Firjan, and Hussun tribes who lived near Ijdabiyya, west of Benghazi.

The political geography of the deportation included the whole eastern region, the southern interior of the hinterland, and the region of the Sirte desert, home of the most brutal camps. The Italian policy was determined from the start to annihilate the population. When I visited the camps and the Green Mountain region, I realized why the fascists chose the desert of Sirte to intern the resisting population of eastern Libya. It is a desert with no trees or water, and it is a land far away from the homeland of the people in the mountains, valley, forests, and camps of northern Barqa. It is also a place where the interned people could be easily locked up and imprisoned and from which escape was impossible. The distance was long, and people were forced to march on foot and travel in old, decrepit ships and were not given water, food, or medicine. And worse, in many cases, their grain and food was burned or confiscated. The most devastating blow to the people was the loss of their livestock which numbered 600,000 in 1929. The destruction of the livestock is a key factor behind the genocide and death of at least 60,000 in the camps in 1934. I am not the first scholar to recognize the significance of this destruction. Evans-Pritchard and Del Boca have brought attention to this inhumane killing, which I call genocide. What I plan to do is to connect the ecological and organic system which integrated the humans with their animals in the seminomadic economic trade and cultural life in eastern Libya. I propose that the destruction of the herds is a major factor behind the death of thousands of the interned in the concentration camps. The archival evidence and the survivors' narrative create a cohesive view on this mass killing of the herds.

The destruction of the livestock: confiscation, massacres, and starvation

The fascist colonial policy targeted not just the resisting civilian population with its genocidal policy, but also targeted their herds as an integral part of their life. The archival and oral evidence of this violent policy showed the intent to destroy both the animals and the people who relied on them. The ecological and economic system in eastern Libya was based on a balance of pastoralism, settlement, and seasonal agriculture which made both animals and their human usage a key to the survival and natural interdependence of the people and their animals. Ottoman, Arabic, and Italian sources agree that the region has a rich economy and a thriving wealth of livestock. Mahmoud al-Shinaty, the Egyptian historian who wrote an important book on Libya, *The Libyan Question*, stated that before the Italian colonial invasion, the Ottoman province, known as Tarabulus al-Gharb, had, in 1910, 1,104,000 animals.[17] British social anthropologist, Evans-Pritchard, who served in the British colonial army and visited Barqa, stated the livestock of eastern Libya to be 600,000 in 1928. Italian historian Rochat confirmed the same statistics provided by Evans-Pritchard for the region of Barqa.[18] Yet, if one compared the number of the livestock between 1910, 1926, and at the end of interment in 1933, a horrific conclusion emerges which proves the decimation of the region's livestock, the source of livelihood and survival for the people.[19] This decimation contributed to the eventual high death rate of the genocide in the four concentration camps. For the people, animals are symbolically significant for their way of life and cohesion, in addition to it being a loss of high quality animals, they are also a source of income, survival, and meaning through hospitality, weddings, and identity.[20] The following records (Table 3.1) show the degree of destruction of the herds between 1910, one year before the Italian invasion, and 1933.

By 1933, 85% of the sheep and goats and 60% of the cattle and camels were destroyed. Such destruction was not an accident of war time. Eric Salerno found letters in the Italian Archives which indicate a specific fascist intention to destroy both the people and their animals. General Mombelli wrote a letter to the troops that stated, "We must eliminate the armed men, their camps, and herds." General De Bono, the colonial governor of Libya, wrote in another report, "We confiscated 20,000 sheep and 8,000 camels, and killed 5,000 others." Another 1,500 camels were confiscated and used in the invasion of the Oasis of Kufra.[21] Evans-Pritchard estimated the total death of animals in the period between 1923 and 1928 and deduced that the Italian army killed 170,000 animals. General Graziani, who was charged with the genocide, boasted about this destruction in eastern Libya. He admitted that the livestock of Barqa was reduced to a critical point that required the import of 160,000 animals from western Libya in 1933–1934.[22] This action is a remarkable addition to the decimation of the livestock of a region known for its rich exports of animals, wool, and local cheese, called kishik, to western Egyptian urban markets and internally to the oases dwellers in the hinterland of Barqa, Jufra,

TABLE 3.1 The Destruction of Native Animal Wealth In Eastern Libya, 1910–1933

	1910	1926	1933
Sheep and Goats	126,000	80,000	22,000
Camels	83,000	75,000	2,600
Horses	27,000	14,000	1,000
Cattle	23,000	10,000	2,000

and Fezzen in exchange for dates. Libyan survivors of the internment present a specific historical and emotional narrative of this destruction of their beloved animals, which were their source of substance and wealth.

Some of the herds were destroyed by the Italian army during the deportation, especially at Wadi al-Kuf, to deprive the mujahidin from using them and to starve them in the Green Mountain. Haj Idris Hamad al-Shilmani from Magrun concentration camp said, "our animals were confiscated, 100 sheep and six camels were taken by the Masswua Askari." He added, "My uncle had 600 sheep, 15 cattle, and three camels, another relative al-Tayyib had 500 sheep and Muhammad Yusuf al-Shilmani had 200 sheep; all were taken." Yusuf Hamad al-Bal'azi said he "lost 90 camels and was left with only five." Haj Atiyya Minana al-Hafi (interned at Agaila) said, "My family lost 500 sheep and 50 goats, and all our camels were lost during our forced deportation to the camps." Haj Muhammad Idris al-Shilmani said "700 camels were killed during the deportation at Wadi al- Kuf when there was a stampede which pushed people and their animals to the bed of the Wadi and died as a result." He added, "His family's herds were lost; 40 sheep confiscated, and the rest died because of starvation and thirst." Haj Murad Abdalhamid al-A'bar said, "The Italian army confiscated our grain and animals." Haj Idris Rizq al-Marimi al-'Abaidi of the Braiga camp said, "We were forced to march with our animals which did not make it as my family lost 20 sheep and 5 camels before we reached the concentration camp."[23]

Haj Yusuf Said Bal'azi from the Agaila camp said, "If the Italians left us alone, we were able to feed and take care of ourselves herding, plowing, planting and harvesting, but our animals were killed like us because of hunger and thirst." He then added,

> The Italian army confiscated our supplies and animals. We had 1,200 sheep and 90 camels. When our herders left, and the animals were left without food and water, and they deprived us from slaughtering our animals, we starved as well.

Senusi Saleh al-'Abdali (Slug camp) remembered his family had 300 sheep, and 500 goats, which all died because of starvation. Haj Jibril Ali al-'Amrani (Agaila camp) said, "We were deported for eight days to Agaila camp. The army confiscated our grain, and our 14 camels, 200 sheep, and 50 goats died outside the camp because of lack of water and food." Haj Hamad Abdalsadiq al-Awami (Slug camp) said,

> We were on our way to Hijra, taking refuge in Egypt, when the army arrested us and forced us to march with our animals from the camp of Ain al-Ghazala for 19 days to Slug. We had 30 camels but were left only with one. We had our own tents, so the Italian army did not provide us with any.

The point here is that the Italian army did not even provide infrastructure to the camps and exploited the people, their money, herds, and food, and, finally, when they lost their animals and had finished their own little supply of food, they let them starve to death.

The survivors' oral history completes the gaps in the official archives of what happened during the Rihlan, the deportation to the concentration camps, the uprooting and the terror, and the killing and robbery of their source of survival, their animals. The narrative sheds light on the significant factor; the impoverishment of the people as they were deprived of their wealth and source of food and economic survival. Furthermore, it contributed to their emotional and cultural trauma, as their animals, especially their camels, were viewed like human beings and not just animals for man to use as a capitalist commodity. The survivors' oral history is full of vivid expressions of such cultural loss and trauma. The memorized folk poetry gives a moving eulogy of the pain of the loss of their beloved animals.

In short, the mass killing of the people was made worse when their animals were destroyed. Without them they could not eat and culturally they were deprived of important symbols of their way of life. The mourning of the loss of the herds permeates all the oral history, testimony, and poetry. Every poem tells the story of a good life with the beloved animals before the internment. One poet at Slug camp said "We are imprisoned at Slug, down and depressed nowhere to go nor sheep around us to make us happy." This destruction took place gradually. The animals were decimated and became the first victims of the colonial genocide, shortly followed by their owners. Thousands of animals and humans died between 1928 and 1934. The Italian genocide therefore represented both a physical and a cultural death for its victims. The Italian colonial policy pioneered the first use, in 1911, of airplane bombing in war. The first time planes were used for surveillance and to drop bombs on fighters and animals. The fascist army pioneered the concept of total war which included collective punishment, exiling, destroying harvests and animals, public hanging, the use of poisoned gas in 1928, and mass deportation and concentration camps in Libya. It is not surprising to know that the Nazi officials looked to the Italian's "success" in the Libyan colony as a model from which to study and learn.

Trauma and death in the camps

By August 30, 1930, most of the civilian population of eastern Libya was interned in the camps in the desert of Sirte. We do not know how many died or were executed during the months-long deportation to the concentration camps. We have reliable cases such as the tribe of 'Abadla al-Bid and the family of Al-Tiif in 'Ain al-Ghazala camp. Others died because they were very young, old, or sick, or the journey proved too perilous for them to endure. The survivors tell detailed stories of people left behind or who died in the ships that transported them from Tobrouq to Braiga and Agaila in the east of the

Sirte region. People were barefoot with few clothes and little food, as the Italian army confiscated their supplies and animals and did not provide them with food. Others, like the Bitnan/Marmarica tribes of the east and the 'Abaidat tribe, were forced to walk for months to the desert of Sirte. It was a painful trail of terror and tears as we learned from the oral history of the survivors and their folk poetry created during the deportation and inside concentration camps. Some women had miscarriages; others died at sea and were thrown overboard without regard for Islamic rituals given to the deceased. Some others suffered insults, whipping, and shooting. The survivors' stories showed that this brutal internment in the concentration camps was indeed comparable to the dead rising from their graves to face God's judgment as cited in the Qur'an. Muhammad Muftah imprisoned at the Tariya Camp said, "we walked barefooted and naked, and 50 people died daily."[24]

When I asked the survivors I interviewed from the five camps why thousands of people died, the answer was the same, we died because of "Shar wa Marad," meaning evil and illnesses. The interned would either have or would borrow a millstone to make bread or a Libyan roasted mixture, Zimita. When I asked them why they did not find animals and fruit to eat, they replied that the desert of Sirte was so barren, that they ate desert rats called Jarbua and boiled a wild desert grass called 'Ansil quill and drank it, but could not find much else in the Sirte desert. People became so desperate that they even ate dead donkeys and searched camel dung for grain. Often, they contrasted life and death in their original homeland and the camps in the desert where many of their families and kinsmen perished.

The ecology and the culture of the rural Libyans connected people to animals and homelands. One has to keep in mind that Libyan nomads view animals as companions and intimate friends and not as a commodity or an object to be used, eaten, or killed en masse for sport or for defeating the enemy. Life is about conservation and basic survival and the animals are key to the nomads' survival, wealth, honor, and identity. Their diet is simple and made up of bread, milk, dates, and, once in a while, meat. The word for bread is *n'ma*, God's generous offering, and sheep are called *sa'ii*, the word for making a living. The stories that follow about starvation and cultural trauma in the camps are heartbreaking.

'Abd al-Hamid al Sabayhi said, "Some of us ate donkeys because we were starving." 'Uthman 'Abdalhamid al-'Abar of the Agaila camp said, "al-Nas Matu min al-shar" (people died because of the evil, meaning starvation). I found one case of cannibalism in an interview with a survivor from al-Marj but could not confirm it. However, after I visited the camps and recognized the harshness of the desert and the sight of thousands of graves, I can imagine that possibility. Muftah al-Shilmani of the Magrun camp said: "Our life is one of shar, Jua, kadar wa marad" (evil, hunger, depression, and disease). Mabruk Ali al-'Amruni (Agaila camp) said "[W]e died because we had no food ... [t]he Italians did not register the names of the dead, whoever died, died forgotten to them." Abdal'Ali al-Fakhri remembered, "People died because of kadar/sadness, shar/evil, and marad/illness."[25]

Yusuf Sa'id al-Bal'azi (Slug camp) said,

> People who had money could buy food from the few shops owned by the Libyan and Jewish collaborators, and Italians, but the majority of us were made poor when they took our grain, starved us, took our property, and decimated our herds.

He continued, "People were desperate and ate anything to stay alive. People became skeletons walking without much power or energy. We wished death because of al-Kadar, depression." Once again, many of them reached the conclusion like Muhammad 'Usman al-Shami that the goal was to exterminate them. Many of the survivors told me the names of their family members who had died in the genocide, saying that they even remembered their eyes and how they died, as if the memory of the killing in the camps never dies.[26]

Nuh Hamad al-Fisi told me he lost his mother and brothers in front of his eyes at Abyar concentration camp. Ibrahim al-'Arabi al-Ghmori al-Maimuni (Agaila camp) stated his family entered the camp with 11 members and by the end only three came out alive. Meanwhile, his Uncle Muhammad's family was almost wiped out completely, except for one person from the internment and three others of his family who were exiled in the prison of Ustica in southern Italy from which many never returned.[27]

Matawal 'Atiyya al-'Abidi (Slug camp) said, "Our family had 26 members and only 10 came out alive after three years of internment." Haja 'Aziza Majid al-'Aquri, also interned at Slug camp, said "I was seven years old when I was interned with my family. Three uncles were hanged, and I lost my seven brothers and sisters and my grandmother at the camp." Jaballa Muhammad al-Minifi (Agaila camp) said, "We witnessed 150 deaths a day." He lost his father, uncle, and cousin. Zahra Jarbu' al-Ya'qubi (Agaila camp) said, "I was young when we were deported to the camp from Benghazi. My mother was pregnant during the forced deportation which caused trauma, miscarriage, and her death at the camp." Haj Muhammad Idris al-Shilmani (Magrun camp) said, "We were forced to leave our homes and to march to the camp of al-Magrun, thirsty, hungry, and without many clothes. At the camp, I lost my sister Karima, and my brothers Muhammad, Hamad, and Ali." Al-Baghadadi al-Shukri (Agaila camp) cried when he remembered his family's ordeal at the camp. His mother died at the camp and his brother was shot, while his father was imprisoned at Binina, near Benghazi. Mirsal 'Atiyya al-'Abdali detailed the decimation of the 'Abadla al-Bid tribe. In October 7, 1930, five members of this tribe escaped the camp of Gyminus and joined the mujahidin led by 'Umar al-Mukhtar. General Graziani decided to punish the whole tribe collectively by forcing its members to march to the terrible punishment camp of Agaila. By the end of the internment in 1934, out of 30 families consisting of about 1,800 people, only 83 people came out alive. Some families, like the

Darman family of the Minifa tribe, were wiped out by the end of the internment in 1934. Once again, the survivors and their children remembered the
names and the way they died.[28]

The highest death rate occurred at the big punishment camps of Slug,
Magrun, Agaila, and Braiga, where 70% of the internment of the population
occurred. Most of the oral history of the survivors confirms that between 100
to 150 individuals died daily at their camps. People were allowed to leave
some of the camps, such as Abyar, Slug, and Magrun, with a permit. Those
who tried to escape were arrested and were put to death either by hanging or
gunfire, as was the poet Fadhil al-Shilmani's wife at the Agaila camp, who
attempted to escape with her brother. They were caught and shot to death.
People who had money could buy food, but they were a small minority.
Women faced severe treatment and sexual attacks, which remain a taboo topic
among the culture of eastern Libya. Still, I found some people who were will-
ing to talk about rape, forced marriage, and women offering sex in exchange
for food or becoming prostitutes to escape shame and their family's punishment. Once again, the camps were not all the same and the worst were Agaila,
Braiga, Magrun, and Slug. I have not done reach on the other camps, which
had 30% of the interned population. Future research should tell us more about
them.

The oral history and folk poetry provide us with evidence of how many
women experienced the period of forced deportation and internment. As is
the case with the men, the oral history of the deportation and internment
was evidenced in the details afforded by the living memory of the children
who were with their families. Zahra al-Yaqubi, for example, came from an
urban merchant family in Benghazi. Her family was interned because of an
accusation by a spy that her family was aiding the mujahidin and, in addition, one of her cousins was a mujahid. The family had money and did not
starve like the majority of the seminomads or Badiya nomads who were
interned. However, she said to me when I interviewed her in Benghazi,
"My mother was hit hard with the arrest of the family." She added that her
mother was pregnant. Sadly, she did not survive the arrest and the forced
deportation to the Agaila camp. She aborted her baby and died in the camp.
Zahra had tears in her eyes when she remembered what happened to her
mother. I asked her if she ever returned to see the camp at Agaila, and she
said, "No, it is too painful for me, and I do not want to see that horrible
place again."[29]

Haja Bahiya Hamad al-Abaidi was a child interned at Braiga camp. She
recounted:

> The Italian army took our food and animals and did not give us any. We
> were forced to walk from our homes in the Green Mountain to Sirte, the
> longest distance from northeastern Barqa to the camp of Braiga. Anyone
> who slowed down was whipped or shot, and the dead ones were left in
> the road without being proper Muslim burial. In addition, when they

forced us to board a ship, some people died, and they were thrown into the sea.[30]

Haja Bahiya added that some women were raped, and others were forced to marry Italian officers and soldiers. She was very open to talking about this culturally taboo topic. She was 14 years old when she was forced into the internment with her family. In Libyan culture, rape is viewed as shame, especially in rural kinship communities, and, consequently, it is not easy for people to talk about it. Poet Rajab Buhwaish must have seen cases of rape but because of cultural shame he just hinted that such a thing was common. Such a cultural view of rape and forced marriage is common. It is based on the concept of honor and protection of women. There's no precise nor even an estimated number of women who were raped or forced into marriage, not to mention others who starved and sold their body in exchange for food to stay alive. The number of women who experienced this fate is surely much higher than what the oral history has shown after four decades of collective oral history in Libya. The historian Sa'ad al-Hayin reported the existence of a camp al-Baggara, near al-Byada, that included women who were raped or left without family support and protection. By 1940, the rise of brothels in Tripoli and some coast cities was a consequence of the colonial displacement and violence and should not be surprising. The late Libyan novelist Khalifa Hussain Mustafa in his daring and brilliant novel *Layali Najma*, (*The Nights of Najma*), captured life in the brothels in Tripoli.

Women faced terror, shooting, and death around them in the camps. Haja 'Aziza Majid al-'Aquri was seven years old when she was interned in the camp of Slug, along with the rest of the 'Awaqir tribe. She showed tears and emotions during the interview. She sang, cried, and expressed her long-lasting pain despite the fact that the internment and genocide occurred 75 years before. Her moving narrative should not be surprising given her tragic experiences while interned in the Braiga camp. Three of her uncles were hanged and seven of her brothers and sisters died in the camp. She said, "Oh my dear, it was horrible what happened to us."[31] Haja Riqiyya al-Fakhri said she knew of cases of women who were forced to marry Italian soldiers in the camp. Another survivor, who was born in 1906, confirmed to the Italian military, cases of rape and forced marriages of Libyan women in the camps, stating,

> A spy came looking for me, and I hid with my mother, but the officer came and had the soldiers take me. I resisted the officer for 12 days and then I got tired and could not resist anymore. I stayed with him for a year, then I ran away and married a man from my tribe, the Fawakhir.

Haja Riqiyya al-Fakhri said she knew two similar cases of girls forced into marriage; they were named Rahma and Riwab. Their father had a heart attack and died from shock and shame.[32]

Aziza al-Niml, born in 1891, said that she remembered a brutal case in the Agaila camp, detailing the shooting and hanging of people who either tried to escape or had relatives still active in the resistance. She witnessed the execution of the wife and daughter of Mujahid Ibrik al-Lawati. The Italian army did not spare women, as the oral and archival sources show women being exiled, executed, and raped. In addition, women were forced to carry water and collect wood while men had to do forced, hard labor inside the camps and in road construction projects for the Italian army. The most depressing news for the interned was the news of the capture and hanging of the resistance leader, 'Umar al-Mukhtar in 1931 at Slug camp.[33]

Haja Haniyya al-Lawati was among the interned people in Slug. She said, "I still remember that horrible day for us. It was an autumn day. They brought him. He prayed twice and was dignified. When he was hanged, people said God is great and some cried. We had mixed emotions." Another survivor, Um al-Izz al-Bal'azi, born in 1918, was interned in the camp of Agaila at the age of 12. She said, with sadness, "You have no idea how horrible what happened to us at Al-'Agaila." She added, "We were forced to be in a line in the morning and the evening, and whoever is absent or tardy was whipped and insulted, including women. We experienced dark years and many of us died." She said the epic poem "Mabi-Marad" was well known and she memorized its opening lines. Haj Abdalhamid Mihammad, born in 1923, said, in some cases, Italian soldiers raped women in front of their families.[34]

The Italian policy began to change after the hanging of 'Umar al-Mukhtar on September 11, 1931. They defeated the resistance and cleared the land of the native people as a crucial requirement for the long-term goal of bringing Italian settlers to the fertile rich land of the Green Mountain region of northern Barqa. The colonial policy, especially under the new governor Italo Balbo, started a school for orphan children at Magrun concentration camp. Yet, this school was not designed out of a humane intent to soften the genocidal internment of the people, but to socialize and educate the young, poor orphans under a fascist ideology and with a military training. In many cases, parents were forced to enroll their children in the fascist colonial schools, so that they could survive and eat. These parents had no choice, as they were dying of starvation and diseases in the four punishment concentration camps. Thousands of these children became colonial soldiers and were used by the colonial military to fight as cheap labor in the invasion of Ethiopia in 1935. The number of these young soldiers started at 12,000 and had increased to 40,000 by 1940 when they were sent to fight in one of World War II's major battles along the Libyan–Egyptian border.

The survivors' interviews confirm the fact that the children and the elderly were the most vulnerable and suffered the highest rate of death, due to the lack of medicine and food. Most of the survivors interviewed were children who lived after the end of the internment in early 1934. Evans-Pritchard, who interviewed Libyan refugees from eastern Libya in the late 1930s and conducted research for two years in Barqa between 1943 and 1945, estimated the number of Libyan survivors of the internment to be 35,000 out of the 100,000 accepted by Italian historian Angelo Del Boca. Children who survived the genocide told vivid historical details about what happened in the four camps and why many thousands died.

Salim Muftah al-Shilwi was 13 years old when he was interned with his family at the Braiga concentration camp. He belonged to the 'Abaidat tribe and was deported from the eastern part of the Green Mountain to Benghazi, where he was put in an old ship with his mother and interned at Braiga camp after coming ashore at the Gulf of Sirte. He told stories, for the first time, about his experience boarding a ship and being seasick, hungry, and frightened. He repeated what others have said in that at the camp people died because the Italian army gave them no food except for a pound of poor-quality barley imported from Tunisia, and that people were prohibited from eating their own herds. Like other, he witnessed the daily deaths of 150 people and cases of insults, whipping, and the execution of six people because of contacting the mujahidin.[35]

The survivors who were interned as children saw their family members die in front of their eyes, as was the case of Mtawal 'Atiyya al-'Abaidi of the Slug concentration camp, from which only ten of his 26 family members emerged alive in 1934. Haj Jaballa Muhammad al-Minifiwas interned at Agaila concentration camp when he was 13 years old. He lost 11 members of his family members due to starvation and diseases in the concentration camp. In 1935, he was drafted into the Italian colonial invasion of Ethiopia. He told me, when I visited him in his home at Rajma, "Son, the Italians did not do us good at Agaila, nothing but evil." Khalid Bubakir al-Minifi, who was nine years old when he was interned, commented,

> I watched my family's death in front of my eyes. My mother and brothers and I were the only ones who survived the internment. I became an orphan and was recruited to join the Italian army to survive in the war in Ethiopia. I was 15 years old.

Haj Said Naji Abdulla al-Badri, who was interned in Abyar concentration camp when he was 17 years old, stated, "I saw my family dying, including my uncle 'Amir and many families perished in the concentration camp." He said,

> What happened to us in Libya, and Barqa in particular, did not happen anywhere else. I was hungry and had no other choices, so I joined the Italian colonial army to eat, and fought in the invasion of Ethiopia in 1935.

This traumatic experience of children witnessing their own parents, brothers, sisters, and other relatives dying because of starvation is a common narrative among the survivors. Haj Nuh Aawadallah Dighaim al-Fisi, who was nine years old when he was interned with his family at Abyar concentration camp, witnessed the slow death of his mother and two brothers because of starvation.

Haj Sa'id Attiyah al-Lafi, who was six years old when he was interned at Agaila, recalled:

> People ate everything because of starvation. One man slaughtered his camel to eat and was punished with 100 whips by the army. When people died, we could not wash nor provide coffins. We were so exhausted and traumatized, we did not pray, nor fasted during Ramadan. We were walking skeletons without any energy. The Italians were harsh and did not distinguish between old and children, men and women and wanted us dead. My larger family was made of 44 people but by the end of the internment [in 1935] only five of us survived.[36]

One survivor said, "As we lost many of our family members to starvation and diseases, we had no option but to walk to the army fascist schools and the older boys were drafted to fight in the army's invasion of Ethiopia. The school provided water, food, and clothes, but also a fascist military curriculum and training." The most recognized school was at Magrun concentration camp. Haj Muhammad Idris al-Shilmani, who was nine years old when he was interned at Magrun concentration camp, remembered, "The camp was about starvation, coldness, and lack of cover. We saw nothing but oppression from the Italians. What happened to us never happened to any people."[37]

Haj Senusi Saleh al-'Abdali was 15 years old when he was interned at Slug concentration camp. The army brought him and they gathered all 20,000 of the interned people. He asked to pray and then said Takbir (saying God is great seven times, a common Muslim prayer when facing death) and, after that, they hanged him. "We cried and said Allah Akbar."

The survivors were aware of the Italian policy of taking orphan children to Italian schools. They said to me, "They wanted to make us Italians." Abdal'Ali al-Fakhri, who was a child when he was interned at Slug concentration camp also said:

> My mother and sister died because of grief and famine. I also lost my three uncles. The concentration camp was prison, and this is the correct word for our internment. I attended the hanging of 'Umar al-Mukhtar and the airplanes were in the air monitoring us during the hanging. We were starved, ill, almost naked, and infected with lice and bedbugs. We thought death would be release for us and better than our hellish prison. All my family died, and I was an orphan.[38]

Culture, poetry, and trauma

The interned people's most reliable sources to document what they experienced during the four years of genocide were their oral traditions and the remarkable folk poetry which allowed them to react to this slow death and suffering and to express their human passions and trauma. It gave them a cultural source of emotional catharsis and creative expression. The Mu'taqalat, or folk poetry, was written during the period of the genocide; therefore, it provides us with a direct cultural record of what happened in the camps. Poetry in literary theory has been viewed as a source for catharsis, or purification and cleansing. In the Libyan case it is a cultural expression of collective identity which in the tragedy and the trauma of internment in the concentration camps took a new meaning centered on the struggle to survive, recover, and heal. Poetry from the camps is recited and sung in social gatherings and everyday communication.

Society was tied to their land, animals, and the trans-Saharan trade between Chad, southern Libya, Egypt, and Benghazi. Folk poetry was an old, creative cultural form of communication and expression which became the most reliable and powerful means of recording the interned people's passions, trauma, and will to record what they were experiencing under the brutal genocide. It became a cultural means for survival and resistance.

The Arabic dialect of the seminomadic Libyans, or Badiyya, is very specific and there is no escape from the fact that some names and concepts have no translation into English. The only way to make sense of it is to understand their society and the historical context of the first half of twentieth century Barqa. For example, the word Arabic word *Shar* means "evil," but the interned used this word to describe the new reality: the imposed starvation, and the lack of food and medicine. This experience of hunger, starvation, and death under the Italian genocidal internment became culturally and historically internalized through oral and poetic narrative. When I spoke with the survivors, they kept saying that the Italians wanted them dead and repeated to me that they died because of "'qadaar, shar, wa marad" or "suffering, evil, and illness." The context of illness is both physical and emotional. They starved to death after their animals were confiscated or killed, or, like them, starved after six months of enclosure without water and pastureland in the desert of Sirte.

This rural and nomadic poetic source of history should be seen as a creative, cultural expression of life in prison. It is a collective expression of suffering through starvation, illness, and death during the period of internment and its aftermath. The poetry was an avenue or tool for fighting imperialism. The interned used poetry as a source of alternative history documenting what they went through and communicating with and uplifting each other to stay alive and resist. The vast majority of this collective poetry serves as a powerful expression of the fight for survival, breaking the silence, and the propaganda of Italian colonial fascism, and serves as a weapon of survival against its inhumanity, violence, and oppression in the camps.

The discovery of this cultural tradition and method of communication among the rural society of eastern Libya was essential for recovering the history of the genocide from the point of view of the victims and survivors. Oral folk poetry, or what is known in Libya as al-Shi'r al-Sha'bi, the people's poetry, preserves the collective memory of the exiled and displaced people of the genocide, especially given that the poetry was composed during the time of mass internment and survived after their death because of the practice of memorization and recitation of oral folk poetry. Folk poetry, then, is the people's history, uncensored and even more than just a reaction to the genocide, it is a cultural, artistic, and psychological expression of people who otherwise have no written history and have only been viewed through the lenses of colonial and Eurocentric scholarship.

Italian historian Angelo Del Boca confessed that only after reading the papers and letters of the anti-colonial leader Muhammad Fekini did he understand the passion and the human feelings of this leader and how he reacted to colonial conquest, the brutality in the western mountains and the southern region in Fezzen, and finally the horrific trail of crossing the desert into exile.[39] Professor Del Boca's admission is moving, because he is one of the few Italian historians who challenged the silence and the reproduction of myths about Italian Fascism and colonial genocide in Libya and Ethiopia. But, had he learned Arabic or been able to read and listen to the narrative and trauma poetry of survivors of the concentration camps, he would have discovered the full reality of the genocide's death and extermination in Barqa, from the point of view of its victims.

The oral poetry of those victims who were interviewed expresses the aesthetic, cultural, and humanistic side of a unique genre. As mentioned previously, while the majority of Libyan society was illiterate, they were nevertheless able to create the most humane and creative poems expressing their feelings inside the concentration camps about the horrors of the Italian occupation. Therefore, I would argue that without the oral history, and above all the folk poetry of the concentration camps, there would be no history of this Libyan genocide, except for what lies in the undisclosed Italian records.

As stated earlier the most famous epic poem is "Mabi-Marad" by poet Rajab Buhwaish. This poem is the most widely known among Libyans. My late mother used to recite its first lines to me and my brothers and sisters. It has been reprinted and read in books and broadcast on Libyan Radio since the 1950s. Libyan historian Salim al-Kubti told me once in Benghazi that, thanks to Buhwaish and his poem, we know about what happened in the concentration camps and the genocide. Buhwaish was born in Zawiyyat al Marsus near Toubuq in 1871 to a family that belonged to the Minifa tribe, the tribe of 'Umar al-Mukhtar. He was educated in Sanusi schools, zawaya, and seminaries and earned the title of faqih, a learned religious scholar and Qur'anic teacher. He was also a talented poet and educated in Arabic and the oral traditions of hinterland culture. In 1930, he was arrested and deported to the Agaila camp like the rest of the civilian population because of their support for the resistance. At Agaila camp he was interned with his family. Broken, depressed, and on the verge of dying he composed this remarkable poem. He came out alive in 1934 and lived to see Libyan independence in 1951, a year before he died in 1952 in Benghazi. I have been trying for many years to find his picture, but without success, yet.

The memory of the genocide is strong in eastern and central Libya. The majority of the interned, as observed earlier, came from the rural tribes of eastern Libya and only a few from the urban centers, such as Benghazi and Derna, what the Libyans called *Hudur*, urban folks. Understanding such social and regional dynamics and diversity, including rural urban history, is essential for capturing the struggle over the recovery and the advocacy of this history of genocide and the indifference and silence of groups who either collaborated or made peace with the colonial state, especially after independence in 1951 and the populist and colonial coup in 1969.

Urban folks were from Benghazi, Derna, and al-Marj, while the seminomads were tribes from the Marmarica: the 'Abaidat, Bra'sa, Drisa, 'Urfa, and Abid, the rest were groups such as 'Awaqir, Magharba, Zuwayya, or the other Marabtin (religiously designated) tribes. There were a few nomads who traveled, such as Fawakhir. Trading tribes such as the Zuwayya lived between Ajdabiyya and Kufra and the Majabra of Jalu and Chad. The rest practiced both agriculture in the rainy season, mostly barley wheat, and animal husbandry, including sheep, goats, cattle in the north and the plateau, and camels in the Burr, or the semidesert of the region. The regional economy also drew in the oases such as Jalu, Oujala, Marada, Jufra, Jikhira, Tazirbu, Jaghbub, Siwa, Kufra, and Tazirbu. The regional economy of Barqa was based on an exchange of the seminomads (animals and grain surplus) and the oases (dates) and goods and tools in markets of western Egypt and Chad. The Sanusi order integrated all these tribes both economically and ethnically into the networks of the trans-Saharan trade between Sudan, Chad, Kufra, Benghazi, and Alexandria and Egypt.

The culture of the interned was oral and poetic to the point where one could call these regions a country of bards. I discovered hundreds of poets of both sexes who composed poems during internment in the camps. These poems were communicated orally and recited many times before they were recorded after 1950. Remaining cognizant to the culture or orality and poetry inside Libya is essential. The keen ability to keep memory alive and recite songs and poems is remarkable.

This oral tradition and folk poetry also preserve the society's values of honor, community, faith in Sanusi Islam, generosity, chivalry, solidarity, and love for their freedom, animals, and homeland. They resisted Italian colonial armies for God, their homeland, and for patriotism. In short, oral folk poetry composed in the concentration camps was an old cultural way of communicating and expressing in the community. It helped the interned survive and resist the Italian Fascist internment and killing by creating and preserving new poems that eased their pain, and became a weapon to check, challenge, and talk back to the Italian Fascist public propaganda. This was their way of spreading truth about the concentration camps, shedding light on their atrocities, and combating the Italian's attempt to cover up these blatant crimes against humanity.

This folk poetry has some specific stylistic commonalities; many poems reference the good life the persecuted lived before their internment, including the prosperity with their herds and the bountiful grain they enjoyed. It also referred to intangible qualities, such as their freedom, their memories, weddings, hospitality, and chivalry. Then, in contrast, the poems often move to recounting the calamity of the Italian invasion and the deportation to the camps. They focus on the details of the camps, on death and illness, and specify the names, places, collaborators, Eritrean colonial soldiers, and the sadistic Italian commanding offices. The poems appeal to God to help their authors endure oppression and suffering. They express the individual talent and diverse style of their creators, including their gender, personality, trauma, and exile. The vocabulary of the poetry is shaped by pastoralist and rural images and metaphors. It is in Arabic, Libyan Arabic, and, more specifically, a Badiyya Arabic, a dialect of Arabic in eastern Libya. Orientalists and colonial anthropologists refer to them as "Bedouin." I find this term ahistorical and orientalist; it is an inaccurate pejorative term that perpetuates falsehood, not a living and changing culture. Oral and folk poetry of the interned shows us specific language used to describe the fascist concentration camps. Before presenting some cases and examples it is important to understand some keywords that are used in this prison or internment culture and poetry.

The concentration camps are called either by the name of the Mu'taqal/ camp (plural Mu'taqalat), or *Shabardaq*, barbed wire. The Italians are referred to as *Tilian* (Italians), *Nassara* (Christians), and in cases of death and killing, *kuffar* (infidels.) The Eritrean colonial soldiers are called Habash, Abasenyians, but after Massawa in reference to the port of Massoā. The Libyan collaborating Banda served as *Cabos*, guards, spies, or soldiers and were called mtalianin, ("gone Italians," collaborators) or Banda which was adopted from the Italian language.

Evil, *Shar* and the symbols of the genocide

Jews refer to the Holocaust as shoah, and Libyans called death in the camps *Shar*, or evil. This, as explained earlier, was a creative way to explain the fact that the Fascist Italian army starved them to death. The term Shar is derived from the holy book, the Qur'an, as the opposite of good. This construction of the term evil from the cultural point of view of the interned Libyan Muslims is different from Hannah Arendt's interpretation of the trial of Adolf Eichmann in Jerusalem. She interpreted his role in the genocide in Nazi culture as "The Banality of Evil." He is an apathetic bureaucrat and, like other Nazi officers whose motives for committing genocide were ordinary, is hence more dangerous.[40] The survivors of Italian Fascism in the concentration camps viewed their ordeal as an evil, Shar in Arabic language. It is the moral economy of the genocide, a proper and brilliant term to describe the horror of the genocide. They saw this genocide and catastrophe from the point of view of their faith in Islam. They faced Shar and their faith allowed them to have *sabr*, patience, in the face of *mihan*, calamities. Poet Um al-Khair 'Abd al-Dayim, of the Braiga concentration camp, described the guards at the camps as "kinsman of the devil." But she saw the death at the camp as the end of the world and God's test of the faithful in the face of such evil deeds. In one poem, she described the devil sadistically whipping the interned without mercy, as if the devil spit in their mouths and turned them into other devils torturing people and starving them to death.[41] Another formal poet named Fatima 'Uthamn expressed the shock, as a teenager, of collective hanging and composed only one brilliant and powerful poem as witness to this colonial injustice. She witnessed of the execution of 19 people in the Oasis of Hun in central Libya as a punishment for the town supporting the mujahidin in the battle of Afiyya in 1928:

> Ruined twice, our home land
> Some are dead hanging in
> The gallows, others are
> Forced to flee in exile we are ruined twice our homeland.[42]

Exile and imprisonment in southern Italy

Poet Fadhil al-Shilmani was arrested by accident when a relative asked him to carry a letter to somebody in the resistance. He was stopped at a checkpoint near Benghazi and was searched by the Italian army who found the letter. He tried his best to tell them that he had nothing to with the message mentioned in the letter and that he was just a messenger. They rejected his story and arrested him. He was tried and sent to prison for 25 years, not in Libya, but in a prison in southern Italy where more than 10,000 Libyan men and women were imprisoned in 13 different prisons. Many of them died due to illness and malnutrition. We know the names of half of them and some of their letters. Many sent letters, but these letters were censored by the colonial authorities. The letters indicate the lack of food and medical treatment. They asked their families to send money, so that they could buy food. Many died and were buried in Italy and only a few returned to Libya after the defeat of the resistance in 1932. Some letters recorded cases of suicide. Nevertheless, we still do not know the story of half of the deportees.

But, once again, thanks to these poets, we know what happened in the-camps. Poet Fadhil al-Shilmani composed many poems during his seven years' imprisonment in a dungeon on the island of Favignana. In 2013, his poems were collected and edited by Libyan scholar Younes Fanush. As a prisoner on a ship to Italy, he described his feelings: "the ship left Benghazi offering a big sound and took us away from our beloved homeland." Given his status as a rural Libyan, he had never seen a ship like the one he was placed in. He described the underground prison cell as "a dungeon in a seventh level inside earth, dark, and we see no sun [but the] closed cell, and everywhere I look, I see Italians." One time he was taken up to the open space and he saw a bird, prompting him to remark, "Oh bird, who is free in sun, gave you wings. Come, so I can tell you about what happened to us. I am a stranger, and you seem to be a friend." After seven years, he became desperate and angry. He expressed his outrage in the opening of "Babur [Ship] to Favignana," writing: "Oh, my hands are so tired of the shackles, as they were bound with time." And in another poem, he writes, "May God ruin you forever, Favignana, you place of depression, bad life, and humiliation." He described the food in his underground cell, writing:

> Damn Faviguana you for your oppression
> Your cell Nasara [Christian] people
> You made our dignified people poor and starved them
> Feeding us just a piece of stone bread
> A little soup and a handful of macaroni without taste or satisfying our
>   hunger.[43]

Poet al-Shilmani was released after seven years and returned to Benghazi; however, he was forced back into prison during the internment of the people and in 1929 was re-imprisoned, ending up again in the collective prison of Magrun,, before his death in 1932. Ironically, this poet lost both his wife and brother-in-law who were interned at Agaila camps. They escaped the camp but were caught and sentenced to death.

Rajab Buhwaish, in his other poem on the deportation, reflects,

> If you ask, I can tell what happened to me. In a ship, we went west for eight nights, and we were seasick and could not sleep. Then, they threw us on a ground near Braiga port, on the ground without money or food, and harsh officers cursing us with their soldiers without mercy.[44]

Poet Um al-Khair described the same period, reciting, "We were uprooted from our homeland in the Jabal. Women and children become seasick for nights because of the waves. We were uprooted, and even babies would be depressed because of what happened to us." Poet Hussain al'Ilwani, interned in the Magrun camp, said about the deportation, "They forced us to walk until we reached al-Magrun. Life was bad, and they built barbed wire around us. Worse, we had to do hard labor using axes, and move stone, and sand for no purpose."[45]

Trauma and terror: they starved our beloved camels

The seminomads who were interned relied on their animals for survival. Their life was organized by an economic cycle. They moved from the north to the plateau and the Burr during the different seasons, looking for water and pasture for their herds. One of the central themes of Libyan genocide is the word *marad*. It refers to physical illness and trauma. The Badiyya, or Badu, seminomads are economically and culturally inseparable from their herds. There is a saying which captures this symbiotic relationship in eastern Libyan Arabic:

"hail al-bawadi, hail al-haiwanis," meaning the strength of Badiyya is their ani-mals. The eminent poet Abd al-Mutalib al-Jamai in his ode "Al-bil (the Camels)" said camels make you proud and are blessed and the horses' role is to guard the camels. He also said, in praise of nomadism and Badiyya, "God blessed my father who made me free like a star in the heart of the sky."[46] Poet Khalid Rmayla al-Fakhri, who was interned in the Agaila con-centration camp, created a moving poem on the destruction of the herds. He referred to the animals imprisoned like him and his people at Barrakat al-Tyir, the camp of the airplanes, where the Italians put the herds of the interned of the Agaila. In six months, the animals died because of starva-tion and thirst like their owners. His poetry commemorates the plight of the herd, reflecting, "Today, at Barrakat al-Tyir, you are imprisoned like us, hopeless, with no good, and we are dying in the concentration camps."[47] Poet Sa'id Shalbi rode his camel to take refuge in Egypt, like many other people who had no choice after the internment of the whole civilian population in the concentration camps. The decision to go into exile was a hard choice for many people. They knew they would either be interned or forced to collaborate, so they fled. Freedom fighters were more eager to leave the region, going into exile in Egypt, which was nearby and open to them. This poet composed the most humane and moving poem, talking to his camel. The poem recounts how he had to continue walking around the Egyptian borders to take refuge, but the camel missed the poet's home camp in the Green Mountain. He spoke in the camel's voice as if it could talk. The camel continuously turned back toward Barqa, as if the camel was homesick as well, like a human! This is an example of where the culture viewed animals as humans and they were treated tenderly like fellow humans. This poem is touching, presenting the camel as if it fights colonial displacement and wants to return to eastern Libya despite the genocide.[48] Another poet, Ab al-Hadi Bukra al-Majari, captured in his poem the deep nomadic love for camels, as they are humans, "Nothing like camels, no cattle, no treasure, and the best of all; better than farming, beautifully created by God to hail no rival."[49]

Still another poet, Jilfaf Bush'rayya, described his life in the Slug concentra-tion camp in a poem that said, "Prisoners in the camp of Slug, we had no sheep or camels to be around us. In Slug, prisoners became poor, doing hard labor without pay." Missing the beloved animals is traumatic because the people and animals are an organic unit and the collective identity of the people and the way they view happiness and autonomy. Their identity and culture are linked with their animals. In a different poem he composed about the intern-ment, the poet's voice reflects,

> The Arabs are dying today. They are fed few grains of old barley from the garbage of other countries. How can we live with a quarter of a kilo? We are dying, some hanged, and others died in one battle.[50]

Poet Um al-Khair, who was interned in Braiga with her tribe, created the 'Abaidat poems about what happened in this concentration camp. In a poem about the lack of sanitation, clothes, and medicine, she spoke about bedbugs and *Baraghit*:

> Baraghit [bedbugs] kept us awake and a sand storm blinded us
> The bad guards of the camp made us ill at heart, depressed
> May God create a rival army who would crush them
> For what they did to us.

> But then, the poet in a moment of human weakness,
> fearing death, depression, and suffering, she turned to God in a poem,
>   saying:

> Muslims, my lord, are weak
> And there is no space left for them to even
> bury their dead ones
> They became ghanima, [booty]
> And their children are taken by the cruel Nassara [Christians]
> They took their money and
> Imposed their rule on them
> You either let them die
> Or get rid of their oppressors.[51]

She described the sadistic commander of the camp Barilla, "Your role is unjust Barilla. You took our money and killed our children." As for the Libyan collaborating guards, she said, "Oh, your bad intentions, you must have seen the devil, who spit in your mouth, and made you a devil."

Poet Hussain al-Alwani, who was interned in the Magrun camp, composed a poem describing the mass death in the camps, saying, "They were forced to walk all the way, and even Kofan could not be found to pay respect to the one dead."[52] The famous poet Hussain Muhammad al-Ahlafi, who was forced to go into exile, described the internment, stating even the number of the interned in the concentration camps:

> People were forced from Akrama to Butnan and left their sheep and cattle
> They were beaten by the army and the whips
> Merciless Habash, Musswa, Somali, and Sicilians soldiers
> Seventy thousand Barqawians died because of the hunger and beating.[53]

Another poet, Sa'id Shalbi, recognized that one Italian army was bigger and better equipped than the mujahidin:

> The lord brought this Italian army a mean and big one more than ours
> With cannons, airplanes, and power.
> What can we do, it is beyond our courage![54]

Al -Ahlafi said in a poem:

> We did not leave Barqa, brother, by choice
> We gave our best
> The noblest knights died fighting.[55]

There are many poems denouncing the collaborators who served in the Italian army as spies, soldiers, informants, guards, and administrators. Fadhil al-Shalmani composed a poem saying, "May God destroy the Italians and the opportunists who finished Muslims with their big army." Meanwhile, poet Musa Hmuda was even more damning in a poem that said, "Our hair turned white and there was pain in our hearts because of the pimps (collaborators) who sold our homeland for money and greed."[56]

The examples above are just a sampling of hundreds of poems that provide the rich voices and views of the victims of this genocide. The most moving and eloquent poem of the genocide and its internment is an epic poem "Mabi-Marad," introduced in Chapter 2. This brilliant poet uses the word marad 67 times and the phrase Mabi-Marad 25 times. Marad means various forms of physical, emotional, and social illness. It is about the whole collective trauma in the concentration camps. Marad, the title and structure of the poem, expresses various sides of an illness and trauma due to loss of freedom, honor, dignity, and self-sustenance which have since passed to many generations of Libyans.

Poet Buhwaish and others are claiming their right to be heard and acknowledged, and for the hidden history of cruelty to be recognized. The poet uses irony and difference, employing the title phrase "Mabi-Marad," "I Am Not Ill, Except," and then he lists 67 lessons or examples of why he is ill, such as: endless agony, loss of dignity, loss of good people, Younis, Mihimmad, and

> Abdalisarian al-'Azaila Bulzsain, al-oud, loss of young men, the absence of my thought, pride, the loss of sons, Musa, Jibril, imprisoned by scoundrels, lack of a cohort to complain to when wronged, the lack of those who rule with fairness, evenness, nonexistent, evil leaning bad or good, dominant, my daughters that serve in the despicable labor, lack of peace, loss of friends, death taken from them, the concept of Al Atati, Azir al-Nussi, Aiyez as well, the loss of day herds, rule by torture, tongue rived and sharpened with pounding abuse, the lack of defenders, the humiliation of the noble, the loss of my gazelle. Like unbridled, bad turn of my stars, the theft of my property, the tightness and misery of where I lie down to rest the horsemen who on days of fray shielded his women folk now begs, struggling after a tailless monkey, every day I miss complaining of subjugation, my spirit disguised and I cannot break my chains, beat shape of my life my lipid wilted tongue. I would not tolerate and now shame has overcome me.

This poem was composed in Agaila concentration camp where he was interned with his family. He belonged to the same tribe as the resistance leader 'Umar al'Mukhtar and, like him, he was educated in the Sanusi order schools and graduated from the order's high college at Jaghbub. He also became a shaykh of one of the order lodges and fought with Sanusi mujahidin defending the order's lodges in northern Chad when the French colonial army invaded.

The epic poem kept the memory of the Mu'taqalat alive. As stated earlier, my own mother, who did not have the opportunity to attend school, learned it by heart and recited the first sections of the poem at home as I was a child growing up in central and southern Libya. The poem is well known to most Libyans. It's the one that broke the silence and prevented the fascist colonial propaganda from completely covering up the horrors of the genocide. The poem countered the colonial narrative and was memorized, recited at social gatherings, broadcast on the radio, and printed in many books inside Libya and among those in exile. This poem was made popular because other Libyan poets replied to the poem using its poetic form and style to continue to add to what the original poet composed about the internment and genocide. The name Agaila was kept in the public consciousness after 1934 due to Buhwaish's epic poem. I met his daughter in Rajma, and have not given up searching for his photo, as he should be recognized as one of the most eminent of all Libyan poets, especially those of the anti-colonial struggle. This is a remarkable case for the power of poetry and for its capacity to keep survivors' histories alive and to oppose colonial silence.

There is no doubt that this ode was brilliant when memorized in Arabic. It used rural and Badiyya images and the vocabulary of everyday life and regional living. However, two other factors made it the most well-known poem in modern Libya: the Libyan tradition of recitation in social events and social gatherings, the cultural traditions inside Libya and in exile, and, finally, the use of modern print and mass media to read and broadcast the poem in clubs, on the radio and television, and now on the internet as well. Yet, the most effective means of spreading the poem was accomplished by other Libyan poets who would use the same meter to add to the original poem. Above all, it was a number of leading, talented Libyan folk poets who should be thanked for making this poem the most popular one. This poem, more than any other, kept the history of the genocide alive.

Buhwaish died on September 18, 1952, just after the country gained independence on December 24, 1951. He was buried in the cemetery of Sidi 'Abid in Benghazi. Poet Musa Hmuda al- Maghribi wrote a poem replying to Buhwaish[57]:

> Your imprisonment at Agaila
> I have experienced something
> Similar for a long time
> Your imprisonment, my dear one
> Written challenge by God as death
> We all humans have to face it All we humans?

Poet Muhammad Zaidan of Wadden also replied to Buhwaish's poem:

> I am not ill except the
> Imprisonment of your noble ones
> The arrest of your children and killing your
> Hope and distance from your homeland.

Poet Hawil Bufraj al-Ghaithi composed a reply poem from his exile in Egypt:

> Oh Buhwaish, the East became a prison in Agaila
> And what happened to you
> Also happened to us.

Poet Haiba Bumariyam al-Maghribi replied in a poem:

> I am not ill except I know your pains,
> The weakness of your arms,
> and your inability to walk.

After the 1951 independence, poets continued to reply to Buhwaish, such as Libyan poet Ali al-Fazani, who composed "A View from the Concentration Camp" for his collection *Death on the Minarat*. Another Libyan poet, Sa'id al-Mahruq, included a poem called "Dar al-Agaila" in his collection, *Poems that Silenced Voice.*[58] "Dar al-Agaila" includes the lines: "I am not ill except for the Agaila camp because I lost documents, and facts and I got lost."

Tunisian poet Ali al-Marzuqi composed a poem in 1997 inspired by Buhwaish that said:

> I am not ill except for my lack of light,
> Suppression of speech, and
> allowing what was illegal.[59]

The poem inspired two plays, one by the Egyptian writer Shawqi Khamis called "al- Mu'taqal" ("The Concentration Camp") and directed by Libyan stage director Salim Fitur, which was performed in Tripoli, Benghazi, Cairo, and the Damascus Arab Theater Festival in 1975. The Libyan novelist Muhammed Salih al-Gamudi wrote a play called "al-Agaila," which was directed in 1977 by Libyan director Muhammed al-Alagai. In addition, the Libyan playwright 'Umar al-Swihli wrote a play, "Mu'taqal," inspired by the Agaila camp and poet Buhwaish's epic poem. The late Libyan writer and later activist Tailb al-Rwaili also wrote a dramatic radio series called "al-Shabardag" ("The Concentration Camp"), which was later turned into a radio drama aired in early 1961 from Libyan radio in Benghazi. In addition to Buhwaish, an urban eminent poet Ahmad Rafiq al-Mahdawi played a key role in keeping the memory of the concentration camps alive.

Ahmad Rafiq al-Mahdawi and his epic poem "Little Ghaith"

The history of the internment was kept alive, as well, by the contributions of the rebellious Libyan poet Ahmad Rafiq al-Mahdawi, nicknamed *Sha'ir al-Watan*, the nation's poet of Libya, who was exiled three times because of his anti-colonial subversive poetry. He was born to a notable family in western Libya, in the town of Fassatu. His father was an Ottoman Libyan Qaim Maqam, an administrator of Fassatu, Nalut, Zawiya, and Misurata, and was active in the anti-colonial struggle after the Italian invasion on October 4, 1911. The family was forced into exile to Alexandria, Egypt, where Rafiq lived and studied before returning to Benghazi in 1925. The fascist plan for the "Reconquista of Libya" forced his family into exile in Turkey, where he lived until he returned to Benghazi in 1934.

In that year, he was able to visit the concentration camp of Magrun and the orphan school, where infants and children who were starving were enrolled. It was after that encounter that he composed a long epic poem he called "Ghaith al-Saghir," "Little Ghaith." Rafiq visited the school and met a boy whose name was Idris Imghaib al-Lawatti . Idris' family was interned at the Agaila concentration camp and his father was a mujahid who fought with 'Umar al-Mukhtar. The poem ends with 'Umar al-Mukhtar's death when he and other fighters tried to cross the border fence into Egypt in 1932.[60]

The poem is 100 lines long and composed as a story with Idris as the narrator. It is one of Rafiq's most famous and detailed epics and offers a haunting portrait of the concentration camps and their impact on children. This poem is remarkable and may rival Buhwaish's "Mabi-Marad." Both of these poems represent the richest record of the history of the internment. Rafiq's poem was composed in modern Arabic, not the Libyan folk dialect. Rafiq came from an urban middle-class educated family, while Buhwaish came from the hinterland rural culture and spoke the everyday language of the rural folks. I should add that, due to the fact most people were illiterate, folk poetry was more dynamic, as it expressed feeling, passions, and everyday life. Modern urban poetry was limited to educated elites in the cities. Rafiq, however, was a militant anti-colonial poet who refused to compromise his view of Italian colonialism and, even though he was at pains to leave Libya in exile, he continued to resist fascism through his poems. He became well known and many of his poems were widely circulated, especially "Little Ghaith." Upon the independence of Libya on December 24, 1951, this poem was assigned as reading for Libyan sixth grade students.[61]

These young students knew about the concentration camps outside eastern and central Libya through this poem, which was recited and even acted as a play in many schools. The founder of modern Libyan theater, Muhammad Abdalhadi, directed and acted in a play called *Watan*, or *Homeland*, in early 1940. The success of Rafiq's poem should be considered alongside that of Buhwaish, who also kept the history of the internment alive. These poets reflected two sides of modern Libyan poetry and culture folk, the modern use of Arabic and literature, and the oral and written modes of expression. Rafiq returned to Benghazi after the Allies defeated the German and Italian armies and he became a member of the Libyan Senate during the monarchy. Rafiq is a national figure because of his brilliant poetic work and his refusal to be bought off by the Italian colonial state and the postcolonial independent Libyan Monarchy. He was a tough critic of corruption and remained a strong and committed nationalist to Libyan unity and independence. Rafiq is honored by many institutions in Libya: the University of Benghazi gave his name to its auditorium, the City of Benghazi named a street "Rafiq Street," and the Libyan post office printed a commemorative stamp in his honor. An international conference was organized by the University of Benghazi, which published the papers and a three-volume collection of his poetry. Rafiq, and before him Buhwwish, are two giant anti-colonial poets who expressed the cultural history of the internment and the genocide. They combine the two sides of Libya's culture, the country and the urban, and provided material for the imagined community of Libya's nationalism. They were remembered after Libyan independence and still continue to be admired.[62]

Many contemporary Libyan novels were also inspired by the genocide experience. The most well-known examples are: Khalifa Hussain Mustafa's *al-Jarima*, "The Crime"; Ahmed al-Fituri's novel *Sirib*, "Old Narrative"; and Abd al-Rasul Uraibi's *Sanawet al- 'Adab al Si'ba*, "The Seven Years of Suffering." And, more recently in 2010, Libyan writer 'Umar al-Kikli dedicated his prison memoirs during 1978–1988 to poet Buhwaish. Two other contemporary writers, Ahmad Yusuf Agaila and Salim al-Awkali, inserted the camp experience into their literary creative writing. Their case is not a surprise. Both their parents were interned as children at Magrun and Braiga concentration camps. Ahmad Yusuf Agaila wrote a moving text called *Sirat al Naj'a, The Biography of the Camp*, (2003). He cited what his mother said to him when he asked her about the camp of Magrun:

> She closed her eyes and shocked her head. It is a long tragedy. May god does not repeat on any Muslim. We ate grass and rats, we even searched camels dung looking for grain but because anything else to eat we became just skeletons, skin and bones. I was just twelve years old girl orphan without my mother and father who died in the camp. I was crying all the time, my bad fate. They did not feed us, just a rationed of half of pound of flour we made a charcoaled piece of bread. Al- Shabardaq, the barb-wired concentration camp had long rows of tents as far as the eye can see and beyond. It had four gates and there were four cemeteries in front of each gate. We were burying the dead all day and at night, some died because of hanging and others because of hunger. There were cruel Banda, Massaoa guards who shut and punish people at any moment. Each of the four gates leads to a cemetery that is my son the Magrun concentration camp.[63]

Salim al-Awkali is a poet and journalist. His parents belonged to the 'Abaidat tribe who were interned at Braiga concentration camp which decimated two-thirds of the tribe. The poem about his father, composed in 2010, is moving.

> My father
> Loves Libya
> Tall and skinny
> Closes his eyes when he remembers the concentration camp
> Watches people pass by him and love silence
> We watch his hands
> And look in our soil seeds of his prayers
> And when we open the windows of the heart
> We see his old face like raining of old homesickness.

Al-Awkali shed more information on his father and the time he spent as a child at the Braiga camps in his powerful essay "Dhakirat al-'alam" ("The Memory of Pain"):

> My father lost his parents. He kept asking to read to him Buhwaish poem all the time until I memorized it as a young child. I learned from him that he lost two brothers, Hussain and Mabruk fighting with the resistance against the Italian army. His brother Hussain was a handsome young man who not killed in battle, his fiancé was forced to marry an Italian officer.[64]

This is the hidden history, a cultural history. It tells us that culture matters and poetry matters, but it is a history of ordinary people, a living history from the bottom up not from the state. This hidden history is mediated and narrated with different generations and people who have various characters, individualism, and creativity. In short, it is a transgenerational cultural history.

The next chapter covers the history of the present, after the genocide inside and outside of Libya. It includes the politics of memory in Italy and the USA, and ends with a new, concluding interpretation of the larger meaning of the Libyan case and its interconnection and impact on the study of genocide, especially the Holocaust, from transnational and comparative perspectives.

Notes

1 Interviews, Muhammad 'Usman al-Shami, June 13, 2007 Agaila and October 23, 2008, Benghazi. Also, Haj Muhammad Idris al-Shilmani, May 5, 2004, Slug, Haj Sa'id Atiyya al-Lafi, November, 2008, Benghazi and Haja Bahiya Hamad al-Abaidi, August 7, 2008, al-Iziyyat.
2 The Italian Archives is silent on the topic of deportation with only one report on the deportation of the
   Awagir Tribe to Slug by The Italian colonial Mutasarif of Benghazi ASAMI, vol.
   v, in ventari e, supplementi, Bacco 5, commissania to regional de Begnasi, Relazione

Sloug, 28 Lunglio 1932. 4. On the nineteenth century American removal of Native American Cherokee known as The Trail of Tears see *The Cherokee Removal: A Brief History with Documents*, (Boston: Biddeford Books, 1995), 160–162, and Amy H. Sturgis, *The Trail of Tears and Indian Removal*, (Westport: Greenwood Press, 2007) 58. On the mass killing of 30 million animals, see Andrew C. Isenberg, *The Destruction of the Bison*, (Cambridge: Cambridge University Press, 2000) 12.

3 On Italian colonial soldiers Ascari (*Askari*) from Eretria, see Uoldelal Chelati Dirar, "Truppe Coloniale e L'individuatione dell' Africa agency: Il Caso degli ascari eritrei," *A fricche e orienti. It ritorno della memoria coloniale*, 1:1 (2007) 41–56, and his earlier article" From Warriors to Urban Dwellers," *Cahiers d'etudes africaines*, 175 (2004) 533–574

 , Nir Arielli, "Colonial Soldiers in Italian Counter-Insurgency Operations in Libya, 1922–32," *British Journal of Military History*, 1:2 (February 2015) 47–66, and Alessandro Volterra, *Sudditi Coloniali. Ascari eritrei, 1935–1941*, (Roma: Franco Angeli, 2014).

4 On the colonial official letters see Giorgio Rochat "The Repression of Resistance in Cyrenaica (1927–1931)" Enzo Santarelli, Giorgio Rochat, Romano Rainero, and Luigi Goglia, *Omar al-Mukhtar* translated by John Gilbert (London: Darf Publishers, 1986), 78–79. This is an undated version of Rochat's 1973 seminal work where he stated that the internment was genocide.

5 The letter with a clear intention and plan for the genocide in Badoglio to Graziani June 19, 1930.

6 Rochat, "The Repression," 78–79.

7 Interviews with survivors, Muftah al-Shilmani, May 23, 2009, al-Magrun, Yusuf Sa'id al-Bal'azi, December 15, 2008, Agaila, and Ali Mijdal al-'Aquri, December 15, 2008, Slug.

8 On the Italian fascist plan to settle to two million Italian peasants and farmers in Libya, see Denis Mack Smith, *Mussolini's Roman Empire*, (New York: Penguin Books, 1976), 37, "Libya is Safe for White Settlers," *The New York Times*, (November 1, 1938), and John Patric, "Imperial Rome Reborn," *National Geographic Magazine*, 71:3 (1937) 269–325.

9 Interview, Haj 'Abdalnabi 'Abdalshafi al-Rifadi, interviewed by Muhammad Mukhtar al-Sa'di, January 23, 2008.

10 Ibrahim al-Ghmari-al-Maimmuni, *Dhikriyat Mu'taqal al-Agaila* [*Memoirs of the Agaila Concentration Camp*] second edition, (Tripoli: Libyan Studies Center, 2006), 91–98.

11 Interview, al-Shami, October 23, 2008, Benghazi.

12 Interview, Haj Idris al-Shilmani, December 15, 2008, Slug.

13 Interview, Haji Bahiya Hamad al-Abaidi, August 24, 2008.

14 Muhammad Abdalqadir al-' Abdali, interview, in Saad Muhammad Abu Sha'ala, *Min Dakhil al-Mu'taqalat* [*From inside the Concentration Camps*], (Tripolli: Al-Munshaa al-'Aamma Lilnshar, 1984), 42–48.

15 Mtawal 'Atiyya al-'Abaidi, interview, December 15, 2008, Slug.

16 Interview, Sa'ad Salim al-'Amruni, November 5, 2008, Al-Abyar.

17 Mahmud al-Shinaty, *Qa'diyat Libya* [*The Libyan Question*], (Cairo: Maktabat al-Nahda al-Masriyyia, 1951)

18 E.E. Evans-Pritchard, *The Sanusi of Cyrenaica*, (Oxford: Oxford University Press, 1949), 189–190.

19 See the study by Rochat "The Repression."

20 On the material and symbolic values of animals for nomads and seminomads in eastern Libyan culture see Emrys Peters, *The Bedouin of Cyrenaica*, edited by Jack Goody and Emanuel Marx, (Cambridge: Cambridge University Press, 1990).

21 Eric Salerno, *Genocide in Libya* second edition, (Roma: Manifesto Librio, 2009) bo, 79–81.

22 Rochat, "The Repression," 99.

23 A common trend is a deep trauma among the survivors for losing their animals and hands as in the cases of my interviews with Haj Muhammad Idris al-Shilmani, Yusuf Sa'id al-Bal'azi, Haj Murad Abdalhamid al-'Abar, Idris al-Marimi, and Jibril al-'Amruni (interview dates for last three December 5, 2008).

24 Muhammad Miftah, interview, in *The Mawsu'at Riwayat al-Jihad. Volume 22*, [*The Encyclopedia of Jihad Oral History*], (Tripoli: Libyan Studies Center, 1991).

25 'Uthman al-'Abar, Muftah al-Shilmani, Mabruk al-'Amruni, Abdal'Ali al-Fakhri, Muftah al-Shilamni, Mabruk Ali al-'Amruni, and Abd al-"Alial Fahkri interview, December 5, 2008.

26 Muhammad 'Usman al-Shami and Yusuf Sa'id al-Bal'azi, Agaila, interview, June 13, 2008.

27 Nuh Hamad al-Fisi, Rajma, interview, May 30, 2008, and Ibrahim al-Ghmari-al-Maimmuni, *Dhikriyat*.

28 Zahra Ahmad Jarba', interview, October 24, 2007, Benghazi, Aziz 'Abdaljalil al-'Aquri, interview, December 15, 2008.

29 Zahra Jarbu' interview, Ibid.

30 Haja Bahiya Hamad al-Abaidi, interview.

31 Haja 'Aziza al-'Aquri, interview, August 10, 2007.

32 Haja Riqiyya al-Fakhri, *Mawsu'at Riwayat al-Jihad*, interview, Volume 37 (special volume on women) *Zainab Muhummad Zuhry*, (Tripoli: Libyan Studies Center, 1995).

33 Interview Um al-'Izz al-Bal'azi, Haja Hania al-Lawati, Slug, December 15, 2008. A critical Italian source on the hanging of 'Umar al-Mukhtar see Santarelli et. al., '*Umar al Mukhtar* and Imran Bu-Rwais, *Waqi', 'Asr, Muhakamat, wa Shanq 'Umar al Mukhtar*, [*The Events, Trial, and Hanging of 'Umar al-Mukhtar*], (Benghazi: Manshurat Solphyum, 2003), also interviews, Ali Burhana, December 30, 2003, Sabha and Abderrahman Ayoub, March 6, 2007, Tunis.

34 "Arresting 'Umar al-Mukhtar, the leader of rebels in Barca," *Bred Barca*, 346 (September 8, 1931). Haj Abdalhamid Mihammad interview in *Mawsu'at Riwayat al-Jihad*, Volume 17.

35 Salim Miftah al-Shilwi, interview, June 10, 2007, 14–114, *Oral History Archives*, (Tripoli: Libyan Studies Center).

36 Haj Sa'id Atiyya al-Lafi, interview.

37 Haj Muhammad Idris al-Shilmani, interview.

38 Abdal'Ali al-Fakhri, interview.

39 Angelo Del Boca, *Mohamed Fekini and the Fight to Free Libya* translated by Anthony Shugbar, (New York: Palgrave Press, 2011), XV.

40 Hannah Arendt, *Eichmann in Jerusalem*, (New York: Penguin Books, 1994 (1963), 52–53, 276, 287, 180–181.

41 Abdali Abu 'Ajailla, in *Um al-Khair: The Poet of the Braiga Concentration Camp*, (Benghazi: Al-Maktaba al-Wataniyya, no date) and Sa'ad al-Hayin, al-Mu'taqatat, 46–47.

42 Fatima 'Uthman, in *Diwan al-Shi'r al-Sha'bi*, Ali al-Sahli, and Salim al-Kubti eds, (Benghazi: Garyounis University Press, 1998), 261.

43 Fadhil al-Shilmani, in *Diwan al-Shir al-Sha'bi*, 167–181, and Sa'ad al-Hayin, al-Mu'taqalat, 48–49.

44 Rajab Buhwaish, in *Diwan al-Shi'r al-Sha'bi*, 131.

45 Um al-Khair Abdaldim, in *Um al-Khair*, 15, 16, 35. Yusuf Salim al-Barghathi, "Al-Mu'taqalat wa al-Manafi," *Al-Shahid*, 10 (October 1989), 260–266.

46 On the cultural significance of camels in Libyan rural culture see ode/poem by the eminent poet Abdal-Mutalib al-Jima'i, "Il-Bill, al-Ibill [The Camels]," in *Diwan al-Shi'r and al-Sha'bi*, 32, 41, and 44 and poet Khalid Rmayla al-Fakhri, 83–85.

47 Poet Sa'id Shalbi, in *Diwan al-Shi'r al-Sha'bi*, 197–198.

48 'Abdalhadi Buqra' al-Majbri described a camel as "resembles nobody, God created it, beautiful forever valuable like gold?" Poet Ahmad Rafa al-shaib-Jama'ii described "camels like humans regardless of the fact they the fact they can't talk." See Ali Burhana ed, *Al-Shi'r al-Sha;bi*, (Tripoli: Al-Lajana al-Shabiyyia al-'Amma, 2000), 153.

49 Poet Jilghaf bush'rayya in Ali al-Shahli and Salim al-Kubti, eds, *Diwan al-Shi'r al-Sha'bi, II*, (Benghazi: Garyounis University Pess, 1998) 81.

50 Awkali, in *Um al-Khair*, 37–38.

51 Poet Hussain al-'Ilwani also described death in the camp of Magrun. See al-Barghathi, "Al-" *Al-Shahid*, 10 (October 1989), 260–266.

52 Poet Hussain Muhammad al-Ahlafi, in *Diwan al-Shi'r al-Sha'bi*, 215–224. See al-Bargathi, Ibid.

53 Poet Sa'id Shalbi, Ibid., 197–198.

54 Poet Sa'id Shalbi, Ibid.

55 Poet Hussain Muhammad al-Ahlafi, Ibid., 215.

56 Poet Musa Hmuda, Ibid., 235.

57 Found in Ali al Sahli and Salim al-Kubti, eds, *Diwan al-Shi'r al –Sha'bi*, (Benghazi: The University Press, 1977) 76, 235.

58 Ali al-Fazani, *Death on the Minaret*, (Benghazi: Al- Makataba al-Wataniyya, 1973) and Sa'id al-Mahruq, *Poems that Silenced Voice*, (Tripoli: Al- Dar al-Arabiyya Lil-Kitab, 1987).

59 The reply to poet Buhwaish's epic/poem came from all over eastern and central Libya, and from exile poets who used the same meter of the poem to support it and add to it. See *Diwan al-Shi'r al-Sha'bi*, 227–249. The epic/poem "Mabi-Marad" continued to have wide impact inside Libya after independence in 1951. The founder of Libyan theater, Muhammad 'Abdalhadi, wrote a play about the camps in Derna in the late 1930s, and the poet Ali al-Fezzani composed a poem with a homage to Buhwaish.

60 For a biography and collections of the poems and letters to poet Ahmad Rafiq al-Mahdawi (1898–1961), see Salim al-Kubti, *Wamid al-Bariq al-Gharbi* [*The Shining of the Western Light*], (Benghazi: Maktabal al-Tumur 5, 2005), 21–28. The best study of his poetry and place in modern Libyan literature is still Khalifa al-Tilisi, *Rafiq Sha'ir al-Watan* [Rafiq Poet of the Homeland] third edition, (Malha; Malta Interunit limited, 1976).

61 The poem/play "Ghaith al-Saghir' ["Little Ghaith"] was based on the real-life story of a child in the Slug concentration camp. His name is Idris Imghaib al-Lawatti. The poem was composed around 1937. The sources are not clear as to when or whether Rafiq visited the camp or if he knew about it since he lived in nearby Benghazi, the capital of the region. The orphan child, like the rest of his family, was interned in the Slug camp designed for his 'Awaqir tribe. He lost his parents and the rest of his family in the Slug concentration camp and then the Italian army put him in an orphanage school for 500 children adjunct to the Magrun concentration camp. Rafiq was exiled outside of Libya twice but his poem/play "Ghaith al-Saghir" became popular all over the country and even rivaled Buhwaish's "Mabi-Marad." The long poem "Ghaith al-Saghir" starts with the lines:

> out of all the orphans
> He stood outstands out,
> quiet yet dignified

After independence in 1951, the poem was required reading for Libyan sixth graders.

62 On the impact of Rafiq as dissident poet, public intellectual, and critic of colonialism and corruption see al-Kubti *Wamid*, and also the papers presented at the

international conference on Rafiq's Legacy, Muhammad Dghaim, ed., *Mahrajan Rafiq al-Adabi*, (Benghazi: Garyounis University Press, 1993).

63 Ahmad Yusuf Agaila, *Sirat al-Naj'a* [*The Biography of The Camp*], (Benghazi: Daral-Bayan, 2003), 60–62.

64 Poet Salim al-Awkali's poem "Abi," ["My Father"] was e-mailed to me by his daughter poet Fayruz Salim al-Awkali via my friend Ahmad al-Faituri, November 5, 2018.

4

AFTER THE GENOCIDE

Hidden and state histories

> We still tell our children and grandchildren what happened to us in the concentration camps.
>
> *Muhammad 'Usman al-Shami, survivor of the*
> *Agaila concentration camp, 2007*

> They wanted to kill and wipe out all of us in the camps.
>
> *Haja Bahiya Hamad al-Abaidi, a survivor of the*
> *Magrun concentration camp, 2007*

This chapter examines a riddle: why, despite the horrors of the genocide, has its memory been erased from mainstream scholarship. I seek to understand the factors behind this silence from 1934 until the turn of the twenty-first century. A second question, which one must raise after realizing the horrors of the genocide in Barqa, is the puzzling matter of why there were no war crime trials in Italy like the well-known Nuremberg Nazi Trial in Germany. Moreover, I shall examine the factors and the process that contributed to the silencing of the Libyan history of colonial genocide until the end of the last century.

There is a growing literature on the factors behind this historical omission in both Italian and Anglo-American scholarship. The apologists produced the myth that Italian Fascism was moderate and not as violent as the genocidal German Nazi state. As critically analyzed in Chapter 2, this Eurocentric claim assumes Nazi examples of genocide as worthy and, consequently, Italian Fascism did not commit such a similar genocide in Europe. But, if one includes the Italian genocide in Libya and later the atrocities in Ethiopia, then this argument is baseless and false. Instead, one has to go beyond Libya and Italy and study both of them from a larger transnational perspective to capture the meaning of this violent history. A second interpretation focuses on Cold War politics and the fear that the war crimes of the Fascist Italian government might help enable the election of the most popular communist party in Western Europe, the Italian Communist Party.[1]

The Allies and the Italian elite decided not to push for war crimes. The consequences led to silence and collaboration, which encouraged the production of the myth that the Italian people were good and moderate oppressors, unlike the German people who were seen as violent and brutal. Because of these complicated Cold War politics, one can explain the survival and the acceptance of the fascist parties in post-World War II Italy and their resurgence in the 1970s and 1980s, as well as why they became legitimate members of the Berlusconi Coalition two decades later, and again in 2018, which brought to power the right wing and pro-fascist Northern League to the coalition government.

I would argue that the Cold War context motivated the Allies to engage in a cover-up, providing the opportunity for them to oppose trials and remain silent, while propagating the myth that Italian Fascism represented a lesser evil than other genocidal regimes or, for that matter, that the genocide in Libya never even happened.

The Allies appeased the Fascists and Christian Democrats in Italy to counter the Italian Communists, allowing Italy to maintain its good standing in public opinion in exchange for its support in the fight in Germany against the USSR. Yet, Italian public opinion continued to be silent about colonial atrocities and to view its brand of fascism as an exception, or as moderate and benign. At the end of the post-1945 negotiations, even the Communist and Socialist parties who had negotiated war crimes trials compromised with the center and pro-fascist parties and refused to turn in fascist generals for trials in Yugoslavia.[2] By 1948, the drive to try Italian Fascists for war crimes had failed. Historian Roy Palmer Domenico, who researched that period's archives, wrote,

> The Anglo-Americans concerned themselves much more with German denazification than they had with Italian defascistization. Through the end of 1945 the matter was the exclusive domain of the occupation forces, and not until 1956 was the work handed off to the German administrators. One reason was that Britain and America considered Germany's position to be more critical than Italy's in the post-war world and therefore events in Germany were subsequently monitored more carefully. In the popular view, Hitler and his SS murderers embodied evil the way Mussolini and his "clownish" black shirts never did.[3]

The American and British governments also decided to oppose war crimes, due to Cold War considerations and the fear of communism. The Yugoslavian and Ethiopian governments tried, through the United Nations, to establish war trial commissions in 1948, but were unable to get the majority vote and succeeded only in submitting detailed war crime files. The most notorious Italian

Fascist general, Rodolfo Graziani, who was in charge of the Libyan genocide and other atrocities in Ethiopia, escaped serious war crimes trials.
Many Italian Fascists were saved from trial and public justice after liberation due to political calculations by Anglo-American policy makers. Domenico, the leading scholar on this topic, described the cover up in the case
of Graziani, explaining, "The Anglo-Americans brought 'The Butcher of
Ethiopia' back to Africa, to Algeria, where he and his American captors
enjoyed 'a bottle of very fine old cognac.'" Graziani stayed in Africa until
February 1946, when the Allies felt it was safe to relocate him in Italy. He
was then placed under Italian authority at Procida Prison.[4] In spite of the
known history, the image of the most brutal fascist general is still positive
among many segments of Italian public opinion. This should not be surprising because there was no serious war crimes trial. The public accepted the
myth of Italy's moderate fascist colonial past, or at least developed
a collective amnesia. It should be no surprise, then, that even the memory
of General Graziani is a positive and honorable one. And it is! On
August 28, 2012, the people of Graziani's birth town donated a bust of the
General as a memorial, honoring him as the most famous of their native
sons. It is not just General Graziani's memory that is honored, Italy, and
especially Rome, is still full of unchallenged fascist movements, in particu-
larones dedicated to colonial wars and atrocities.[5]

It is also important to keep in mind that Libya was still an Italian colony up
until 1943, and thereafter ruled by British and French administrations until
1951. Aside from the documentation provided in two books by active Libyan
leaders exiled in Damascus, there was little historical record to hold Italians to
account for the atrocities in Libya. The first book, published in 1931 by Bashir
al-Si'dawi, is titled *Fadi' al-Isti'mar al-Itali al-Fashisti fi Tarabulus Wa Barqa
(The Horrors of Italian Fascist Colonialism)*, and the second, published in
1932 by a group of authors, is titled *Al-Fadi' al-Sud al-Humr (The Black Red
Horrors on [or of] Italian Colonialism)*. An updated third edition of the latter
was published in Cairo in 1948.[6] The three editions were published only in
Arabic and were widely read in Arab and Islamic countries. However, no similar Libyan files were produced in English or other major European languages
as occurred in Yugoslavia and Ethiopia, simply because those states were independent after 1943, whereas Libya was not. The Libyan documentation of
colonial war crimes occurred only after Qadhdhafi and the young pan-Arab
Nationalists took power in 1969. Subsequently, the state-sponsored Libyan
Studies Center organized committees which filed and documented colonial war
crimes through many reports, journals, and publications produced between
1984 and 2008.[7]

It should not be surprising that anti-fascist Italian intellectuals, filmmakers,
and leaders focused on criticizing fascism inside Italy, while keeping silent
about the genocide in Libya and Ethiopia. The silence on Italy's fascist and
genocidal past was reproduced even in the mass culture, including by the inter-
nationally celebrated Italian realist and neorealist cinema created by talented

leftist filmmakers such as Fellini, De Sica, Visconti, Pasolini, and Pontecorvo. It may be possible that they were duped by the state and the common view inside Italy.[8]

The most famous film on colonialization and the struggle for independence, the classic *The Battle of Algiers* (1966) by Gillo Pontecorvo, should have portrayed the atrocities in Libya and Ethiopia. Is it because Algeria was known all over the world while Italian Libya was obscured and unknown? It is a puzzle. For Pontecorvo, was Algeria a safer case, or was it hard to make such a film inside Italy? He admitted that the Italian pubic would not have liked a film on Italian colonialism.[9] More research must be done to find out why. However, there is no escaping from the consequences of this silence on Libya's genocidal history. It opens the door for an uncritical setting for the cultural and artistic production of the misleading myth, of moderate Italian Fascism. A cinematic genre invented this myth and popularized it. Italian soldiers have been depicted in a new genre made popular by Italian, English, and American films such as *Mediterraneo, Tea with Mussolini,* and *Captain Corelli's Mandolin,* while critical films like *Lion of Desert* were being banned, and critical documentary films like *Fascist Legacy* were being purchased by the Italian RAI television channel and shelved to restrict their distribution.

Fascist Legacy was deemed dangerous because it revealed the secret and hidden history of fascist atrocities, genocide, and war crimes. I spent three years trying to find the film, and to contact the historian, Michael Palumbo, who provided the historical research and primary material that became the basis for the film, and I failed to find either. I discovered, to my surprise, that there exist only five copies worldwide. I could not locate historian Michael Palumbo despite the efforts of my colleagues and my university library staff. An Australian university agreed to mail me a copy of the film. Palumbo, who had discovered declassified files on the Allies' cover-up, had disappeared for two decades and I could not locate him. The case of the BBC documentary film on Italian Fascist war crimes and atrocities is significant. *Fascist Legacy* was an attempt by the BBC producers to show the dark side of Italian Fascism and break the silence, but it was thwarted and defeated by the Italian state. What an irony that the BBC, a public organization, supported by taxpayers in England for informing public opinion, was thwarted by power and politics, resulting in the censorship of its work. I did not know that there was a cover-up and censoring of the film, and it has been difficult to find the people behind this remarkable documentary. In March 6, 2018, I finally found the address for Ken Kirby, the BBC producer behind the film, who answered my questions and talked about the politics behind the shelving of the film and its puzzling disappearance from Western Libraries. Mr. Kirby wrote the following answer:

> Michael Palumbo told me that he discovered the original documentation in the Public Records Office in London. I think they were open to view

initially probably because people knew very little about Fascist Italy's war crimes. I don't think historians within the PRO understood the significance of the documents and they were open to be viewed. When Palumbo spotted the documents, he thought he would copy them but when he went to the photocopier there was such a queue that he almost gave up, but he decided he would wait and managed to copy them. It was a good job he did because when the Public Records Office found out we were making a film based around them many were withdrawn. I don't think this was due to any kind of conspiracy but the PRO, just being prudent, perhaps withdrew them temporarily to absorb their importance or significance. I am not sure if the documents were returned to public access. There was one large Black book in the PRO that Palumbo told me about which contained all the prosecutions of Italian War Criminals post war. All those prosecuted are listed, their crimes detailed, the sentence detailed (To be hung, jailed or released) When the two-part Timewatch *Fascist Legacy* was aired on the BBC it came down to BBC Enterprises – the commercial arm of the BBC – to do what it does best and sell them. I believe that The Italian TV RAI 3 was first on the waiting list and bought the film for a substantial amount of money. (Sorry can't remember the figure but for several years the films held the record for the highest amount paid for two BBC Docs) RAI 3 was keen to construct an entire evening's programming around the films and as the deadline came closer to handover and agreement to transmit the BBC got cold feet. BBC Lawyers, I'm led to believe, were afraid that despite the deaths, of people like Badoglio and Graziani, uniquely in Italy, the relatives can possible sue the BBC for the impact the films had on "Family Honor." The BBCs lawyers hesitated to the point where on the morning of the RAI 3 broadcast RAI 3 got cold feet and backed out. By the afternoon the BBC decided it was probably OK to let the film be transmitted and they would take the chance. Next on the waiting list was RAI 1 which, in the words of an insider RAI producer, "Buried it in the RAI Deepfreeze!" I suppose with the conflict in Yugoslavia its fate for being broadcast in Italy was sealed.[10]

It is not surprising that there were no academic departments of postcolonial studies in Italy before 1990. Only a few critical voices, such as the historians and journalists Del Boca, Rochat, Salerno, and Labanca stand out. Many Western scholars have bought this myth about moderate Italian Fascism, while others did not know of the existence of concentration camps and a genocide in Libya. After visiting several American universities, I reached the conclusion that there is a widespread acceptance of Italian Fascism as moderate and those propagating this myth have, until now, largely succeeded. The real challenge is to examine the actors and processes behind this collective amnesia so as to once and for all break the silence regarding the Libyan case of genocide. But, this is no small challenge. Italy still has not confronted its legacy of the colonial genocide and, even today, fascist movements, symbols, political parties, and even the celebrations of colonial soldiers persist. To expose the cover-up, break the silence, and debunk the myths about Italian Fascism one must challenge the fascists who are part of legitimate government today and other public figures, parties, and state institutions.

In the spring of 2000, I began my research on the history of the Italian fascist colonial internment in Libya. I had no idea what I might discover regarding the attempt to cover up the history of the internment. As I learned, the cover-up was signified by the destruction of archives and an attempt to silence this forgotten genocide. Both the fascist regime and the post-fascist regime kept silent about their actions, and also went so far as to invent and reinforce the myth of Italian Fascism as an aberration of Italian culture and society, as well as the myth of Italian colonialism as a civilizing regime. The colonial assumptions and production of these myths and narrative can be traced back to colonial policy. First, there was the military attack against the anti-colonial resistance and, second, a campaign to eliminate the civilian social base of that resistance. The censoring and destruction of the evidence and the production of the myth of a civilizing and modernizing colonial regime in Libya are the third dimension of the covering up of history and of the consequences of the Libyan genocide. The destruction of the archives and the rewriting of the history represent another integral stage of the colonial regime and its silencing of the genocide and its victims.

The archival research in multiple countries was frustrating, leading me, at times, to dead ends. I discovered that there were limited files on the internment, and encountered intentionally misleading language, statistics, and figures. I had to track down the survivors, as best as I could, and read all the documents, written letters, and archives, knowing that the survivors were nearing the end of their natural lives. In fact, by the time I began my research few were still alive. After a decade and a half of researching the internment, my view of that period has changed and, more than before, I believe that what happened in the period between 1929 and 1934 was not only one of the most brutal genocides after World War I, but was also one of history's most extensive cover-ups, which lasted until the late 1980s when a few studies started to challenge the myth, starting with a significant 1973 article by historian Gorgio Rochat calling what happened in eastern Libya a genocide. Despite this early study, and a few others such as Eric Salerno's *Genocide in Libya* and Angelo Del Boca's extensive work, the myth of moderate Italian Fascism continued to persist.

The question, then, is how to understand the process behind the success of the myth of Italian Fascism that until recently has been considered moderate and benign and to understand why most scholars and people did not know about the concentration camps in Libya. This collective unawareness is consistent in most recent books and scholarship on comparative and forgotten genocides. A few examples illustrate this. When I visited the Holocaust Memorial

Museum in Washington, DC, I looked for the section on colonial genocides. I found the case of the Italian internment of Libyan Jews in Jadu, but the wider Libyan case of the internment of hundreds of Libyan Muslims was missing. Italian censorship and Cold War politics and cover-up contributed to the same silence on the question of what happened in Libya. The questions then became: who is responsible for this historical amnesia and silence? Moreover, what happened after 1934 to those who were interned and survived? Who kept their history alive? What happened in postcolonial Libya, officially and unofficially? And, finally, why were there no criminal trials for the Italian Fascist leaders and the perpetrators of the atrocities in Ethiopia and Yugoslavia, in contrast with the Nazi war crime trials?

These questions regarding language and the writing of history are not just about the past, but also about the history of the present, to use Michael Foucault's famous argument about history, language, and power. Foucault argues that power produces knowledge and normalizes it as truth through institutions, including universities and scholarship. American political scientist James Scott builds on Foucault's critique, adding that this is not just a question of power, but also one of agency, and resistance by the dominated groups. He presented a critique of Foucault's method on challenging Western liberal modernity and epistemology as only a one-sided conceptualization.[11] Instead, Scott theorized about the dynamics of language and power using on- and offstage metaphors and transcripts. The onstage public "transcript" is advocated by elite and dominant groups, and an offstage behind-the-scene discourse of resistance he calls "weapons of the weak" everyday forms of resistance, or hidden transcript. Scott is right in his critique of Foucault's silence on the role of agency and resistance, but Scott equally overlooked how the ruling classes and dominant elites repress and silence the subaltern histories and the hegemony of colonial knowledge in the social sciences, which emerged during the age of empire and colonial domination.[12] To apply this theory to the Libyan genocide, one has to recover the hidden connections between Germany and Italy. I was not aware, until two years ago, of extensive Nazi interest and visits to Italian Libya between 1934 and 1940. The Nazi elite were not interested in British and French models of colonialism and settlements. Instead, they looked to Fascist Italy to learn from the "successful model," especially in the colony of Libya. This is a significant discovery, but it was not surprising to me.

The German Nazi interest in the Italian Fascist model in Libya

First, one has to recover a hidden connection between the German and the Italian states between 1933 and 1943. Recent German scholarship pointed to an overlooked collaboration where Nazi leaders looked to Italian colonial settler colonies, especially in Libya, as a model for conquering and settling around 15 million Germans in Eastern Europe. Historian Patrick Bernhard discovered in his archival and diplomatic research from Rome, Berlin, and

Tripoli, a long record of Nazi admiration and of Nazi visits to Libya to learn from the efficiency and the success of the Italian colonial model in Libya. These visits included Nazi scientists, urban planners, biologists, and agronomists, who were fascinated by the Italian model in Libya. Numerous German books and press articles were published between 1938 and 1941 on the success of the Italian colonial settlement program in Libya and, after 1935, in Ethiopia. German state officials who were responsible for planning policy began an active program of fieldwork examining the Italian colonial experience through contacting Italian officials and conducting fieldwork visits to Italy and the colony of Libya.[13]

Bernhard stated that German interest in the Italian colonial model became serious to the degree that the Third Reich Commissariat under Himmler's leadership organized special training programs for its staff. These culminated with the visits to Tripoli in 1937 and 1938 of high Nazi leaders such as Robert Ley, Rudolf Hess, the head of the SS Heinrich Himmler, and Marshal Hermann Göring. This led to the signing of an agreement to train 150 SS officers in the Italian Colonial School in Tivoli or Rome in 1937.[14] This so-called success led to the settlement program and the massive building of 40 villages, aided by scientists, geologists, and agronomists, for Italian settlers in the aftermath of the genocide of 1929–1934. The plan was for the arrival of 20,000 Italian settlers in October 28, 1938 who were to be settled in Libya and given the stolen land of the native people. Many German high officials, including the German labor attaché in Rome, were invited to travel with the ships that carried settlers with tremendous fanfare and propaganda by the Italian Fascist state. There is strong evidence that the Italian genocide, which is linked to the settlement plan after 1938, was the most attractive model for the Nazis. Consequently, it should not be too far-fetched for the Germans to have seen the genocide in Libya as a model for their own Holocaust, in addition to the earlier German Herero and Nama colonial genocide in South West Africa at the turn of the twentieth century.[15]

I shall address this argument and these questions inside Libya, Italy, and the USA, through an examination of the hidden and silenced state memories of transcripts from 1934 until now. It is a narrative of the struggle over regional, national, and transnational histories that focus on Libya, Italy, and the USA, using comparative and transnational perspectives, but keeping in mind the view of the Libyan survivors and the larger dynamics of Africa and the Arab Muslim world.

After the genocide, 1934–1951

By early 1934, the 30,000 to 40,000 estimated survivors of the genocide were freed but put under surveillance for two years. Most of the survivors were ill, poor, and weak, while others suffered from debilitating conditions, like blindness, as a result of the camps. They were not allowed to return to their homes, as their land had been given to the Italian settlers who had begun to settle in eastern Libya. The end stage of the internment resulted in the arrival of about 20,000 more settlers from Italy. The fascist state's goal was the settling of 500,000 poor Italian peasants in Libya and one million in Ethiopia after 1935. The oral history of the survivors spoke not only of poverty and their lack of land and their animal loss, but of people struck ill with disease and infertility for years. The communal trauma became transgenerational as each generation interpreted and preserved a new identity based on the context of the time under the monarchy, and the republic after 1969 and 2011. The testimony and the culture of the genocide is mediated by each generation. It is a process of living history which is communicated and contested in the eastern and, to a degree, the southern regions, while the West was not impacted nor aware of this brutal history.

The survivors spoke of not having children for four years, in some cases. Fu'ad Shukri, a notable Egyptian historian, was the leading scholar in Libya and an advisor to the Libyan Nationalist Movement in the 1940s. Shukri estimated that Libya lost half of its population because of the internment and its aftermath. He based this on the fact that in 1911 Tripoli, the name of Libya under Ottoman rule, had a population of 1.5 million, but, in 1951, the population stood at 779,072. Barqa had only 197,000 people, and there were only 570,929 in Tripolitania. Barqa lost half of its population and a majority of those losses were in the concentration camps.[16]

What happened to the 40,000 survivors after they were released from the camps in 1934? The survivors tell vivid stories of inhumane treatment, starvation, horrors, and death during the four years inside the concentration camps and enduring trauma for the ones who emerged alive in 1934. Abdal-Khaliq al-Fakhri of Slug concentration camp recalled, "We left the camps poor, ill, and without our herds and money." Haj Muhammad Idris al-Shilmani the Magrun camp said, "We lost men and money. We became poor and have lived in fear. Even today our families live in Zingo, or shacks; no, I do not want to have relations with the Italians after what we went through." Abdalhamid Ismail Hussain said, "Many of us were pressured to escape to Bilad al Hijra, or Egypt." Haj Hamad Fraj al-Awami al-Sha'ri of Braiga camp said,

> I was three years old when my family was interned, where I lost my parents and three siblings, and I had no option but to enroll in the Italian school for orphans. As a grown-up man, I worked for an oil company near the concentration camp of Braiga. I have gone to the cemetery and repaired the damaged tombs of my lost family, caused by wild animals and storms. Every year I have gone there for a visit to pay respect where I would read and reread al-Fatiha [Qur'anic verse] and ask God for mercy and a blessing for the dead ones of the concentration camps. I have done that because I owe them respect by remembrance. Remember son, I lost all of my family at Braiga concentration camp

Muhammad 'Usman al-Shami of Agaila camp told me,

> We tell our children about what happened to us at al-Agaila. These years
> were horrible years for the Libyan people. After we were released,
> I received no compensation. My mother died in 1940 and my father was
> poisoned by the Italians after being captured 1931. Even today we are still
> poor and destitute. We deserve recognition and reparation.

It is clear that many survivors and their children in eastern Libya kept the
memory of pain and suffering alive.[17]

Oral narrative of the internment kept alive; and this was important, con-
sidering that the genocide affected the majority of the population in eastern
Libya. One other group that played a major role in keeping history alive
was comprised of those who were exiled to Egypt, Tunisia, and Syria. In
addition, the Arab and Muslim independent press in these countries gave
the Libyan exiles support and allowed them to publish and advocate their
cases for Italian war crimes, including the mass killing in the concentration
camps.

The active exiled Libyans organized themselves in a creative and effective
new coalition which proved to be significant in countering Italian propaganda
and keeping the history of the concentration camps alive. The most significant
political organization was the Al-Lajna al-Tanfidiyya Lil Difa an Tarabulus and
Barqa (Commission for the Defense of Tripolitania and Barqa). This committee
was founded by educated Libyan leaders Bashir al-Si'dawi, Fawzi al-Na'as,
'Umar Fa'iq Shinib, Abdal-Ghani al-Bajigni, Abdalsalam Adham, and Hussain
Dafir Ben Musa in 1928, in Damascus, Syria. It established branches in east
Jordan, Egypt, and Tunisia. The Tunisian branch was led by the dynamic exiled
Libyan Ahmad Zarim al-Rhaibi. The well-educated and active group in Damascus was led by a respected veteran and Ottoman-educated Tripolitanian nationalist, Bashir al-Si'dawi. He had been active in the anti-colonial struggle since
1911 and was a member of the Ghawyan and the Tripolitanian Republic from
1918 to 1920. After the defeat of the anti-colonial resistance and the internment,
this anti-colonial and anti-fascist organization proved to be well organized and
effective in mobilizing Arab and Islamic support for independence and unity
through educating those in exile, keeping the Libyan case public, and by speaking about the Libyan case and against fascist atrocities. This activism kept documentation of the Libyan case alive from 1929 until 1943. As stated earlier, in
note 6, the most important documents printed by the group were published in
the book *Fadi' al-Istimar al-Itali Fi Tripoli and Barqa* in 1932. This book was
updated in 1948, first under the title *Al-Fadi' al-Sud al-Humr*, and then under
the title *aw al-Tamadin bil Hadid wa al-Nar'* (*The Black, Red Horrors* and
"*Modernizing*" *with Iron and Fire*). It presents a detailed record of Italian colonial atrocities and crimes from 1911 until 1932, including a chapter on the concentration camps with information pertaining to the number of people interned,
and the mass deaths due to execution, torture, and death due to a lack of food

and medical care. The committee also lobbied through the Arab and Muslim press by publicizing articles on Italian atrocities, including the concentration camps. They were unable to reach the Western press; thus, Libyan exiles' anti-colonial and anti-fascist activism and documentation is still unknown by most of the scholarship in English, with the exception of a book by Italian historian Anna Baldinetti.[18]

The black red horrors

The Libyan people who survived the internment reacted in various fashions, including oral history, folk poetry, memoirs, documentation, and activism beyond Libya, especially in other Arab and Muslim countries. The most organized and influential were the Libyan exiled activists in Damascus, Syria, who organized their efforts through the Commission for the Defense of Tripolitania and Barqa. The Commission published the remarkable book, mentioned earlier, first under the name of *Fadi' al-Isti'mar al-Itali al-Fashisti fi Tarabulus Wa Barqa* (*The Horrors of Italian Fascist Colonialism*) authored by the leader Bashir al-Si'dawi in 1931. This book is significant for two reasons. First, it is the first organized reply to Italian colonial and fascist propaganda covering up the genocide and claiming what happened in Libya was a small price for disciplining and modernizing the nomads and seminomads of eastern Libya. Second, the book is a clear and direct critique of fascism and documents atrocities, including the genocide. In Damascus, exiled Libyans found a sympathetic Arab and Muslim public opinion and were able to mobilize and send the book to their offices and supporters in east Jordan, Lebanon, Tunisia, Egypt, Arabia, and even to India.[19] The 1948 edition included a new section on World War II and the Libyan struggle for unity and independence. This edition was published in Cairo, Egypt, the new center for the exiled activists. Cairo became the hub for the activists after the 1945 formation of the Arab League, which called for the independence of Libya.

Al-Si'dawi and many exiled Libyan activists moved to Cairo for this reason and found in Abdalrahman Azzam Pasha, the Egyptian first Secretary General of the Arab League, a strong advocate in the Libyan struggle against Italian atrocities and the call for Libyan independence. Azzam Pasha was no stranger to the Libyan struggle. He was a strong Arab Nationalist during his youth and grew up as a supporter of Mustafa Kamel and the Egyptian Nationalist Party. He joined the party during the Ottoman fight against the Italian forces in Libya, and when the Ottoman Empire signed a peace treaty with Italy in 1912, he decided to remain in Libya where he joined the resistance. In 1918, he became an advisor to the Tripolitanian Republic. He married a Libyan woman and, after the defeat of the Republic, returned to Egypt and became the strongest advocate of Arab Nationalism and the anti-colonial struggle, highlighting the Libyan case. The book was reprinted in Cairo and became an influential shaper of Egyptian public opinion, evidenced by the fact that Egypt supported the Libyan struggle and opened its borders to thousands of Libyan exiles representing all walks of life and regions.

The 1948 Cairo edition of the book was published by Hai't Tahrir Libya (The Commission for the Liberation of Libya) and mocked colonial claims about modernization and progress. This book presents a remarkable documentation of and arguments against the horrors and atrocities of Italian Fascist colonialization in Libya from 1911 until 1943. The later edition included a section on World War II and the case for Libyan unity and independence. The book was dedicated to future Libyan youth, and the second page has a photo of 'Umar al-Mukhtar. The caption under the photo is a one-line poem by the famous Egyptian poet Ahmad Shawqi. It was an eloquent eulogy poem for al-Muhktar that became famous all over the Arab world:

> The Captive came,
> Dragging his chains,
> A Lion drags a black snake.[20]

The book includes a preface on the Italian economic and diplomatic activities in Tripoli to prepare for the invasion in 1911. The preface reveals that the main goal of the book was to expose the Italian lies and cover-up Libya's history. The second goal was aimed at emphasizing the Libyan people's right to self-determination and the need for Libyans to focus on unity and independence. The book makes a remarkable argument against the misconceptions pertaining to the horrors of colonialism and fascism by Italy. It continues by documenting all the atrocities committed against the Libyan people. The sources of the book include eyewitness accounts, along with Arab and foreign press coverage of the brutal history. The authors state that what happened in eastern Libya is a case of *Fada'ia, Ibada, wa Ifna* (horrors of genocide and extermination). The book relies on the Arabic language press in Egypt, Syria, Palestine, Lebanon, and Tunisia. The end of the book contains an index on reporting and analysis of the Italian policy of military services in the colonial army; it states that 40,000 Libyans, many of them orphans from the concentration camps, were forced to fight on the side of General Franco and the fascists in Ethiopia and Spain during the civil war. Sadawi first published a book in 1931. One has to remember that the first edition or second was published in Damascus in 1932 and that the second or third was published in Cairo as a result of the creation of the Arab League in 1945 and the movement of the Libyan Nationalist's activities to Cairo, the new center of anti-colonial struggle for all North African movements. In retrospect, this book is significant in cultivating a unified program, a critique of the colonial narrative, and a blueprint for the next fight centered on unity and the struggle for postcolonial independence. It is clear that the Nationalist group behind the makings of this book were clearheaded and rational about what occurred during the "Ibada, Ifna," or

"Genocide and Extermination." They were aware and well informed about fascism and colonialism and presented an alternative narrative for the genocidal history. They had a plan to translate this book into European languages, yet the Iraqi journalist Younes Bahri, who was commissioned to translate the book, took the money and failed to complete the translation task, a pity because had he delivered on his task, the fascist policy of cover-up and silence might not have been as successful as it has been. Emir Shakib Arslan, the fiery Arab Nationalist activist and editor of the anti-colonial newspaper *Nation Arabe* in Switzerland, published many articles in support of the Libyan resistance and exposing Italian atrocities in Libya before 1929. Unfortunately, he ultimately lost his commitment to the Libyan struggle after making peace with Mussolini and the fascist state and, ultimately, advocating for a compromise between Mussolini and Libya.[21]

Recent Western scholarship has focused on cases of some Arab sympathy and collaboration with the Nazi and fascist regimes, especially the cases of Palestinian Haj Amin al-Hussaini and the Iraqi Nationalist Rachid Ali al-Kilani. Such cases are used out of context and presented as part of a narrative to discredit Arab opposition to Zionism. While there are some cases of such collaboration in the region, such as Young Egypt, the Lebanese Phalange Party, and the Syrian Nationalist Parties, such cases are isolated and taken out of the historical context of anti-colonial nationalism against the so-called liberal colonial countries, including France and Britain.[22] What is overlooked is the Libyan struggle and fight against fascism, as in the case of the exiled Commission for the Defense of Tripolitania and Barqa.

The committee participated in the Islamic conference in Jerusalem in 1931 led by Bashir al-Sa'dawi and made a strong presentation against Italian Fascist crimes in Libya. The conference led with a moment of silence in memory of the Libyan leader 'Umar al-Mukhtar. Egyptian pan-Arab Nationalist Abdalrahman Azzam Pasha, who fought in Libya and was an advisor to the short-lived Tripolitanian Republic, made a critical speech on the Italian crimes in Libya, but the Italian government protested to the British mandate colonial administration in Palestine, who arrested and deported Azzam during the conference. Libyans exiled in Damascus were successful at engaging public opinion, not only having rallies and publishing articles, but also publishing books, such as the three authored by Libyan Nationalist, 'Umar Fa'iq Shinib. Of these three books, the second was *Andalus Muslim Spain*, which referred to Libya as "the mother of the last part of the Muslim World." This trilogy was aimed at assuaging Arab and Muslim international opinion at a time when Arabs and Muslims were still haunted by the loss of Muslim Spain, called the Andalus.[23] Equally significant was the 1937 publication of the first modern Libyan novel, *Mabruka*, by Hussain Dafir Ben Musa in Damascus. The novel was censored by the French colonial officials immediately after a protest by the Italian Embassy.[24]

Postcolonial Libya: the politics of the official and public memories, 1951–2015

Libyan state and public reaction to the genocide of the colonial period was complex due to the consequences of the Cold War alliance between the Libyan royal elite and the Western powers between 1951 and 1969. After the anti-colonial, pan-Arab military coup on September 1, 1969, a new state was formed as a republic from 1969 until 1977, and then a populist regime called the Jamahiriyya existed between 1977 and 2011. This populist dictatorship was defeated by a coalition of urban dissidents, defeated members of the regime supported by Gulf State monarchies, the USA, and NATO military intervention. The key question that will be examined in this text is how these regimes, the monarchy, the republic, and the Jamahiriyya viewed and reacted to the genocide. In addition, the question arises about how the civil society in the three regions of Libya reacted to and remembered this case of mass internment and extermination perpetrated by the colonial fascist regime. In other words, how did state and society struggle over this history and keep the memory alive, and how did the silence about it arise? What are the claims for representation and when did they become a national issue after 1969? And who and what was revisited and how did such demands lead to the 2008 Italian apology for the atrocities committed against the Libyan people, including for the internment? My main argument is that history is contested and fought over by the state and various regions and groups in Libya. Hence, the focus is not on memory or remembrance, but rather the politics covering the history of these memories and the present. Let us consider the name used for the country and its flags, the National Anthem, and the universities; in 1951 Libya was called the United Kingdom of Libya, but, in 1969, it was renamed the Libyan Arab Republic, in 1977, Libyan Jamahiriyya, and, in 2011, the State of Libya. I shall discuss the different social contexts in which the genocide is remembered and the politics affecting each context.

The Sanusi Monarchy and the memory of the genocide, 1951–1969

The Libyan nationalist movement that began in 1920 fought to achieve two goals: independence and exercising the right to natural self-determination and national unity of the three regimes of Libya, collectively combined under al-Istiqlal wa al-Wahda, or Independence and Unity. By 1943, most of the anti-colonial resistances' educated and charismatic leaders had been killed in combat, captured, and executed or had escaped into exile. The ones who had been either executed or killed by the Italian army or civil conflict were 'Umar al-Mukhtar, Yusuf Bu-Rahil, Fadhil Buomer, Ramadan al-Swaihili, Khalifa Ben 'Askar, Farhat al-Zawi, Ali Ben Tantuch, Sa'dun al-Swaihli, 'Usman al-s, 'Umar Saif al-Nasr, Ghadwar al-Suhuli, Muhammad Ben Abdallah al-Busaifi, and Muhammad Salih. The remainder of the leaders of the Tripolitanian Republic and the Sanusi movement were forced into exile. Many of them died, among them Abduljalil Saif al-Nasr, Muhammad Fkayni, Muhammad Hasan al-Mashi, Salim Abdal-Nabi al-Zintani, Sulayman al-Baruni, and Sayyid Ahmad al-Sharif al-Sanusi, the militant leader of the Sanusiyya, who was forced into exile under British and Italian pressure following his war against the British in Egypt in 1916. Sayyid Ahmad al-Sharif was exiled to the capital of the Ottoman Empire in Istanbul and then to Hijaz in Arabia, where he died and was buried.

The military defeat of the resistance decimated the educated leaders. Many of them died in battle, were killed by Italian jets, or died of hunger and thirst. Others managed to flee into exile. The exiled leaders played the main role in keeping the story of the genocide alive and the fight for self-determination for the Libyan people. Thanks to these exiled leaders the Libyan hidden history and cause was polarized in Arab and Muslim countries and the credit has to go to this active group of Libyans exiled in Syria, Jordan, Tunisia, Egypt, and Chad. Libyan independence was made possible as the Allies, especially the British, wanted to secure their place in Egypt and the Suez Canal. In addition, their goal was to have a moderate leadership that would secure British interests in exchange for granting independence to Libya, under the moderate Amir Muhammad Idris al-Sanusi, the fourth leader of the Sanusiyya and the King of Libya.

The Nationalist Congress Party of Western Libya, led by Bashir al-Sadawi, agreed to accept the Sanusi's royal leadership in exchange for keeping Libya unified. The new state was declared in 1951, a result of the public protest for independence, the advocacy of the exiled, and the larger geopolitical consideration which is behind the collaboration between the British and Sayyid Idris. However, this modern conservative state did not tolerate dissent outside the limited parliament, and when the National Congress Party became a threat in 1953, election to the elite political parties, including the National Congress Party, was banned. Its leader, Bashir al-Sadawi, was stripped of his citizenship and expelled to live in exile, as was the case with the radical historian of pre-Libyan resistance, Shaykh Ahmad Tahir al-Zawi, who spent most of his years exiled in Egypt. The main point here is that the Sanusi Monarchy excluded most of the nationalist figures and was dominated by urban and rural notable Libyans who made peace with the Italian state, such as the first prime minister, Mahmud al-Muntasir. His father and grandfather had collaborated with the colonial state and served as advisors and administrators within the state. In short, the historical context is essential to reading and examining the place of the internment and the genocide as it was perceived by the new Sanusi Monarchy.

These pragmatic and collaborative nationalist leaders must be placed in the limited choices they had in the 1940s. King Idris I's pragmatic policy is based on an argument that the country was very poor and that the eastern region infrastructure was destroyed during World War II battles. He and his royal elite decided that the time was not conducive for serious negotiation with Italy

over the war crimes of genocide. The Libyan Monarchy did though start negotiations in early 1952 with the Italian government on the legal transfer of settlers' ownership of land. The negotiation was led by Italian-educated minister
Muhammad al-Saqzli in the government of Prime Minister Mahmud al-
Muntasir. The Italian side refused the delegation's demand for reparation
for the destruction and suffering during the colonial period. The Italian side
argued that Libya was part of the Italian state; hence, the Libyan delegation
had no legal rights to reparation. Once again, opposition members of the
Libyan parliament asked the government to pressure the Italian side to compensate the Libyan people for their suffering and the crimes committed. On
April 6, 1956, al-Saqzli became prime minister. He pursued the case, but
his request did not lead to any action by the Italian side, which by then
was emboldened by the fact that the Allies had allowed Italy to refuse
demands for war crimes trial by the Ethiopian and Yugoslavia governments
at the United Nations. The Libyan attempts were kept alive because of the
opposition in the parliament, but the government was not keen on pushing
the issue.[25]

The major reason the issue wasn't pressed is that Libya needed financial support from the Allies, especially since it was one of the poorest countries in the
world, with a $35 per capita income. When Libya signed a treaty with Italy in
March 1955, it had only limited success. The new treaty indicated that Italy would
pay a million Libyan pounds for reconstruction and an additional 1.75 million
Libyan pounds to buy goods from Italy. According to Libyan historian Miftah al-
Sharif, who is an expert on the negotiations of that period, the Italians interpreted
this treaty as a final closure to the Libyan claims for reparation from Italy for the
colonial period.[26] There was no mention of the internment or the genocide in the
agreement. The Libyan side demanded 13 million Libyan pounds, but their
demand was rejected by the Italian side. The Libyan official policy was weak and
nobody with power was seriously interested in pressing the Italian side hard for
the war crimes. The discovery and the exporting of oil from Libya by 1961 gave
the Libyan royal elite some leverage in establishing the state infrastructure. This
conservative elite needed Wstern expertise and support, including the Italians, to
build the infrastructure of the new, poor state and ensure its security. The royal
elite were not interested in opening the question of the genocide and the war
crimes.[27]

As stated earlier, Libyan society has not kept quiet, especially when the
anti-colonial revolutionary movement was on the rise next door in Egypt after
the 1952 Revolution and during the Algerian Revolution from the period of
1954 to independence in 1962. The anti-colonial, pan-Arab military coup led
by Mu'ammar Abu Minyar al-Qadhdhafi revived the radical anti-colonial
resistance movement of 'Umar al-Mukhtar and the Tripolitanian Republic. It is
no accident that the first announcement made by the leader of the coup,
Qadhdhafi, included references to corruption and the tool of colonialism as
reasons for the needed change mentioned specifically by 'Umar al-Mukhtar
and the militant exiled leader of the Sanusiyya, Sayyid Ahmad al-Sharif. The

ideology of Qadhdhafi and the nationalist officers who toppled the Sanusi Monarchy should be interpreted as a delayed reaction to the crimes of Italian colonialism. Some of Qadhdhafi's early officers even made radical and outrageous speeches, invoking memories of the concentration camps, especially after Qadhdhafi recanted and condemned the silence of the monarchy regarding the Italian atrocities, continuously repeating, "Remember what happened at Agaila concentration camp."[28]

Qadhdhafi was born near the city of Sirte, not far from the Agaila and Braiga concentration camps. His small tribe was historically a smaller unit of the tribal alliance of Saff al-Fughi, the upper alliance which fought both the Ottoman and the Italian colonial states. He mastered the history and the decentralized traditions of central Libya and used them against his rivals inside the Revolutionary Council, and against what he regarded as the urban population that had collaborated with the Italian state. By the end of the 1970s, his faction had removed his rivals and, as a result, anti-colonial populism became a tool to establish a cult of leadership that systematically reread Libyan Jihad to target his opponents inside and outside Libya.

In the 1970s, the new nationalist regime started to put specific pressure on Italy to compensate Libya and apologize to the Libyan people for war crimes. The strategy was so strong that it became embodied in Libyan state education and cultural media, led by Qadhdhafi himself. The Libyan Studies Center was named to collect and record the history of the resistance and thus became the face of the resistance. The founder and the director of the Center, Dr. Mohamed Jerary, granted the regime the materials on the resistance it required. In addition, Dr. Jerary used state funds to build a first-rate academic center. Radio and television in Libya interviewed veterans of the anti-colonial struggle, and Shaykh Ahmad Tahir al-Zawi was invited to come back from his Egyptian exile and was appointed as the new mufti of republican Libya. The bodies of anti-colonial leaders who died in exile were brought back and reburied in al-Hani National Cemetery in Tripoli. The two most visible cases were the bodies of Sulayman al-Baruni and Bashir al-Si'dawi, whose remains were returned in 1970 and 1973. They were given a national ceremony, which was covered by Libyan newspapers and television. Monuments were built to signify battles against Italian colonialism. All these nationalistic symbols were promoted by Qadhdhafi himself, and often he would give an anti-colonial speech retelling the history of the event and the national struggle. The objective was to boast about the regime's nationalist credentials and his legitimacy as an heir to the leaders of the Libyan struggle for independence and unity. These symbols and policies were aimed specifically to appeal to the poor and rural, and the interior and eastern communities that were interned or who fought against Italian colonialism.[29]

The regime's anti-colonial populism began to lose support by the end of the 1980s. The regime's erratic economic policies, political repression of dissent, and the Qadhdhafi cult of leadership led to a crisis that lingered until 1988, when the regime freed political prisoners and dissidents. In addition, the Regan administration's sanctions against the regime caused economic and social hardship and black-market activities and corruption. The regime reacted with further repression and purges of the universities and professional associations. These policies backfired and led to radicalization of the youth, many of whom joined radical Islamic movements that spread across the region, a result of the crisis of the nationalist military regimes in Egypt, Iraq, Syria, and then Libya.

Italy's ambiguous apology and the treaty of 2008

The demand for compensation and apology by the Libyan regime paid off when the Italian billionaire prime minister, Silvio Berlusconi, agreed to give Libya a vague apology and to pay five billion dollars as compensation for the crimes of the Italian colonial period. The language was not very clear, mandating a simple "sorry" for what had happened, but the Libyan leadership hailed this as a clear victory for the Libyan people. To be fair it was a major accomplishment and Qadhdhafi should be given the most of the credit for it. No other European state has apologized for the colonial atrocities in Africa, except for Germany, which apologized for the genocide committed against 80,000 people in German South West Africa (now Namibia) between 1904 and 1908. By that measure, the regime did achieve a victory greater than that of any other postcolonial states, including Algeria, Egypt, India, and Congo. The survivors of the camps did not receive any compensation, nor were there trials for the Italian war crimes committed by the Italians and their loyalist colonial soldiers from Libya. There was no attempt to educate the illiterate or open a debate about either the silenced history, the rebuilding of the camps, the honouring of the dead through new monuments or memorials, or a demand to reopen the archives and record the names of all the victims of the genocide. In the end, it was a step forward but not much more than a public relations campaign for the regime and a business deal for the Italian government, as the Libyan government agreed to grant Italian corporations' big investments in the Libyan economy. Libya also agreed to cooperate with Italy in stopping illegal immigration from Africa south of the Sahara through Libya into Italy.[30] Yet, the most positive outcome has been the start of collaboration between Italian and Libyan scholars on rewriting the history of the concentration camps. There have been four meetings in Tripoli, Rome, and London between 2003 and the present. These meetings may lead to more collaboration on the Italian and Arabic secrets of the genocide.[31] Given Libya's more recent role in diminishing blame for Italy's brutal fascist colonial history, how has Libyan society itself reacted directly and indirectly to its higher expectations for a resolution that will meet its national and cultural demands?

I investigated the societal reaction of Libyan college and university students' reactions to this question during the period between 2007 and 2009 using a survey of comparative colleges in different locations (see Appendix A 5).

The questionnaire comprised five questions on how they first heard of the internment, at home, or school, or from other sources and I also wanted to know what their most significant story was about the internment and what should be done in the future to address it. I distributed these questions to seven universities in the four regions of Libya to find out how the Libyan youth reacted to this significant debate. University mass education included all Libyan youth, so surveying and assessing college students' views is representative of the views of much of Libyan youth. The questionnaire answers were very helpful and interesting and can be used to interpret the history of the present.

Libyan university students' views of the memory of the colonial internment and genocide

The question now is how have young generations of Libyans remembered and viewed the 1929–1934 genocide? I chose to investigate the reaction of undergraduate college students in the four regions of the country – the east, the center, the south, and the west. The responses provided by university students on the seven campuses of the three eastern regions were as I expected, but with some surprises. Undergraduates in the eastern region where the internment took place were largely as expected. Eastern students knew of the internment and cited what happened to their grandparents and relatives, in detail. That was the result of my survey of the reactions of the students of Garyounis, now the University of Benghazi, and 'Umar al-Muhktar University in Bayda. It is safe to say that this awareness of the history of the internment is not the result of state education and media, but rather from family socialization and a strong oral history. Students responded from the colleges of arts and sciences' departments of economics, political science, and history at the University of Benghazi, and from the sociology and history departments at 'Umar al-Mukhtar University in Bayda. My guess was that this trend would be representative even at the colleges of medicine and engineering as well, due to the role of the family and of the community's strong oral memory of the colonial period, including the dramatic deportation and internment. Here are some samples of the students' answers: "I learned about the Mu'taqlat from my grandparents who were interned in Magrun camp," "We learned about it through our elders whenever we get together for social events," "We learned about the genocide at early age through our families who were interned." The students at 'Umar al-Mukhtar University were very specific in their answers and they said that their parents or grandparents were interned at Agaila or Braiga. This reaction should not be surprising because the majority of the students are from the region that was massively deported and interned. They did not mention the other death camps, Slug and Magrun, because they were populated by the 'Awaqir tribe who live west of Benghazi. The answers of the University of Benghazi students also echoed the same role of their families, but they included Slug and Magrun. The family and the community kept the young informed about the concentration camps' terrible history.[32]

The responses to my survey at the four western Libyan universities were different. I passed my questions through colleagues at the following institutions: al-Fatih University, the University of Tripoli's departments of history, political science, public administration, and history; Zawiya University; and two universities on international relations at al-Taqadum, Nasir; as well as the foreign ministry's Diplomatic Institute; and, last, the Center of Libyan Studies Center in Tripoli. The responses from these western universities share a common lack of specific knowledge of the internment, aside from information based on the film, *Lion of the Desert*. This film seems to be the most influential source of awareness and knowledge by non-eastern Libyan students about the genocide in the concentration camps in eastern Libya.

Only a few of the students from western Libya remembered the poem "Mabi-Marad," "Except," however, and not as well as the students in the eastern region, who remembered it and recited its first lines. This finding was surprising, especially among young Libyan college students. The Libyan regime boasted of making the history of the Italian colonial period the key element of its mass media and populist anti-colonial ideology and education in schools and universities after 1969. Despite few students knowing details about the internment, they were very eager to learn more and they all praised the film *Lion of the Desert*, recounting that they had, in many cases, watched it several times. A third of the students at the universities of Tripoli and Zawiya Uwere unaware of the Mu'taqalat history but also, they were critical of the educational policy and the failure to educate them about this history. Here are some of the answers: "I have not heard of it and you'd be surprised this is the first time for me to hear of it," "I have never heard of the poem Mabi-Marad due to the lack of good education, they did not teach us."[33]

The answers of the college students in central (Waddan) and southern Libya (Sabha) are similar to those of the east – very strong knowledge due to the impact of the family and community, but a new factor is mentioned, the role of teachers and schools. The public school curriculum is the same all over the country, and that is why this factor is significant. Here is some of what the students said: "My family told me and in school," "We learned about it in elementary and middle schools, "We read about it in a book on history and in elementary school," and one student said, "I first [learned] through a speech by brother Colonel Qadhdhafi when he spoke about the horrors of Agaila concentration camp in 1999."[34]

One takeaway from these findings is the state's failure in making documentaries and films to educate the young about the atrocities of the colonial period. This reaction should be placed within the context of wider alienation from the Qadhdhafi regime. The regime used the heavy ideology of anti-colonial populism history as a weapon to mobilize support and punish its opponents when needed. This policy alienated many of the young, who had to receive military education, but felt limited with no social clubs, libraries, cafes, or entertainment. The male students became alienated from the heavy state media culture of ideological mobilization, hero-worshiping, and the lack of specific scholarly study of the internment. The female students benefited from state policy and the opening of schools and universities for Libyan women, and thus took full advantage of it to the point that the majority of undergraduate students, especially in the humanities, were female. The female population dominated males by at least 70%.

The Libyan students in central and southern Libya presented some interesting findings, which showed a wide variance on how they remembered the genocide compared to the students in western Libya. Students in central and southern Libyan universities were aware of the genocide due to their having more interaction with the east and a greater sense of common history. The social alliance emerged during the anti-colonial struggle, built through the strong ties to the Sanusiyya movement, the main organization which led the anti-colonial struggle. The leaders of the resistance in central and southern Libya were the brothers Abduljalil and Ahmad Saif al-Nasr, who were Sanusi followers like 'Umar al-Mukhtar. The two Saif al-Nasr brothers led a strong confederation of tribes, peasants, and merchants known since the nineteenth century as Saff al-Fughi. One has to keep in mind that tribesmen, town peasants, and merchants have been linked through economic exchange and integration during the date season; in the fall, northeastern tribesmen will travel to central Libya and be hosted by specific families and barter in exchange for dates, grain, and animals. These regional memories existed until the end of the colonial period and made migration and the conveyance of news accessible to people in central and southern Libya. In addition, many people from those regions fought alongside 'Umar al-Mukhtar and some were interned at Agaila concentration camp. This historical background shed light on the fact that young Libyan college students in central and southern Libya knew more about the concentration camps than people in the west.

Another interesting finding from the survey questionnaire is on the role of pre-college education in teaching the history of the genocide, especially the role of teachers. In central and southern Libya, teachers played a larger role in discussing this history than it seems teachers did in the western regions. Many students referred to their families but, above all, both males and female said that their teachers were aware of and passionate about the anti-colonial struggle, acknowledging the concentration camps, the al-Mu'taqalat, or Mu'taqalat al-Ibada, the camps of death. The answers by the College of Economics and Banking in my birth town, Waddan, in central Libya, indicate a different view and the answers confirmed this conclusion regarding the role of education and teachers. It's essential that I explain the significant role of teachers in central and southern Libya, which can be explained through both geography and history. Libya is a large country, which creates very large distances between eastern, western, and southern Libya. Geographical distances are a factor, but the history of regionalism is a second factor as well. Libyan hinterland people maintained a culture of decentralization and semiautonomy from the central government even after independence in 1951. True, Libyans were unified in calling for unity and independence, but they wanted a minimal state and valued the decentralized social and cultural management of their affairs. This interior culture of autonomy is even more evident after the end of the colonial period. It confirmed the distrust that the people of the hinterland harbored toward the modern state and their view of it as violent and to be feared as a necessary evil. The coming of Libyan independence in 1951 and the institution of the federal system between 1951 and 1963 enhanced the regional autonomy of central and southern Libya and the establishment of schools in Fezzen and the capital city Sabha. Even Libyan and Arab teachers who were hired to teach in Fezzen found a climate of more freedom and autonomy to teach. Both the distance from Tripoli and the leadership of the region made this relatively open social and political climate in Fezzen possible, especially if one keeps in mind the wise role played by the first walii, the governor of Fezzen, the anti-colonial leader Ahmad Saif al-Nasr. He returned with the French army and with other exiles from Chad and was joined by others from Egypt.[35]

My own maternal grandfather, Ali, and my mother, aunt, and uncle, returned to Libya from exile in Faya, Chad in 1940. Sabha was a rising, modern Libyan city with bookstores, newspapers, bands, a high school, and the only cinema in southern Libya. There was a UNESCO library, a high school library, a teachers college library, and an American cultural center in the middle of the desert. These regional, free institutions and their distance from the central government were most impressive. The state of Fezzen also hired some outstanding teachers from all over the country and other Arab countries. The state of Fezzen had a printing house and weekly newspaper, which was relatively free, to the point that it attracted the most gifted Libyan journalists and writers who were censored in Tripoli but found more freedom and a more open press in Fezzen. There were police and high school marching bands as well. Ustadh Faruq al-Diib was recruited to teach the police marching band of the state of Fezzen and after five years the governor of the state asked him to teach students in middle school as well. He chose 20 out of the 60 students, and I was lucky to be one of them, as a member of the school marching band. My teacher taught us music for six years. He was a brilliant Egyptian man from the city of Alexandria, who was hired, as he told me, by a committee from Fezzen that traveled to Egypt. The historical social history of the Fezzen is yet to be written and it matters in explaining the living memory of the internment in central and southern Libya.

Below is a summary of the students' answers to the survey in western, central and southern Libya:

1. **Progress University, Tripoli (10 students)**
    They remembered the camps, particularly the Agaila camp, from elementary school education, and also the film about 'Umar al-Mukhtar, *Lion of the Desert.*

2. **Nasr International University, Tripoli (6 students)**
   They learned about the history through families, school, and the film about 'Umar al-Mukhtar.
3. **April 7th University, Zawiyya (now Zawiyya University, 29 students, female)**
   The film about 'Umar al-Mukhtar is the main source of information for the concentration camps. Only one student knew the poet Buhwaish and his epic work Mabi-Marad, and that was through her father. Students asked that Italy apologize to the Libyan people.
4. **College of Economics and Banking, Waddan (40 students, 24 faculty)**
   The majority of the students (38) knew about the internment. They stated that this was through their families at home, their teachers, and television programs on the topic. Also, I discovered from the answers that there were a few Arab faculty from Egypt and Iraq who stated in their answers to my questions that they knew about 'Umar al-Mukhtar before coming to Libya and that the film enhanced their view of him as mainly an Arab and Muslim hero. Yet, the students stressed the role of their parents and teachers for making them aware of the internment and the atrocities of Italian colonialism. All students were aware thanks to their parents and teachers, except one who said that he knew about the concentration camps through Qadhdhafi's speech in 1999 about the Agaila camp. One must bear in mind that Colonel Qadhdhafi was talking about the camps, especially Agaila, as early as the 1970s. Qadhdhafi spoke loudly and repeated for many years the phrase, "Remember what happened at Agaila concentration camp.' This was repeated time and time again through Libya. I found this to be the most commonly repeated theme in his speeches, which are available in the multivolume al-Sijil al-Qawmi, The National Record.
5. **Sabha University, Sabha (121 students from the colleges of humanities, social sciences, science, agriculture, medicine, and engineering)**
   Students' answers identified an awareness of the concentration camps and they attributed this awareness to the role of their teachers in elementary and high school, in fact only one student did not know about the camps. This exceptional role of education and teachers in central and southern Libya is indeed the key factor, as the students' answers indicated that about 100 more students knew about the camps in central and southern Libya than in western Libyan universities, where there was limited knowledge of the camps, and some students even stated that they have never heard of them.

It is safe to conclude that the memory of the concentration camps varied from one region to another in the four regions of Libya. The survey shows that Libyan college students have strong memories in the east, central, and southern regions, but weak memories in the western region. The film *Lion of the Desert* was significant all over the country and is shown annually on

Libyan television. However, the role of the family made the biggest difference in the eastern region. This is not surprising as most of the students there lived in extended families and had grandparents who had survived or died in the camps. What is surprising is the role of both the family and the teachers in central and southern regions. Teachers made the extra impact on their students' knowledge of the history of the concentration camps in central and southern regions. The survey contradicts the claims of the Qadhdhafi regime as a revolutionary anti-colonial state which recovered Libyan resistance history. The students were very critical of the educational system and recommended a more in-depth educational curriculum on the history of the concentration camps, the building of a museum, and the organization of student visits to the camp locations. Finally, the empirical survey of Libyan university undergraduate students' perceptions and knowledge of the camps shows the complexity of this social memory, which is varied because of geographical and historical reasons. The Libyan elites, after independence in 1951 and up until now, have neglected this terrible history of genocide. This brutal phase of Libyan history was not a top priority for the monarchical and populist regimes. Instead, the task of keeping the memory alive was taken up by social initiatives and non-state actors.

In addition to the variance created by regional identity, after 1969 anti-colonial nationalist officers spread awareness of the history of the genocide. These anti-colonial nationalist officers made the history of the Libyan Jihad a top priority, at least in the first two decades. Qadhdhafi later took this anti-colonial view of history and used it along with the symbols of the anti-colonial struggle, including the heroes of this struggle, as a tool to consolidate his regime and remove his rivals inside and outside the country. Ironically, Qadhdhafi's populist dictatorship's most positive investments, which will last for a long time, were the building of an academic research center, the Libyan Studies Center, and the financing of the international film, *Lion of the Desert*. One may ask why these two, an academic center and a film, became the most lasting legacies of the populist period after 1969.

One factor is the role of leadership. Mohamed Tahir al-Jarary, the founder of the Libyan Jihad, was an effective administrator and scholar. He accepted state funding and created some symbolic rituals to keep Qaddafi quiet, but also used the money to build a first-rate scholarly academic research center by international standards. The wise Libyan Minister of Foreign Affairs, Muhammad Abulqasim Al-Zuawi, promoted the agreement behind the production of the film on 'Umar al-Mukhtar. He chose the talented and critically minded Mustafa Akkad, a Syrian-American filmmaker who had made a career in Hollywood by producing major blockbusters, such as *Halloween*. Al-Zuawi gave Mustafa Akkad total freedom to hire top-notch people while he made the film between 1979 and 1980. This film did not do well in the USA but was a hit overseas – especially in the Arab and Muslim world – and continues to be popular today. The Center and the film kept the memory of the Libyan anti-colonial resistance alive inside Libya, even though the state claims to have done more for this struggle while ignoring the terrible atrocity of the genocide at the camps between 1929 and 1934. In addition to the role of the Center and the film, certain individuals, especially in Benghazi but above all in the small town of Hun in central Libya, are worth mentioning.[36]

The people of Hun founded an association called "The Association of the City Memory on Hun" in 1992. The leaders of the initiative were the late Libyan poet and political prisoner Senusi Habib and writer and folkorist Abdallah Zagub. The Association stated the following:

> Collecting the oral history of "Jalwa", the people of the town [who] in 1928 [faced] a collective punishment for their support of the Mujahidin, who attacked the Italian army at the battle of 'Afiyya in November 14, 1928. The following day, the Italian army hung 19 elders of the town, and deported the whole of the town on foot to Misurata and Khums.[37]

The Association not only collected the oral history of the Jalwa but also began an annual program to educate the young by reenacting the hanging and the deportation, visiting schools, and holding a series of lectures. The Association also invited the people of Tripoli and Benghazi to attend the annual commemoration of the suffering of the people of Hun under Italian Fascist rule. These activities have been taking place annually since 1992. Furthermore, the Association made a documentary film about what happened and asked some lawyers to draft a legal suit against the Italian government, which was given to the Libyan Studies Center and the Italian Embassy in Tripoli.

Abdallah Zagub, the director of the Association, provided me with the history and publications and the aforementioned legal document. I interviewed him, and he was gracious enough to e-mail me all the needed documentation of the work done by this remarkable small town in central Libya, using not state money, but voluntary contributions from civilians. Hun is an impressive example of civil volunteerism, the basis for the history deriving from a brilliant poem written by the poet Fatima 'Uthamn in 1928 when she was 20 years old. The poem is called "Our Homeland Ruined Twice." In conjunction with the poem, the Association's work, which began in 1992, focusing on preserving history has made the case of Hun one that is alive, current, and everlasting. The Association also drafted a petition, which was approved by the community, requesting reparation from Italy. The text raised a central question regarding the suffering and the crimes of Italian Fascism against the town of Hun and the need to heal the open wounds of colonial history and to restore normal healthy relationships between the Libyan and Italian people, based on respect and acknowledgment of what had happened to the town between 1928 and 1930. The text specifically included the following grievances: killing, exiling, stealing property, deporting people, and psychological and traumatic abuse in the painful collective deportation of the year of "Jalwa," 1929. Italy, the text stated, must offer recognition of both material and physical crimes against the people of Hun. The document requested a house, a farm, and two years' salary to all the 550 families who were victims of the colonial deportation, exile, and loss of property. These are just demands and would go a long way toward healing the wounds of colonial crimes against the people of Hun. The text was submitted to the local popular committee and the Libyan Studies Center, the Libyan foreign ministry, and the Italian Embassy in Tripoli, on January 20, 1992. Unfortunately, the Italian government refused to reply to this civil initiative by the people of Hun. What mattered most, though, is the fact that people took matters into their own hands and tried to record their own history and the pressures of both the Italian and the Libyan state governments through their community initiative.[38]

The view from the American state and society

Recently, I had a discussion with one of my political science undergraduate students at the University of New England, in southern Maine, about her image of Italian culture and society. She replied that the American view of Italy has been largely positive. Growing up in northern Maine, she said her perception on Italy included pizza, *The Godfather* film trilogy, soccer, and as a bucket list vacation spot. This is vastly different from the American view of Germany as militaristic, harsh, and dreary. She admitted to knowing nothing about Italian Fascism, and certainly nothing about the internment in Libya.

The view of Fascist Italy was impacted by geographical distance, the Red Scare, the view of Italian Fascism as a modern and developmental ideology, and American society's acceptance of the dominant view of moderate fascism after World War II and the start of the Cold War. Critical scholarship of Fascist Italy shows strong positive views of the regime. David Schmitz, a leading historian, investigated the American National Archives and interviews with State Department officials conducted between 1922 and 1940, and concluded that American leaders perceived the rise of Italian Fascism "as meeting of qualifications for supporting political stability, anti-Bolshevism, and promised increases in trade[39]." Thus, Washington welcomed Mussolini's rise to power in 1922 and established policies that aided his regime because it believed that fascism would bring equilibrium and strong government to Italy, work against Bolshevism, aid Italy's economic recovery along acceptable lines, and provide American businesses with favorable investment opportunities. And he added that Mussolini was viewed as a "moderate" leading a progressive administration that would help modernize Italy.[40]

There was silence about the war crimes and no critique of the war crimes in Libya. However, the American Archives on the American Embassy reports from Rome show a different view and clear understanding and documentation of the repressive policies in Libya, which clearly did not persuade the Roosevelt administration to rethink its moderate image of the regime even after it invaded Ethiopia in 1935. The archives show that the American government stayed neutral and refused to condemn the fascist regime's aggression that led to the end of the League of Nations.

If the American state in the 1920 and 1930s supported and engaged the fascist regime, it follows that the view of the American public was not much different. I examined *The New York Times* coverage of Italy and colonial Libya between 1911 and 1940 and found only one vague reference to pacification of the rebels and the capture of 'Umar al-Mukhtar. Not only did *The Times* take the fascist side and language it did not even mention the concentration camps. Here is the only reference to the resistance on January 24, 1930:

> The rebellion really was crushed last year when General Graziani Stretched 180 miles of barbwire across the weeping sands separating Egypt and Libya and blocked off tribesmen from food and water. After unsuccessful attempt to pierce the barrier, Jusuf Bu Rahil [Yusuf Bu Rahil] chief aide of the rebel leader 'Umar al-Mukhtar and his band were pressured into the desert and virtually wiped out.[41]

Furthermore, the coverage was short and uncritical of the Italian colonial and orientalist language representation of the native people, such as "Bedouins," motivated by "religious fanaticism," and "holy war." The reporting accepted uncritically the colonial claims and policies, such as the use of "pacification" or the positive reporting of the big fascist celebration of shipping 20,000 settlers to the colony on October 31, 1938: "sixteen ships carrying 1,800 families of agricultural workers to the Italian colony of Libya." In short, the reporting did not question the colonial claims, its violence, atrocities, or the genocide in concentration camps up to 1934.[42] There is one exception to this historical silence and amnesia; the only well-informed reports came from the American Embassy in Rome, but even this reporting took the Italian side for granted. This is striking if one keeps in mind that the American Embassy in Rome was informed about the camps. One can conclude from this investigation that the leading American paper, *The New York Times*, not only did even mention the camps, accepted the colonial fascist narrative, and contributed to the making of moderate or benign Italian Fascism.[43]

The *National Geographic Magazine*, which was founded in 1888, had close ties to the American government, as many diplomats and businessmen contributed articles to it. It is the third most popular magazine in the USA and had a high subscription of 37 million readers in 1989.[44] I discovered 24 articles on Italy and Libya between 1922 and 1940. The magazine published three main articles on Libya. All three accept fascist claims and even the myth of reviving the Roman past by linking it to long-ago Libya. Furthermore, the articles are silent on the brutal Italian history of the internment and the military and cultural atrocities including the genocide. Instead, the articles suggested that the regime's colonial policies helped modernize Libya and developed and civilized the fanatical and savage "Bedouin" natives. The first article was written by Gordon Casserly in 1925 and titled "Tripolitania Where Rome Resumes Sway." The author takes for granted and supports the Italian claim of a Roman past as justification for invading Tripoli. He had no words for the resistance.

The second article was written by Harriet Chalmers Adams in 1930 and titled "Cyrenaica, Eastern Wing of Italian Libya. It is another apology for Italian colonialism. The author repeated orientalist gazes such as "a primitive land" inhabited by "fanatical Muslims." The third article was authored by John Patric in 1937 with a propaganda title of "Imperial Rome Reborn." He celebrated the great fascist celebration of the rebirth of the new "L'impero Italiano." No moral or critical question was raised but the right for empire and conquest by fascism was taken for granted.[45] This coverage by *National Geographic Magazine* was silent about the concentration camps and the mass killing. Instead, the three articles constructed well-produced, edited photos and exotic images which contributed to a positive image of fascism and colonialism and the absurd myth that it was benign and modernizing.

Thus, Italian Fascism and its genocidal policies in Libya was accepted and even viewed as a modernization period. This myth of moderate and modernizing Italian Fascism became an influential interpretation among some American social scientists who accepted the claims of pro-fascist Italian historian De Felice, whose defense of fascism became a well-respected view and was defended by his students, and the *American Journal of Historical Studies*.[46] In addition, American political scientist James Gregor made a career for himself teaching at the University of California, Berkeley, in the department of Political Science. There, he advocated Italian Fascism as an aid to development during most of the 1980s. His book *Italian Fascism and Developmental Dictatorship* (1979), published by the Princeton University Press, supports his view of fascism.[47]

Even the eminent political theorist Hannah Arendt and many German academic refugees from Nazi Germany advocated this myth of moderate Italian Fascism, as compared with the genocidal German Nazi state. Perhaps Arendt did not know what was going on in Libya; we know she was very early on in her career, writing her second book on totalitarianism in which she took a moral stand against imperialism and even argued that the route to the German genocide, including the Holocaust, originated in the European genocides in the colonies, especially the Congo and German East Africa. Arendt was clear about the impact of genocide, but not so for fascist practices in Libya, or the Native American genocide in North and South America between the sixteenth and nineteenth centuries She was also wrong about Fascist Italy when arguing that there was no Jewish question and no anti-feminism in Italy, and also silent about Libya, Ethiopia, and Yugoslavia, to the point that she repeated time and time again that Italian Fascism was just an ordinary dictatorship under fascism.[48]

Popular American culture also portrayed a positive view of Fascist Italy, and one should not forget that some American icons were supporters of Mussolini and his regime, such as American businessman Henry Ford and the American poet Ezra Pound, who not only lived in Italy but worked in fascist Italian Radio, advocating for fascism and Mussolini.[49] It should be surprising that the Italian election in March 2018 witnessed not only the continued neo-fascist movement, but also many small fascist parties including one called Casa Pound, in reference to the pro-fascist American poet Ezra Pound.[50] Historical and geographical distances, as well as lack of knowledge and awareness, allowed certain policy makers and mass media such as *The New York Times* and the third-most widely read magazine, *National Geographic Magazine*, with its 37 million readers, to reproduce the myth that Italian Fascism was not genocidal but was a moderate, positive force aiming to modernize. In the post-script, Chapter 5, I shall theorize on the conclusions about the Libyan genocide in the study of modern genocide through the Holocaust and offer a new reading of the three main Western political theorists on genocide today: Arendt, Foucault, and Agamben.

Notes

1 Martha Pertrusewitz, "Hidden Pages of Contemporary Italian History: War Crimes, War Guilt and Collective Memory," Special Issue, *Journal of Modern Italian Studies*, 9:8 (2004), 269–270, and in the same issue Filippo Focradi, "The Question of Fascist Italy's War Crimes: The Construction of a Self-Acquiring Myth (1943–1948)," 330–348. Also see Nicola Labanca, "Colonial Rule, Colonial Repression and War Crimes in Italian Colonies," *Journal of the Modern Italian Studies*, 9:3 (2004), 300–313. For a defense of the Allies policy not to try Italian Fascists for war crimes see Effie G. Pedaliu, "Britain and the Handover of Italian War Criminals to Yugoslavia", *Journal of Contemporary History*, 39:4 (October 2004), 529.
2 Neelan Srivastava, "Anti-Colonialism and Italian Left," *Interventions*, 8:3 (February 18, 2007), 427, 420, 425.
3 Roy Palmer Domenico, *Italian Fascism on Trial, 1943–1948*, (Chapel Hill: University of North Carolina Press, 1991), 10, 114, 154.
4 Domenico, Ibid., 154, 160.
5 Ruth Ben-Ghait, "Why Are So Many Fascist Monuments Still Standing in Italy," *The New Yorker*, (October 5, 2017) and Krystyna Von Henneberg, "Monuments, Public Space and Memory of Empire in Modern Italy," *History and Memory*, 16:1 (2004), 37–85. Also, Mia Fuller, *Moderns Abroad*, (New York: Routledge, 2007).
6 Bashir al-Sa'dawi, *Fadi' al-Isti'mar al-Itali al-Fashisti fi Tarabulus Wa Barqa* [*The Horrors of Italian Fascist Colonialism in Tirpoli and Barqa*], (Damascus: Manshurat Jam'iyal al-Difa' an Trabulus Wa Barqa, 1931). A revised and updated version was published by a collective committee of Libyan exiles in Syria under the title *Al-Fadi' al-Sud al-Humr: safahat min al-Isti'mar al-Itali fi Libia* [*The Black Red Horrors on [or of] Italian Colonialism in Tripoli and Barqa*], 1932. Finally, a later edition was published in Cairo in 1948 by a new organization Ha'at Tahrir Libya [The Commission for the Liberation of Libya] headed by Bashir al-Sa'dawi.
7 Angelo Del Boca, "The Myths, Suppressions, Denials and Defaults of Italian Colonialism" in Patrizia Palumbo, ed., *A Place under the Sun* (Berkeley: University of California Press, 2003), 17–19 and *Gli Italinani in Libia: Dal Fascismo a Gheddafi*, (Roma-Barie: Laterza, 1988), 440, 459.
8 In the early 1990s, Libyan and Italian scholars collaborated in a few important conferences which I participated in, such as the ones in Siena (2008) and Rome (2005), as well as the conference inspired by Mia Fuller at UC Berkeley, "Writing and Speaking Libya's Histories" (2009), and a conference in Tripoli which I helped organize at the Libyan Studies Center, "Libyan Concentration Camps and the Study of Colonial Concentration Camps" 2006.

9 See Joan Mellen,"An Interview with Gillo Pontecorvo," *Film Quarterly*, 26:1, (Autumn 1972), 2–10 on the making of his film *The Battle of Algiers*.

10 For an overview of the controversy over the critical BBC documentary film *A Fascist Legacy*, see "Italy's Bloody Secret," *The Guardian* (June 25, 2003).

11 Michael Foucault, "Two Lectures" in Nicolas B. Dirks, Geoff Eley, and Sherry B. Ortner, eds, *Culture/Power/History: A Reader in Contemporary Social Theory*, (Princeton: Princeton University Press, 1994), 201–221.

12 James C. Scott, *Domination and the Arts of Resistance*, (New Haven: Yale University Press, 1990), XI.

13 Patrick Bernhard, "Borrowing from Mussolini: Nazi Germany's Colonial Aspirations in the Shadow of Italian Expansion," *Journal of Imperial and Commonwealth History*, 41:4 (2013), 617–643, and "Hitler's Africa in the East: Italian Colonialism as a Model for German Planning in Eastern Europe," *Journal of Contemporary History*, 51:1 (2016), 61–90.

14 "Marshal Goerhing in Tripoli," *Libia al-Musawra [Illustrated Libya]*, (Benghazi 1939) 15, and Bernhard, "Hitler's Africa in the East," 78–90.

15 On the Herero genocide, see Jan-Bart Gewald, *Herero Heroes: A Socio-Political History of the Herero of Namibia, 1890–1928*, (Oxford: James Curey, 1999), and Horst Dreschsler, *Let us Die Fighting: The Struggle of the Herero and the Nama People against German Imperialism (1884–1915)*, (London: 2ed press, 1980). On the impact of the Hereros genocide on the Nazi Holocaust see Benjamin Medley, "From Africa to Auschwitz," *History Quarterly*, 53:3 (2005), 429–464, and Jürgen Zimerer, "The Birth of the Ostland Out of the Spirit of Colonialism," *Patterns of Prejudice*, 39:2 (2005) 115–134. On Germany recent apology for the Namibian genocide see Andrew Meldrum, "German Minister Says Sorry for Genocide in Nambia," *The Guardian*, (August 15, 2004).

16 Muhammad Fu'ad Shukri, *Libia al-Haditha wathi'q Tahrurha Wa Istiqlaluha, 1945–1947 [Modern Libya: Documents of its Liberation and Independence]*, (Cairo: Itihad Press, 1957), 157–164.

17 Abdal-Khaliq al-Fakhri, Idris al-Shilwi, Hamad al-'Awami al-Sha'ri, and Muhammad 'Usman al-Sha. All encountered in my interviews of the survivors, such as al-Shami, in 2008. Children and grandchildren were also present, interested, and remembered the history very well.

18 See al-Si'dawi, *Fadi' al-Isti'mar* and Mahmud al-Sayyid Dughaim, "Jihad Bashir al-Sa'dawi Dida al-Fashiyya," *Jihad Bashir al-Sa'dawi against Fascism al-Hayat*, (February 27, 1995).

19 See Ahmad Shawqi's poem on the first page of al-Si'dawi's, *Fadi' al-Isti'mar*.

20 For the scholarship role of Shakib Arslan's anti-colonial activism in detail or his complicated relationship with Fascist Italy and Mussolini with regard to the Libyan people, see MDL, Shukri Faysal files, Arab documents, document November 27, 1934, from Arslan to Sa'dawi, 30, 31a collection. Also, Muhammad Rajab al-Za'idi, *Shakib Arslan wa al-qadiyya al-libiyya [Arslan and the Libyan Question]*, (Al-byada: Maktabat al-Wahda al-Arabiyya, 1964).

21 For a critical overview of the literature on Islam, the Arabs and Fascism, and the Nazi State, see Gilbert Ashcar's essay "Fascism in the Middle East and North Africa" The Oxford Handbooks online (September 2015). www.oxford books.com.

22 'Umar Fa'iq Shinib, "Libia Mahdal Butula wa'Arin al-Ausud" ["Libya Place of Courage and the Den of Lions"], *Majalat al-Ikhwan al-Muslimin*, 91–94 (February – March 1946).

23 Hussain Dafir Ben Musa, *Mabruka*, (Damscus: Makatabat Dimashiq, 1937).

24 Angelo Del Boca. "The Myths, Suppressions, Denials and Defaults of Italian Colonialism" Ibid., 25-27

25 Miftah al-Sayyid al-Sharif, *Masirat al-Haraka al-Wataniyya al-Libiyya* [*The Path of the Libyan Nationalist Movement*], (Beirut: Dar al-Furat, 2011), 162–171.

26 Ruth First, *The Elusive Revolution*, (London: Penguin, 1974), 87–98 and 99–118.

27 All Qadhdhafi speechs are published in the Libyan record call al-Sijil al-Qawmi, the National Record.

28 I address this topic in the postscript, Chapter 5, of this book.

29 For an Italian view of the apology see Claudia Gazzini, "Assessing Italy's Grand Gesto to Libya," *Middle East Report* (March 16, 2009) and Mustafe A. Khashiem, "The Treaty of Friendship, Partnership and Cooperation between Libya and Italy," *California Italian Studies*, 1:1 (2010) 1–14.

30 The most important meetings took place between 2000 and 2009 in Rome, Siena, and Tripoli.

31 'Umar al-Mukhtar University in Bayda and the University in Benghazi survey.

32 Al-Fatih University, Zawiya University, the Private University of al-Majd, and the Diplomatic Institute, survey, April 7.

33 College of Banking, Jufra University, and Sabha University survey.

34 Teachers played a strong role in central and southern Libya as indicated in the student's survey in 2008–2009.

35 Sabha, the capital of the state of Fezzen after Libyan independence in 1951 emerged as a modern city with five libraries and civic organization and schools such as a teachers college, a high school for boys and girls, a nursing school, marching bands, and five soccer clubs and Boy Scout organizations.

36 Abdrahamn Shalqam, interview, May 15, 2012, New York.

37 Abdallah Zagub, interview, May 16, 2016.

38 The Association Dhakiral al-Madina [City as Memory] of Hun publication.

39 ANA, Internal Affairs Italy 130–139, Decimal 865, Roll 31. The USA refused to impose sanctions on Italy after invading Ethiopia, and David F. Schmitz, *The United States and Fascist Italy, 1992–1940*, (Chapel Hill: University of North Carolina Press, 1988, 1, 4, 60, 213. This is a well-researched book from the State Department and American Archives.

40 Ibid.

41 I surveyed all the articles published by *The New York Times* on Italian colonialism and Libya between 1911 and 1943.

42 "Arabs in Libya Bellicose," *The New York Times*, November 23, 1914.

43 "20-Year War Ended by the Italians in Tripoli" *The New York Times*, January 27, 1932.

44 The *National Geographic Magazine* is the third most popular magazine in the USA with 37 million readers. For a critical analysis of history, representations of the third world, captions, photos, and articles from the magazine, see Catherine A. Lutz and Jane L. Collins, *Reading National Geographic*, (Chicago: Chicago University Press, 1993), 10.

45 On De Felice's defense of Italian Fascism and Mussolini see Australian historian Robert Bosworth, "Coming to Terms with Fascism in Italy," *History Today*, (April, 24, 2012) 4. Also, Colonial Gordon Casserly, "Tripolitania: Where Rome Resumes Sway," *National Geographic*, 48:2 (1925), 131–161, H.C. Adams, "Cirenaic, Eastern Wing of Italian Libya," *National Geographic*, 57:6 (1930), 689–726, and John Patric, "Imperial Rome Reborn," *National Geographic*, 71:3 (1937), 269–325.

46 Ibid.

47 See James Gregor, an American Political Scientist, who taught at the liberal University of California, Berkeley and his book, a defense of fascism as a developmental model, *Italian Fascism and Developmental Dictatorship*, (Princeton: Princeton University Press, 1979), IX–IV, and Jon S. Cohen, "Was Italian Fascism a Developmental Dictatorship? Some Evidence to the Contrary," *Economic History Review*, 41: 1 (1988), 95–113. Gregor and the critic Cohen are both silent about the

colonies and the genocide in Libya, as well as the atrocities in Ethiopia and Yugo-slavia. On Italian atrocities in Ethiopia see Richard Pankhurst, "Italian Fascist War Crimes in Ethiopia," *North East African Studies*, 6:1–2 (1999), 83–140.

48 Hannah Arendt made an error and was blind to the horrors committed by Italian Fascism and was also silent about the Native genocide in North America; see her book *The Origins of Totalitarianism*, (New York: Harcourt, Brace and Jovanovich, 1973), 257. The same silence continued in her book *On Revolution*, (New York: Penguin Classics, 1951).

49 Ezra Pound was one of the most visible American propagandists for Fascist Italy. See Matthew Feldman, *Ezra Pound's Fascist Propaganda, 1935–45*, (New York: Palgrave, 2013) and David Motadel, "The United States Was Never Immune to Fascism, Not Then, Not Now," *The Guardian* (August 17, 2017). Recently, a new fascist political party emerged in Italy, Casa Pound. It took its name as a homage to the American fascist poet, see Elisabetta Povoledo "Anti-Fascist Protestors Rally in Italy as Mussolini Heirs Gain Ground," *The New York Times*, (June 20, 2018).

50 The 2018 Italian election brought to power the right wing Northern League which changed its name to The League. It's leader, Matteo Salvini, has not hid his admiration for Mussolini and fascism, see Elisabeta Poveledo and Gaia Pianigiani, "Italian Minister Moves to Count Roma, Invoking Memories of Mussolini," *The New York Times*, (June 20, 2018).

5

POSTSCRIPT

Rethinking postcolonial state formation, crisis, and collapse

You cannot take down a mountain with a hammer.

Libyan proverb

The long specter of settler colonialism

The reader may ask a legitimate question about how the unearthing of the hidden history of the Italian geoncide in Libya may inform us about the politics of the country after independence in 1951 and its recent unraveling after the 2011 uprising. This is the reason behind a postscript chapter with a focus on how the recovery of the missing history can help us read the politics of the country since 1951. Let us first start by recovering the violence of the colonial history. Libyan history has been affected by colonialism beginning with the colonial state that was imposed by the Italians from the period 1911 until 1943. This period was followed by British and French administrations from 1943 until 1951. Two postcolonial states followed: the Sanusi Monarchy that lasted from 1951 until 1969, and the Qadhdhafi regime that lasted from September 1, 1969 until February 14, 2011. The February 17, 2011 uprising opened a new era of optimism, but, after 2014, Western, Turkish, and Arab Gulf interventions allowed the support of counterrevolutionary militia, criminals, smugglers, and extremists despite the fact that the Libyan people voted three times for a civilian government.

The Italian colonization in Libya may have been comparatively brief (1911–1943), but it was exceptionally brutal and bloody. Its brutality cast a dark shadow across the decades that followed. Half a million people were killed as a direct result of the prolonged military campaigns across the country, including those who perished in the concentration camps set up as part of the Italian counterinsurgency programs. The impacts of Italian Fascist colonial rule were quite radical, including the destruction of long-standing institutions of governance and education, and the utter degradation of life in agricultural areas. Yet the Italians unified the three former Ottoman provinces of Fezzen, Tripolitania, and Barqa into a single state, which is, of course, modern Libya.

Libya won its independence only with the Allied military advances across North Africa in 1942–1943. Even after the war, the British and American military presence became a central fact of post-Italian Libyan history, and provided the necessary force and support for the installation of a pro-British and American monarchy under King Muhammad Idris al-Sanusi (1951–1969).[1] The upper class that led Libyan independence made a compromise with the UK and the USA. In exchange for security, economic assistance, and independence the royal elite signed agreements, in 1954, granting military bases to the USA and the UK. This elite group, which included some collaborators with the colonial state, such as the first prime minister Mahmud al-Muntasir, overlooked Italian colonial atrocities such as the genocidal internment and the mass killing in Mu'ataqalat, and the exile and the uprooting of over thousands who were forced into exile outside of Libya. In other words, King Idris' rule did not end the trauma of the colonial period, since his policies – mirroring those of his British and American benefactors – suppressed the more difficult questions of the past atrocities including the genocide in the Mu'taqalat, concentration camps.

This brutal colonial history, and the neocolonial rule of the Sanusi Monarchy of King Idris that kept generally silent about that history, is the immediate backdrop to understanding the anti-colonial populism that has been at the core of the post-monarchy regime from the outset. Outside observers might be surprised by the regime's tenacious focus on events of a colonial past that ended nearly 70 years ago, but it is crucial to understand that Libya's stubborn anti-imperialist ethos is rooted in the modern colonial experience of the Libyan people, and their very reasonable feeling that their suffering and historical justice has yet to be fully recognized.

Processes of modernization, urbanization, and, especially, education began as early as independence in 1951 with the support of the United Nations, which helped to accelerate social change. In 1954, a new Libyan university with two campuses in Benghazi and Tripoli created new educational opportunities which then led to the expansion of colleges and universities all over the country. New educational policies led, by the late 1960s, to the rise of a new salaried middle class, a student movement, a small working class, trade unions, and modern intellectuals. The number of students increased from 33,000 in 1952 to 300,000 in 1970. By 2010 there were two million students in all levels of education in Libya, including 300,000 at college and university levels.

The question is how to rethink the history of the present that is the formation of the Libyan state up until today based on the new history of the colonial genocide? I propose to read this postcolonial history from below, from the point of view of the culture and institutions of the local people who were interned and the larger subaltern society. As stated in Chapter 1, both prior to colonial conquest and under its domination, society continued to live and resist through its own local organization, as the innovative leaders and followers of the Sanusiyya did during the second half of the nineteenth century and up until 1932. The local native society created a voluntary and self-governing autonomous organization, one not based on the nation-state model. The lodges and Zawayya were neither nationalist nor ethnic but pan-Islamic and inclusive, and reflected from the bottom-up the local values of the community while keeping away from the Ottoman and Italian states through regions of refuge and the frontiers of the Sahara. These local institutions and movements reflect the hinterland traditions of autonomy, a desire not to be governed by the state in Tripoli and Benghazi and were often misunderstood as dated and tribal, or anti-modern. Instead, they should be read as a creative way of life and local culture, and an ability to resist and survive before, during, and after the colonial period. Here, we face an interesting situation where Libyan society has no army or police force and, yet, the local elected municipalities keep life going despite all odds. The history of self- governing values such as trust, interconnectedness, and social capital that existed before the modern state allow people to survive and continue.

The problem of the modern state is the fact that, as in many other places, it was imposed on the people through violence and brutality and, consequently, it was often seen as lacking legitimacy, especially when it tried to discipline and normalize its policy through claims of progress, civilization, and modernization. Resistance to this violence and elitism varies from kinship organization, to orality, folk poetry, and avoiding the state as much as possible. When the modern Libyan state was created, the challenge was what type of state it should be and whether it respected the values, culture, and religion of the local society, particularly in the hinterland as the coast cities were dominated by the central state. Anglo-American scholars of modern Libya mistake these problems and contradistinctions as fragmentations and a lack of cohesive modern institutions. They also read Libyan modern history through the Westernized models of the Tunisian state and the paradigm of modernization and Westernization.

This narrative, which accepts colonialism as a form of modernization, assumes that Libya was a country created by European Italian colonialism, but in an unsatisfactory way. The country is viewed as a failure when compared with what the French did in Tunisia, which Europe found easier to colonize. If only Libya was just like Tunisia! Instead, the contradistinctions should be read as forms of resistance and signs of a living society which has long and rich traditions of anti-state and colonial struggles. In other words, checking the model of the nation-state and insisting on creating a state that is consistent with its own culture and experiences is what at stake; this is what is interesting about Libyan history from below.

The study of the state by Western political theory has to be reexamined. The first problem is the assumption of Eurocentrism; political theory is mainly centered on Western political theory. It assumes and takes for granted the idea that European experience is the model and that other models are either catching up or deviating from the norm of modernity and progress. The second problem is ignoring the history of empire and colonialism, as if it has nothing to do with the formation and politics of the modern state. There are though critical and self-reflexive cases. I make the argument that we need to rethink these assumptions, including the division between the evil Nazism in Germany and the benign fascism in Italy. Libyan history suggests that there was not much difference between the two. Futhermore, bringing to attention the repressed history of genocide in Libya should change our way of thinking. It is simply no longer possible to just mention that there were concentration camps in Libya and move on, as is the case with much current scholarship on Libyan politics and culture.

The right question then is not to take the nation-state as normal and given, but rather as a problematic and investigate when it was normalized around the world. The state in Libya and the rest of Africa and the Arab world is a product of violent history, hegemony, and resistance. Yes, its heritage is Western, native, and Islamic and, in addition, the history of the state is both of domination and resistance, process and content, and cultural models and institutions. Only when the theory of the state is decolonized can one capture a different narrative of subaltern history from the point of view of local society not as a victim but as an agent of living culture.

This poses the question: who writes history? It is not just historians but also journalists, cartoonists, poets, politicians, university lecturers, religious figures, novelists, and bureaucrats hired by the state to write school text and set exam questions. However, the quality of the writing of history rests on the quality of the evidence and the ethical perspective of the interpretation. In short, colonial and national histories are problematic as they normalize race and take the modern state for granted.

The main objective of this postscript chapter is to present a new reading and analysis of the historical and structural causes of state collapse in Libya after the February 17, 2011 uprising and the crisis of transition after 2013. This analysis will present the reader with an overview of the current crisis, highlighting essential information pertaining to the crisis, and will prepare the reader for the genealogy of the making of the silenced and forgotten genocide under Italian Fascist colonialization. This mapping of the postcolonial Libyan state is linked to the larger context of the genocide. In short, the current contradictions and unresolved conflict in Libya are rooted in the colonial period and, especially, the genocide.

The final challenge of the postscript of this book is to present a new reading of the social origins of the postcolonial state, the factors behind the early success of the revolution and the toppling of the Qadhdhafi dictatorship, which resulted in a crisis of transition, the collapse of the state, and the mini civil wars in many regions of the country, in spite of the United Nations brokered agreement in Morocco of December 2015. The chapter will also seek to determine who was responsible for the state's early success, and the crisis and failure after 2013, and will examine the roles of NATO, the USA, the European Union EU, the Arab countries and Turkey, and transnational organizations, especially al Qaida, Da'esh (Islamic State), and their local affiliates.

I will make three main arguments in the chapter. First, the crisis of the current state in Libya did not occur overnight, but rather is structurally rooted in the contradictions that the modern Libyan state created in the shadow of settler colonialism. In addition, today's crisis was caused by the long process of undermining political and social institutions in the late 1980s and 1990s, especially with the reliance on informal institutions. Second, the leadership failed to tackle the security and the arms challenge and the rebuilding of the army and the police forces after 2011. Last, the Obama administration, the European Union, the regional Gulf States, Sudan, and Turkey played a negative role by supporting various factions, and militated against compromise in reaching agreement to disarm the militia groups and rebuild the army and police forces. There was lack of a clear vision to recognize Libyan historical and cultural traditions and institutions, all of which contributed to the collapse of the state and the persisting weak institutions. The postcolonial Libyan state has not resolved the problem of weak, fragmented institutions which opened the doors to authoritarianism and the rise of strong leaders before 2011, and with the collapse of the state after 2013 there was the temptation and lure of a new strong authoritarian leader, which would explain the rise of General Khalifa Haftar in eastern Libya. This current crisis created Libya as a body without a head, or two heads that are fighting each other. In short, the current crisis is one of transition, not of an old segmented tribal society or tribalism, as claimed by most Western media and Libyan policy experts.

It was not an inevitable crisis. Had the Obama administration, the European Union, and the United Nations stopped the flow of money and arms to the various armed groups in both the east and the west of Libya, a compromise could have been reached and the crisis could have been avoided. Instead, the two most powerful military groups became entrenched: the Libya Dawn political Islamic organization, led by the City of Misurata Brigade in the west, and the Government of National Accord in Tripoli and the Libyan National Army led by General Haftar in the eastern region. Consequently, as long as Western intervention continues and until the rival forces in the east and the powerful factions of the west agree political compromise, the crisis will continue, the state collapse may last longer, and Libya will become another Somalia or Iraq.

Alternatively, a good start to solving the current crisis would be an admission of responsibility by both the USA and the European Union, followed by a reining in of their clients/allies in the Gulf. Next, a firm action plan by the United Nations is needed to stop the flow of arms, money, and media wars between the various factions in the country. Only then can one talk about institution building and national reconciliation. There is a need for a truth and reconciliation commission to heal society from the long injuries of war and repression, and the curse of revenge and retaliation, especially against the supporters of the Qadhdhafi regime. Killings and severe human rights abuses have taken place in all regions of the country. Next, three factors will be addressed: conceptualizing and defining the problem of institution building; the social and external origins of the colonial and postcolonial state of Libya; and the persisting of weak national institutions and the crisis of transition after 2011.

Defining the problem and the genealogy of the state crisis in Libya

Two scholarly theoretical debates – one, comparative social revolutions, the other, fixing failed states – have addressed the problem of state collapse and institutions that are relevant to the Libyan case. The literature on modern social revolutions evolved from the theories of social revolutions, and it helps to explain the Libyan case from a comparative perspective. These theories, whether they are the national history of revolution, the social mobilization and institution building, or the structural theories of revolution (which include the impact of war and outside forces), help us understand the stages of institution building after civil strife. Since the French classical revolution in 1879, five stages were recognized, two of which included the crisis of the state, alienation, and coalition building, and the struggle over the future, and pragmatism. The twenty-first century Arab Spring revolutions and uprisings have introduced new factors, such as the role of social media, demography, youth, and transnational communication. While these factors are useful, and highlighted in the analysis of these uprisings, the literature and the media coverage suffer in silence about the fact that revolutions have been defeated and appropriated by counterrevolutions.

The Libyan case is unique given that the revolutionary coalition succeeded in defeating the old regime, while in the other cases in Syria, Tunisia, Egypt, and Yemen, the old regime is still a factor in the conflict. On the negative side, the Libyan uprising started with the rebellion in the city of Benghazi when it became militarized. The failure of all the leaders who managed the transition can be seen in their inability to disarm the militias and their becoming hostage to these interest groups. There are around 23 million weapons in a country of only 6 million people. The number of armed militias increased from 20,000 to 30,000 in 2011, and from at least 200,000 to 250,000 in 2014. Consequently, despite the remarkable Libyan participation in the 2012 and

2014 national elections, elected officials, unfortunately, were unable to represent their constituencies because the armed groups did not recognize the results
of those elections. I would argue that the failure that produced the crisis of
transition and state collapse can be attributed to, first, the leaders who led the
transition inside Libya, and, second, the USA and the European Union who
stood by silently while regional powers and transnational extremist organizations filled the vacuum and blocked the Libyan democratic transition to a post-
uprising state and institution building.

The current analysis of the state collapse and the narrative of the simplistic
invention of tribal ideology is misleading. It is an easy excuse to cover up the
lack of knowledge and the lack of a deeper understanding of the complexity of
the Libyan social and historical reality. The tribal-based narrative fails to make
sense of the participation of the Libyan people in the 2012 and 2014 elections,
and of the fact that society has been managed remarkably well by the 113
elected municipalities in the absence of police, security, and armed forces.
These elected municipalities are remarkable but escaped many observers of the
Libyan impasse today. The society is self-governing despite the absence of the
army, the police, and the state. As if Libya is a body in search of a new head!
Still society is resisting all challenges of violence, fighting, crime, and outside
intervention.

Again, a serious national dialogue and the building of a lasting constitution with good governance will not work without understanding the social
origins of the state and public institutions based on Libyan political traditions. These political traditions include strong values and a culture of
decentralization, regionalism, and local Ottoman and Sanusi public institutions. Above all, what must be taken into consideration is the Libyan living
memory of the brutal genocide under Italian colonialism. Libyan independence under the Libyan Sanusi Monarchy in 1951 was a major achievement
for the Libyan people, despite the fact that it created a client state dominated by Western powers. The Libyan Sanusi Monarchy created new West-
ern-like institutions, such as the parliament, the federal system, the civic
courts, the army, and the police forces. At the same time, indigenous institutions were based on local traditions, such as the majlis al-shyukh, Council
of Elders, the zawayya lodges, the Islamic Sanusi schools and universities,
Islamic family courts, and traditional 'urf and Mi'ad that reflect the autonomous decentralized traditions of the hinterland. The Qadhdhafi-led anti-
colonial, Arab nationalist coup in September 1969 broke the silence on the
genocide under Italian colonialism. This populist military coup became
a dictatorship by 1977. In short, understanding the social and political origins of the Libyan state is an essential context for capturing the history of
the present and the current state collapse.

State collapse takes place when institutions, authority, and legitimate power,
law, and political order fall apart, leaving civil society facing armed militias to
fill the vacuum. The decline of the state is linked to the breakdown of social
order. Without the state institutions and the ability to use legitimate violence,

as Max Weber argued, society breaks down. Contrary to public perceptions, state collapse does not happen overnight, nor is it caused in the short term. Rather, it is the result of an accumulative, long-term process like a festering wound. Consequently, when a state becomes unable to satisfy its citizens' basic social demands, rival groups try to fill the vacuum, as in the case of Libya today, when in the last three years armed groups and criminal elements use illegal activities such as kidnappings, ransoms, smuggling, and imprisonment as a source of revenue to satisfy their followers.

The next question is: what are the historical and structural causes of the February 17, 2011 Libyan uprising, its early success, and the current crisis of transition since 2013? I will make three arguments to analyze the causes of the current revolution and its success in liberating Libya from the control of the Qadhdhafi forces: the Qadhdhafi regime's failure to address the question of political reform and its alienation of important elite groups; the impact of demography, urbanization, and global social media; and, the success of an enterprising rebel leadership that was able to obtain diplomatic and military support from the United Nations, the Arab league, and NATO. The inability of the Qadhdhafi regime to make serious political reforms appropriate to the changes in the economy, education, and society eventually led to conflict between a dynamically changing social structure and a rigid political system that, in turn, inhibited new social forces – especially unemployed youth – from having their social demands and grievances met. The gap between the Libyan youth and the ruling elite undermined all the gains achieved by the regime during the 1970s and eventually led to the formation of a revolutionary coalition that became alienated from the regime. Had Qadhdhafi responded with openness to the calls for reform and not overreacted to the uprisings in Tunisia and Egypt, the urban elite in Libya might have been placated and the violent rebellion avoided. Qadhdhafi miscalculated and overreacted. Once his army and police shot at protesters, the pent-up disaffection of Libyan society was unleashed, and it was too late for the regime to contain it. In August 2011, the revolutionary forces liberated the southern region of Fezzen, which historically was both rural and pro-Qadhdhafi, and only two cities remained under his troop's control: his home city of Sirte and the city of Bani Walid. The regime lost moral, diplomatic, and military battles, leading, by the end of October 2011, to ultimate defeat in the war. Furthermore, the revolutionary coalition that led the opposition and was supported by regional Arab countries, NATO, and the American military, created a proxy war inside Libya's civil war. This compounded Libya's crisis of transition, which made Libya an open country for jhadi and Salafi groups ranging from al Qaida, to Ansar al-Shari'a in Benghazi, Derna, and Subrata, and to ISIS, which took over the city of Sirte in early 2014.

The irony is that the regime could have been spared if reform had been serious and if the regime had addressed the key popular social, political, and human rights abuses. Instead of implementing real reform, the regime fired on peaceful protesters in Benghazi and Bayda on February 15, 2011 and Qadhdhafi, and his son Saif al-Islam Qadhdhafi, made speeches declaring war against the protestors, even calling them rats, drug addicts, and brainwashed by Osama Bin Laden. By then, the majority of Libyans realized that the regime was hopeless and needed to be removed by force.

Populism, cult of hero, and the marginalization of institutions

On September 1, 1969, 12 young pan-Arab and Nasser-inspired officers in the Libyan Royal Army were led by a 27-year-old charismatic officer named Mu'ammar Abu-Minyar al-Qaddafi to overthrow the monarchy of King Idris in a bloodless coup d'état. The officers came from lower-middle class backgrounds and represented the three regions – i.e., the formerly separate Ottoman provinces – of Libya. This group had formed the central committee of a secret organization within the Libyan army called the Libyan Free Unionist Officers Movement. It subsequently renamed itself the Revolutionary Command Council (RCC) and declared the creation of the Libyan Arab Republic. The RCC's rhetoric was firmly anti-imperialist, anti-communist, and anti-corruption, while making ideological references to Arab nationalism and Islam as well. The RCC, however, did not have clearly delineated policies and looked for guidance from the 1952 Egyptian revolution. The 1969 revolution was not an anomaly, as so many Western journalists and scholars have claimed. Rather, its ideologies and style of governance were rooted in the hinterland social history of the Sanusiyya resistance and the Tripolitanian Republic. The Sanusi movement was founded by an urban Algerian scholar, Sayyid Muhammad b. Ali Al-Sanusi (1787–1859); it was a reformist movement built on modernist Islamic interpretation and two innovative institutions, trade and education, which continued until 1911 when Italy invaded Libya. The Italian colonial forces faced a well- integrated, unified, and cohesive society in eastern and southern Libya (and northern Chad) and hence the Libyans were able to resist the modern Italian armies until 1931. In western Libya, the leaders of the region organized their groups under the first republic in the Arab world, The Tripolitanian Republic, in 1918. This republic had a four-person collective leadership, a *Shura* (or parliament council), a flag, a newspaper, and an army. But, by 1922, the Italians had managed to defeat it, when Mussolini and the fascists decided to reconquer the colony and abrogate all agreements with the resistance. These two early political cases of state formation of the Sanusi movement and the republic provided the genesis of Libyan modern nationalism. The new Libyan state was a unique blend of pan-Islamic aspirations, skepticism toward central state rule, and social linkages based upon fluid and far-reaching family-based organizations.

After the 1969 revolution, Libyan society experienced major social, political, and economic advances, but the new government initially enacted its policies without significant popular participation. Qadhdhafi's faction within the RCC did not consolidate its power until 1976. At that point, it began to experiment with creating what it called an "indigenous pastoralist socialist society." While trying to attain this objective, the state benefited from significant petroleum revenues that provided steady employment not only to Libyans but also to a large expatriate workforce.

If Qadhdhafi can be credited with anything, it was that he was able to create a state ideology that resonated strongly with the entire spectrum of pan-Arab, pan-African, and third world national liberation movements. He did all this while employing language understood by ordinary Libyans and while referring to a common history that could be understood by all. He spoke, dressed, and ate like ordinary *badawi*, rural folks in the hinterland, at least during the first decade. Above all, Qadhdhafi was able to mobilize nationalist cadres effectively and attack his Westernized urban opponents and rivals inside and outside the country. At the core of his self-presentation was the image of the *badawi* tribesman. He led prayers like an imam. In fact, he was a shrewd politician to use these symbols of Islam, anti-colonial jihad, and the hidden atrocities history of Italian colonialism and fascism including the concentration camps to mobilize his social base in central and southern regions.

The new regime also began to pursue a cultural policy of "Bedouinization" by attacking urban culture and encouraging rituals based on "tribal values," as evidenced in dress, music, and festivals. Students, intellectuals, and the urban middle class in the big cities were compelled to shift their own self-presentation as they found themselves on the cultural defensive. They were not wrong to imagine the regime's Bedouin policies as being aimed at undermining their prestige in society. As a result of deliberate de-urbanization policies, for instance, the city of Tripoli (the most urban and cosmopolitan in the country) lost much of its relative importance even while its population increased to two million people.

Behind the rhetoric of a pure "Bedouin" identity unsullied by Western modernity, however, lurked a more mundane reality. The Libyan population had increased from one million in 1950 to six and a half million people by 2010 with a very large youth cohort where the median age was 24. Sixty-five % of the population was under the age of 30, but the unemployment rate was very high at 30%. Today, the vast majority of Libyans (80%) live in towns and cities. The supporters of the regime – like those of the democratic uprising – included lawyers, judges, journalists, engineers, writers, academics, officers, and diplomats. The oil-driven economy was complex, and Libyan citizens participated fully in it. The literacy rate was the highest in Africa (68.05%), and life expectancy was 78, years ahead of life expectancy in Tunisia. The United Nations 2010 Human Development Index ranked Libya as first in Africa and number 53 in the world. In other words, those who wanted to talk about tribalism in Libyan society would have to account for the disconnect between the official regime image of Libyans as timeless Bedouins, and the more complex reality on the ground. Moreover, they would also have to confront the fact that the representation of Libya as inherently tribal had its roots in the Qadhdhafi regime's battle to ideo-logically disenfranchise the urban, middle classes of the country – that is, most of the population. The anti-Qadhdhafi revolution included 6.5 million people who were globally connected to international education, travel opportunities, social media, and international television stations such as Al-Jazeera and Al-Arabia. These products of globalization played important sympathetic roles in supporting the revolution.

While Qadhdhafi's regime was able to restore its standing in the inter-national community during 2003 by providing reparations to the families of those murdered in the bombing of Pan Am Flight 103 over Lockerbie, Scot-land, the regime was failing domestically. Despite being allegedly strong mili-tarily, the regime was domestically weak because of internal dissent. Qadhdhafi's core of support came from his diehard allies, foreign mercenaries, and the loyalty of the residents of the two central cities of Sirte and Bani Walid.

The revolutions that occurred in neighboring Tunisia and Egypt may have been precipitating events for what occurred in Libya, but the Libyan Revolu-tion drew its core motivation from its brutal experience of colonialism. The young protesters in Benghazi raised the independence flag and the photo of 'Umar al-Mukhtar, the hero of the anti-colonial resistance. Other young men in western Libya raised photos of their own local anti-colonial resistance leaders in Nalut, Zintan, and Misurata. What is most striking about the rhetoric of the Libyan Revolution is how Qadhdhafi's anti-colonialist themes, such as state-ments from 'Umar al-Mukhtar before he was hanged, were turned against Qadhdhafi on the media of cell phone text messages, television videos on Al-Jazeera, and posts on Facebook. Even while assaulting Qadhdhafi's forces, the rebels resisted calling for forceful Western intervention, while nevertheless asking for the imposition of a no-fly zone. Libya's history explains the reason-ing behind this decision. Qadhdhafi's nationalist populism was rooted in the traumas of the colonial era, traumas which were papered over during the mod-ernizing but out-of-touch monarchy that ruled from 1951 to 1969. This popu-lism appealed to Libyan women who took advantage of the regime's new opportunities in education and public space. The reactions of women to the new regime are rooted in what I call gendered nationalism. They advocated anti-colonial nationalism but, in their voices and style it is a case of gendered nationalism.

Gendered nationalism

The role of Libyan women has been remarkable. This is a country that, in 1943, was one of the poorest with an illiteracy rate as high as 98%. Thanks to Libyan women's social movements and the spread of education since independence, today millions of Libyan women are educated. Such progress in Libyan women's education made it possible to see active young women in the February 17, 2011 uprising. This uprising, which removed the regime, began when the mothers of political prisoners killed in the massacre of Abusalim and who marched every year, on February 15, 2011 demanded justice and information about the 12,000 loved ones who were killed in 1996. Libyan women played many roles in the revolution, such as taking care of the wounded, documenting the regime atrocities, making videos and sending messages over the internet, cooking for the fighters, taking care of the children, speaking to the media, and sewing the revived independence flag of the monarchy. Today, there are more women in Libyan institutions of higher education than men. In the humanities and social sciences departments in Libyan universities, female students make up 80% of the enrollment.

Well-paid jobs in Tripoli and Benghazi and the oil fields attracted many rural people to move north to these cities. The population of Tripoli increased from 130,000 in 1951 to 213,000 in 1964, and to 400,000 in 1970. Benghazi grew from 70,000 residents to 137,000, and then to 300,000 during the same period. By 2010, Tripoli had a population of 1.8 million and Benghazi 650,000. But one has to be aware that thousands of poor rural immigrants lived in shanty towns outside these two cities, such as Bab Akkara, the Brarik, and the Campos outside Tripoli, and al-Sabri in Benghazi.[2] In summary, in 1951, while 80% of the population lived in the countryside, this statistic had reversed by 1967, with 80% living in urban areas. A small but well-organized working class emerged in the cities and near the oil fields.

In its first two decades, the Qadhdhafi regime brought many benefits to ordinary Libyans: widespread literacy, free medical care and education, and improvements in living conditions. Women, in particular, benefited, becoming ministers, ambassadors, pilots, judges, and doctors. The government received wide support from the lower and salaried middle classes. Beginning in the 1980s, excessive centralization, greater repression by security forces, and a decline in the rule of law undermined this experiment in indigenous populism. Institutions like courts, universities, unions, and hospitals weakened. Civic associations that had made Libyan society seem more democratic than many Persian Gulf states in the 1970s withered or were eliminated. A hostile international climate and fluctuations in oil revenues added to the pressures on the regime. The Jamahiriyya government received wide public support from the lower and middle classes that allowed it to engage in a major transformation of the economy as well as of social and political structures. Education and health care were free and energy, basic food materials, and water were subsidized by the state to all Libyans. But these educational and social achievements were contradicted by excessive political control and the development of a cult of personality centered upon "Leader-Brother" Qadhdhafi who became president for life. Power became a personal matter.

The regime responded by transforming its rituals of hero worship into a rhetoric of pan-African ideology and turned to violence to repress dissent.

After repeated coup attempts, it tortured, imprisoned, and exiled dissidents. The regime staffed security forces with reliable relatives and allies from central and southern Libya. During the 1990s, as externally imposed economic sanctions took their toll, health care and education deteriorated, unemployment soared to 30%, the economy became ever more dependent on oil, and the regime grew increasingly corrupt. Qadhdhafi's sons, including Mu'tasim, Hanibal, and Sa'adi, dominated the oil industry, communications, and most of the state-controlled contracts. They spent millions on wild parties that many young Libyans viewed through the internet and YouTube videos, while at the same time most Libyan educated professionals were paid a mere $300 a month and had to borrow money to travel to Tunisia for medical treatment. In 2010, Transparency International ranked Libya as one of the most corrupt countries in the world, at 146 out of 178. While the use of social media in Libya is not as wide as in Tunisia, Egypt, and the rest of the Maghrib, thousands of people still used cell phones, had access to independent websites, and relied upon Al-Jazeera and other television stations. After the resolution of the Lockerbie crisis and Libya's renewal of contacts with the international community, more media and newspapers were allowed to circulate, helping to accelerate reformist and dissident forces within Libya, especially among the youth who increasingly interacted with the outside world.

The move toward centralization and reliance on informal and security organizations such as the security apparatus, Revolutionary Committees, al Rifaq (a new organization comprised of Qadhdhafi's school contemporaries, Boy Scouts, secret organizations, and the military academy), Ahl al-Khaimah (comprises his close loyal friends, elder kinsmen, relatives, and tribal and regional allies), and invented unofficial tribal organizations, at the expense of formal institutions and the rule of law, undermined earlier reforms and led to the decline of the experiment in indigenous political populism. A hostile international climate, as well as declining oil revenues from the late 1970s onward, compounded the crisis of legitimacy for the regime and further weakened important public institutions such as courts, social clubs, universities, unions, hospitals, and banks. Thus, a confluence of internal and external dynamics weakened the state's ideology that had been based upon populist authoritarianism and a cult of personality centered upon Qadhdhafi's persona. These changes began primarily after Libya's defeat in its war with Chad during June 1983 when 10,000 Libyans were killed. Also significant in this process was the regime's confrontation with the USA in April 1986, which involved a bombing, under the Reagan administration, on targets in Tripoli, including Qadhdhafi's headquarters. Conditions worsened after 1992, when the United Nations Security Council imposed sanctions against Libya after evidence was produced linking Libyan agents to the terrorist bombing of the Pan Am Flight 103 that exploded over the town of Lockerbie. Furthermore, the regime killed 1,200 Islamist political prisoners in the massacre of Buslaim in Tripoli in 1996. According to human rights organizations, the victims were Islamist political prisoners who opposed the Libyan regime in the early 1990s. When they protested against their guards and demanded more rights, General Abdullah al-Sanusi, head of intelligence and brother-in-law of Qadhdhafi, ordered the troops to open fire, which led to the killing of the 1,200 prisoners. The regime buried the corpses in a secret location and refused to say anything about their faith. However, this horrific massacre haunted the regime and was one of the leading issues for the 2011 uprising.

The 2011 uprising started as the families of the victims of the 1996 massacre protested in Benghazi and many residents in the city of Benghazi joined the original group of protestors. Fathi Terbal, the lawyer representing the aggrieved families, was arrested on February 15, 2011. His arrest led to a social media announcement asking for "the Day of Rage" on February 17. When the regime's troops fired on the peaceful demonstrators, the cities of Bayda and Benghazi rebelled, and those protesting stormed the Qadhdhafi security garrisons and many soldiers and officers defected to the side of the protestors, including General Abdul Fattah Younes, the Minister of Interior, and Judge Mustafa Abdel-Jalil, the Minister of Justice. Younes and Abdel-Jalil would become leaders of the newly formed Interim Libyan Transitional Council in Benghazi.

The Libyan state under Qadhdhafi's leadership was an authoritarian state that was reliant on its income from petroleum and natural gas rents. Like other petroleum-producing states, such as Algeria, Iraq, and Syria, to name a few, Libya has attempted to deploy both formal and informal institutions to address its citizens' material and moral demands in return for a modicum of allegiance and their obedience.[3] After 1986, the Libyan regime used corporal punishment, incarceration, and forced exile for thousands of dissidents to maintain its power; it staffed its security forces with reliable relatives and longtime allies so that their interests became intertwined with Qadhdhafi's aspirations to stay in power. The regime also employed legitimizing strategies in order to rule; this is what some social scientists consider the "normative" dimension of compliance.[4]

The new regime consisted of institutions and forces such as the Inner Circle of Rijal al-Khaimah (his trusted close advisors and confidants), the Revolutionary Committees (the feared zealous ideologists), the tribal alliances of Sufi (the tribal allies from central and southern Libya), and the al-Rifaq organization that included most of Qadhdhafi's friends and classmates from the southern city of Sabha prior to the revolution in the early 1950s. Qadhdhafi invented a policy of "retribalization" and used a divide-and-rule strategy of old Libyan traditional rural institutions like Mi'ad (a tribal negotiating form), Jabr al Khawatir (a traditional Libyan conflict resolution form), and Sufuf (nineteenth century tribal alliances). The institution of Mi'ad is a meeting of tribal leaders to deliberate; Jabr al Khawatir is a tribal meeting to reconcile differences and make peace.[5] Qaddafi often assigned the task of mobilizing tribal support or making peace with rivals to his kinsman and tribal advisor Colonel Khalifa Hanish, who was dispatched informally to these institutions to resolve differences. In the Libyan hinterland, peasant and tribal alliances, called Sufuf, filled a political void where the colonial state lacked a real presence. Even though Libyan society is detribalized and most people live in cities, Qadhdhafi revived old tribal alliances in order to recruit his troops and security forces from Sirte and Sabha and to ensure loyalty to the regime.[6]

From 1975 until 1993, the regime sustained itself by creating a military force with officers being recruited from three important tribes: the Qadhdhafa, Migarha, and Wurfalla. When a plot to overthrow the regime was discovered in 1993, Qadhdhafi reduced the size of the Libyan army to 50,000 men, and only 10,000 were trained and possessed equipment.[7] Instead of strengthening a central army, the regime increasingly relied on the security brigades that were trained, equipped, and paid for by Qaddafi. These brigades and security forces were led by his brother-in-law General Abdullah al-Sanusi, his sons Khamis, Sa'adi, and Mu'tassim, and his cousins, including General Mus'ud Abd Hafidh, Mansur Dhawu, and the brothers Ahmad and Sayyid Qadhdhaf al-Dumm. In addition, Qadhdhafi created a 2,000-person Islamic African legion with recruits obtained from Chad, Niger, Mali, and Sudan. The leader's second wife, Safiyya Farkash, was from the powerful Sa'adi tribe Bra'sa, which gave him some support in the home region of the Sanusi Monarchy.

What went wrong? There are at least three original sins: first, the dominance of security and informal institutions, such as the leadership and Revolutionary Committees, over formal institutions; second, the lack of a national constitution; and third, hostility toward institutionalization. The cult of personality, corruption, the abortion of political reform, and the focus of security over institution building have all contributed to the alienation of lower- and middle-class Libyans and the defection of many reformists, military officers, and diplomats who led the democratic uprising. The Jamahiriyya experiment was over. The fight itself was almost over; Qadhdhafi's regime lost moral legitimacy when it fired on the peaceful protesters in Benghazi, Bayda, Misurata, and Zintan in May 2011, then it lost regional support, the United Nations and international support, and, finally, military support. It was the courageous Libyan youth who confronted the regime and the whole world watched it through the television stations of Al-Jazeera and Al-Arabia, and then CNN. The Arab League had to condemn the killing of the civilians, and the United Nations Security Council resolutions of 1970 and 1973 had to protect civilians and destroy the regime forces. That was crucial in preventing the Qadhdhafi army from crushing the uprising and to save Benghazi from a possible massacre. In other words, the NATO forces led by the UK, France, and the USA allowed the uprising forces to survive, organize, and fight the battered and demoralized Qadhdhafi forces.

The geography and the history of the opposition

The history of Libyan opposition to the regime goes back to the early 1970s, and the strongest regional base for opposition could be found in the eastern region of the country. The regime repressed various opposition movements, including the military and student opposition of the 1970s, the opposition in exile of the 1980s, and the Islamist-inspired opposition of the 1990s. During the 1970s, it first retaliated against those who led a failed military coup by executing over 120 junior officers. Later, on April 7, 1976, the regime suppressed the Libyan Student Union at the main university campuses in Tripoli and Benghazi, executing the leaders of the student revolt and torturing and purging dozens of students and faculty. During the 1980s, resistance to the regime was led by an opposition group in exile that was called the Libyan Salvation Front, which allied with the governments of Sudan, Morocco, Saudi Arabia, Iraq, and the USA.

Finally, during the 1990s, a new wave of opposition arose, which was a radicalized Libyan youth who fought in Afghanistan, Bosnia, and Iraq as jihadists who expressed a more militant form of political Islam. The Libyan Islamic Fighting Group (LIFG) and other Islamist groups in Eastern Libya initiated armed struggle and challenged the regime. The majority of the radical Islamists came from the eastern cities of Ajdabiyya, Benghazi, Bayda, Derna, and Tobrouq, which had also been the traditional geographic base of both the Sanusiyya movement and the Sanusi Monarchy. Some residents from this region had viewed Qadhdhafi's 1969 coup as illegitimate. Yet, by 1998, the regime had managed to crush this armed Islamist insurgency. The consequence was that by early 1990 there were approximately 100,000 exiled Libyans living abroad.

In February 2011, the Qadhdhafi regime's brutal reaction to the peaceful protesters in Benghazi, Bayda, and other eastern Libyan cities led to moral outrage among many people including military officers, diplomats, and even ministers. Minister of Justice, Mustafa Abdel-Jalil, Minister of Interior General, Abdul Fattah Younes, Ambassador to the United Nations and longtime Minister of Foreign Affairs, Abdul Rahman Shalqam, and ten other Libyan ambassadors quickly rejected the regime. Two months later, more members of the elite defected, including Musa Kusa, a longtime intelligence chief and Foreign Minister and former Minister of Energy, Fathi Ben Shitwan, Governor of the Central Bank, Farhat Ben Gadara, and former Prime Minister and Head of the Libyan National Oil Company, Shukri Ghanim. In addition, many soldiers and army officers defected, not only in the eastern region but also throughout the rest of the country. The sole exception was in Libya's southern region, where many communities were isolated and without allies in Egypt or Tunisia.

This combination of opposition forces, which arose in the eastern region of the country, was subsequently joined by defectors and exiled groups who all formed the revolution's new leadership. These leaders met in Benghazi on March 5, 2011 and created the Libyan National Transitional Council (NTC).

For a listing of the known members of the NTC, refer to Appendix A 5. The council included more than 40 members representing all regions of the country. The NTC is a coalition of professionals, academics, doctors, lawyers, reformers, defectors, Islamists, and royalists, and a few traditional tribal figures from rural areas. The Chair of the Council is Judge Mustafa Abdel-Jalil, who was the justice minister under the old regime. His deputy is Abdel Hafidh Ghoga, a lawyer and former head of the Libyan Bar Association. The youth were represented by lawyer Fathi Terbal, the women by Professor Salwa Deghaily, and political prisoners by Ahmed Zubair al-Sanusi, who spent 31 years in a Libyan prison.

The NTC established military and judicial committees, and an executive board chaired by Dr. Mahmoud Jibril, an American educated political scientist who, until last year, was the head of the Libyan Planning Council. Dr. Ali Tarhouni, an exiled Libyan and a professor of economics at the University of Washington in Seattle, became its finance minister. Mahmoud Shamam, another exiled Libyan who was educated and lived in the USA, became the press and communication minister. The NTC has begun functioning as a parliament. The social base of the uprising was the urban Libyan youth under 30 years of age who joined the rallies and became the voluntary liberation army fighting the regime troops and security brigades. They were trained and led by the defected Libyan soldiers and officers. The anti-colonial resistance heroes and symbols came back, and both sides fought over who should own them.

The return of anti-colonial history: culture, symbols, and institutional mobilization

One of the most remarkable topics that escaped so many observers of the Libya crisis is the return of the anti-colonial symbols and memories. They tell us that history and culture are not static nor a one-way street, but rather a changing process that will be contested from the top and below. Three symbols were used to mobilize popular support against the regime: first, the image of anti-colonial resistance hero 'Umar al-Mukhtar; second, the flag of the Libyan Monarchy, which was adopted and viewed as the flag of independence; and, third, the old national anthem, which was adopted after the name of the king was replaced by 'Umar al-Mukhtar's name. It is remarkable that after four decades of the Qadhdhafi regime, rituals, particularly those representing 'Umar al-Mukhtar, are presenting themselves as the legitimate culmination of the Libyan anti-colonial movement. In other words, the national question, which is linked to the brutal colonial period, is still persistent in Libyan society. Yet, this successful mobilization was followed by a military civil war against the regime with unexpected consequences, especially the spread of arms that came to the cities of Misurata and Zintan. Groups such as the jihadi and militant Libyan fighters from Afghanistan, and the previous Islamist fighters such as the LIFG, all gained strength. The armed militias became the power brokers in Libya, even though the Libyan people participated in two impressive civil elections in 2012 and 2014. These groups had no interest in giving up their arms and found Arab and Western allies who supplied them with arms and media support.

Libya has two parliaments, one in Tobrouq in the east, and another in Tripoli in the west, and three competing governments. On December 15, 2015, the United Nations brokered an agreement signed in Skhairat, Morocco that unified the two parliaments. However, the Tobrouq parliament has not voted on the Fayez al-Sarraj Government of National Accord yet, and the Libyan army, led by General Khalifa Haftar, who controlled most of the eastern region, including the region known as "oil crescent" complex, rejected the political agreement. Haftar became a force in the Libyan conflict to the point that he visited Russia, Egypt, and Algeria as a Libyan statesman. I argue that the rise of a new strongman like Haftar is problematic. His army is popular in the eastern region as people are eager to have security and stability. Yet, his history and lack of clarity in assuring Libyans of his support for the democratic process should worry most Libyan people who revolted against the Qadhdhafi dictatorship in 2011.

The struggle over the new Libya

The upsurge in fighting in Libya after 2014, which continued until 2018, has been the most intense since the overthrow of Qadhdhafi in 2011. In addition to pitting various militias against each other, Haftar has proclaimed his intention to seize the reins of power throughout the country. Haftar is a serious player and his operation, Karama ("Dignity"), has gathered broader support both inside Libya and abroad. He expresses the frustrations of many Libyans. Public opinion has become disillusioned with many things, including the elected General National Congress, the Government of National Accord and the parliament in Tobrouq; its own government; high levels of corruption; and the violence and lawlessness by unrestrained militias competing for resources and positions. In other words, Haftar is riding a wave of public frustration inside Libya despite the fact that his motives and integrity are questionable, particularly given his past work for the American CIA and the fear of the rise of a new strong military man. Haftar did not create the crisis; the crisis created Haftar.

Saudi Arabia and the United Arab Emirates are supporting Haftar's movement, as are Egypt and Algeria. The Saudis and Emiratis consider Haftar the Libyan arm of their regional campaign against the Muslim Brotherhood, while Egypt and Algeria – both of which share long borders with Libya – have more pressing security concerns such as arms smuggling, terrorism, and stemming the flow of jihadists. A number of groups, such as the Egyptian Muslim Brotherhood and al Qaida in the Islamic Maghrib, have established a presence inside Libya. On the other side of the equation, Qatar, Turkey, Sudan, and the Egyptian Muslim Brotherhood are supporting various Libyan Islamists. These include a broad range of organizations and militias such as the Libyan Muslim Brotherhood, the jihadist Wafaa' block, and the old Libyan Salvation Front. This broad coalition of Islamists has become more powerful despite the fact that it lost the July 2012 elections to the "liberal" National Democratic Coalition.

The Islamists achieved these gains by relying on the power of regional and religious militias which exercise real power on the ground. They were further assisted by the resignation of more than 40 members of parliament, most of whom belonged to the National Democratic Coalition. Consequently, the General National Congress became dominated by Islamists, and they were able to oust Prime Minister Ali Zaidan in March 2014, and replace him with the Islamist-leaning Ahmed Maitig, and later by 'Umar al-Hasi, and Ibrahim al-Ghwail. This is the larger context of Haftar's movement.

The uprising has been hijacked by extremists, armed militias, and warlords who publicly oppose rebuilding the army and the police, and have created a climate of fear, kidnapping, and assassinating anyone who opposes them and their Salafi jihadi agenda. I asked a family member why some people now support Haftar. She replied "our life became worse and people would support anybody like him, anybody who helps us to create army and police force capable of fighting terrorism, crime, kidnapping, and ending lawlessness." A Libyan friend who edits a leading newspaper told me that around 512 people have been assassinated so far, including journalist Muftah Abuzaid in Benghazi and Nasib Karfada, a female correspondent for the Libyan al-Wataniyya television station in Sabha. The defeat of the old regime, the opening of Libya's borders, and intervention by militant jihadi groups enjoying Arab and international support has blocked the transition. There is a refusal to rebuild the armed forces and police. An unintended consequence of the uprising has been the rise of regionalist militias such as the Misurata and Zintan brigades, as well as jihadist groups which are powerful in cities such as Derna, Sirte, and Benghazi. The army took over Benghazi and Derna, and Misurata forces had cleared Sirte from Islamic extremists by 2018.

Back in 2012, these armed groups used their power to force a weak parliament to approve the Exclusion Law, which they have used to remove rivals and opponents from the political process. Thus, Mahmoud Jibril and Muhammad al-Magariaf were ousted from office, as were most top officials who worked for the Qadhdhafi regime between 1969 and 2011. Weak governments are effectively held hostage by armed groups who control key ministries and demand salaries for their 250,000 members – even though only 20,000 people fought the old regime in 2011. In other words, weak post-uprising governments created this problem by appeasing armed groups who, for economic reasons, oppose efforts to rebuild the army. At the same time, groups such as Ansar al-Shari'a have publicly proclaimed their opposition to elections, democracy, and a standing army. Libya currently has two contending governments: Fayez al-Sarraj, appointed by the 2015 Sikhairt political agreement and claiming to be the legitimate prime minister; and

Colonel Abdullah al-Thinni, who has been at the post in the east at Bayda since March 2014. A third government was led by Ibrahim al-Ghwail, and supported by the Islamist political groups from the old but expired 2012 National General Congress. This last government is out of the picture now after a military defeat in 2016. Haftar has denounced the parliament as an illegitimate body and asked the Constitutional Assembly and Supreme Court to govern the country. When both declined, he asked the Supreme Legal Counsel to manage the country. The General National Congress, in turn, accused him of staging a coup to depose an elected parliament. Needless to say, the country is still split.

The larger dynamics driving what is almost a civil war are a fractured political process, incompetent leadership, and a weak formal government, while regional, religious, and clan-based militias and political groups fight for power, positions, oil, and money. Corruption and patronage became endemic. The elected leaders became tools for the armed militia who demanded salary and money. In addition, the actions of many Libyan opposition leaders after they returned to Libya in 2001 from exile were negative. Some of these exiled Libyans were hungry for power, position, and money, which led many Libyans to react negatively to all Libyans exiled in Western countries. This reaction is understandable, but often unfair because not all returning exiled Libyans participated in corruption and, after 2011, sought mainly to enrich themselves and their families. Many did, though, offering, for example, full government scholarships to their children to study abroad, and appointing themselves ambassadorships and to cultural attaché positions. Also, some paid themselves salaries retroactively as compensation for the years since 1969 that they had spent in exile.

Both the elected leaders and the Libyan civic activists who have been the driving forces for this early democratic uprising must learn from the mistakes of the post-2011 failed transition. These leaders failed to resolve the security and military problems and have to compromise for the sake of the entire country, an essential foundation for building state institutions. Haftar and the powerful Misurata militias have to compromise, recognize the General National Assembly, respect the voters' choices and rebuild the national army and the police force after dismantling the armed militias, as well as open the process for national reconciliation, including with the supporters of the old regime inside and outside Libya. Libya is a case of failed transition, not a failed state. In addition, the Arab Gulf states, Turkey and Sudan, the USA, and the European Union have been guilty as well, and they can help the process by putting a lid on the flow of arms and jihadists into the Libyan civil war, both directly and through their allies and client states. The challenges of building a stable civil and pluralistic democracy are indeed formidable and much harder than defeating the Qadhdhafi dictatorship.

The lessons for resolving the Libyan crisis of transition require a deep knowledge of the scholarship on comparative social revolutions, failed states, and, above all, a deeper grasp of Libyan social, institutional, and political struggle for national independence from colonialism and for the rule of law and democratic governance. Libya is not an isolated island and is integrated in the regional Arab, African, and Mediterranean worlds. The problem of transition is complex and formidable and requires a bold new leadership and creative and imaginative solutions. The lure of authoritarianism and support for a new strongman in the name of law and order is real. But this is only one option and there are alternatives to this old form of leadership and governance. The Libyan people fought for two goals: unity and independence from colonialism. They are again, ironically, being betrayed by failed leaders and regional and greedy foreign interests who lost Libya as a client state in 1969 and now want to incorporate it again. Libyans are, as in 1950, debating who is a Libyan and what type of a state we should build.

After the war is over, I would argue that they should learn from the culture and the history of the people in the concentration camps. They were open, creative, human, and inclusive people who valued self-governance and not being controlled by the nation-state. This heroic and human culture should be the model to look at and emulate for this new opportunity to do it right. But yes, the challenge now is how to end the senseless war and free the Libyan people from the violent control of the armed criminal militias and their outside patrons. The culture of the survivors of the camps gives a good example in how to create a decentralized system and to be governed through the native institutions and values as a counterforce to the colonial and postcolonial state. Perhaps it was good that the genocide was not ideologically packaged as a state-organized story or industry, or told in an orthodox way to school children as many modern nation-states have done. Instead, it has remained in the possession of the ordinary people with its richness, diversity, and local fluidity preserved. This is the lesson of the Libyan case.

The United Nations can still play a constructive role if it realizes the obstacles and the negative factors behind the persisting paralysis of the crisis, and the stalled process of rebuilding the state and civic institutions after 2012. However, in the future, after the end of armed criminal and private militias, and the end of outside invention, Libya will need a commission for truth and reconciliation to record the truth about all the abuses from 1969 until today, in exchange for pardoning and forgiveness. Only then will Libya be able to heal the open wounds of the past and achieve justice for the survivors. In summary, the challenge is formidable, but with the right leadership and international unified support, success in building peace, stability, and democratic institutions in Libya, as well as good governance, is possible, despite the fact that it may look bleak and remote today. Libyan people have to be defended and if they can outlast genocide they can overcome warlords, criminals, neocolonial manipulation, and corrupt and selfish leaders.

Notes

1 Ismail Raghib Khalidi, *Constitutional Development in Libya*, (Beirut: Khayyat's College Books, 1963), 62–63, and for UN Commissioner Adrian Pelt's own account see his book, *Libyan Independence and the United Nations*, (New Haven: Yale University Press, 1970).

2 On the impact of oil on Libya see J. A. Allan, *Libya: The Experience of Oil*, (Boulder: Westview Press, 1981) and Dirk Vandewalle, "The Libyan Jamahiriyya Since 1969," in Dirk Vandewalle, ed., *Qadhdhafi's Libya*, (New York: St. Martins Press, 1995), 3–46, and Stace Birks and Clive Sinclair, "Libya: Problems of a Rentier State," in Richard Lawless and Allan Findlay, eds, *North Africa: Contemporary Politics and Economic Development*, (New York: St. Martin's Press, 1984).
3 Ibid.
4 Ali Abdullatif Ahmida, *Forgotten Voices: Power and Agency in Colonial and Postcolonial Libya*, (New York: Routledge, 2005), 65–85.
5 John Davis, *Libyan Politics: Tribe and Revolution*, (Berkeley: University of California Press, 1991), 71–91.
6 Ali Abdullatif Ahmida, *The Making of Modern Libya*, (Albany: State University of New York Press, 1994, second edition 2009), 51–54.
7 Said Haddaadt, *The Role of the Libyan Army in the Revolt against Gaddafi's Regime*, (Doha: Al Jazeera Centre for Studies, March 16, 2011), 2–5.

CONCLUSION

Toward a paradigm shift, decentering Italian Fascism and genocide studies

This book has examined the history of the pretext regarding the Italian Fascist colonial genocide in eastern Libya and the politics of that memory from 1929 until our present time. I examined the genocide from the point of view of the victims of this forgotten tragedy using a comparative and transnational perspective. My critical examination employed a double critique. First, I examined the Eurocentric, colonial, and fascist scholarship that has been silent on genocide outside Europe, and the false myth of Italian Fascism as a lesser evil, or *"Italiani, brava gente."* Second, I examined modern Libyan historiography and the politics of postcolonial history, which include the origins of the Libyan state but also contrast with the subaltern view of society, especially that of the survivors of the concentration camps and their families, during the second half of the twentieth century. This conclusion reflects my thinking on the recovery of the history of the concentration camps based on the survivors' oral and folk histories. This new history from below, grounded in people's indigenous hidden history, challenges both colonial racism, fascism, and the nationalist elitism perspective that has dominated the writing of history since World War II. In summary, this book calls for a larger critique of the silence around colonial genocides, the Eurocentric study of modernism and fascism, and the assumptions that the nation-state is the inevitable culmination of the historical process.

This double critique of colonial and nationalist canons of the study of genocide, as well as capitalist modernity, is challenged in two ways. First, it investigates the assumptions of colonial and modernist archives and the context of power and the production of knowledge. It is not based on nationalist ideology nor takes the nation-state paradigm for granted. Second, it recovers subaltern voices that are viewed alongside living, cultural, and historical processes, in the case of Libya, the Arab/Muslim, African traditions, values, and institutions. I assume an equal historical agency to the survivors of the camps and their counternarrative, and the colonial and Eurocentric paradigm and justification of silence and genocide.

In these remaining pages, I shall focus on four areas that are relevant to the lessons and findings of this book: the politics of memory inside Libya and Italy; the factors behind the cover-up and silencing of the crimes of Italian Fascism; the crisis of historiography; and, finally, the challenge for the study of genocide, especially the Holocaust in Anglo-American studies, and an examination of why colonial and Eurocentric scholarship needs to be rethought in terms of the assumptions regarding identity, modernism, and violence. Ultimately, this discussion ends with a call for a transnational and comparative critical paradigm that engages not only subaltern voices, but examines the silence of an empire, colonial genocides, and the political theory associated with them. This double critique of Eurocentric and nationalist colonial paradigms is grounded in the recovery of the living history of concentration camp survivors who retained their voices and culture despite colonial and nationalist silence and politics. Their human agony and trauma reject the colonial myth of moderate Italian Fascism and its misleading depiction as a lesser evil in Western public media and in the scholarship of fascism. In short, history and memory create an arena for the politics of the present. Consequently, assumption, silence, and language reflect the dominant and obscure the subaltern, hidden narratives, and discourses of power and representations. Colonial genocides are linked to and interpreted in relation to European genocides. The Libyan case contributes to our understanding of the other two cases of genocide in Africa: the Congo and the Herero. The Armenian genocide took place during World War I. Thus, the Libyan case is the only one committed by a fascist European regime in its colony, and the first genocide after World War I.

How to think about forgotten genocide

When I started researching and writing this book, I faced a methodological challenge: I could use the nation-state and current assumptions behind disciplinary area studies and treat the Libyan case in isolation within its region and African boundaries, or, I could frame this as a transnational case within its Arab-Muslim and African dynamics. If I had chosen the first option, I probably would not have been able to understand the reaction of the people of eastern Libya, their culture, and living history. The nation-state is a problem not a solution. Listening and reading the survivors' narrative of those affected by the internment pushed me to reexamine modern education in Libya, Egypt, and the USA. The survivors have their own culture within the larger Libyan culture and, above all, they have a living culture deeply rooted in rural Islamic and Arab traditions. Only when I began to listen and critically examine my own modern education did I come to understand their cultural reaction, language, and worldviews. This book became a critical examination of language, identity, and the politics of cultural survival. I also started to recall the culture and values of my mother and grandmother's generations and reminded myself that this rural and regional culture is not traditional, nor anti-modern, but is a living and significant subculture with Libyan and Arab Muslims. The survivors narrated their history through their rural and regional values and language. They knew that their colonial and fascist enemies were planning to exterminate them, crush their resistance, and replace them with colonial settlers. It is this agony, expressed through their language and their culture, which allowed me to understand the survivors' narratives and hidden history, the deep trauma they carried with them and passed to their descendants after 1934. One must confront the double challenge of living history among Libyan survivors and postcolonial society on the one hand, and on the other understand the construction of silence and invisibility of the Libyan case inside Italy and its resulting spell over modern Anglo-American scholarship and Italian Fascism and genocidal studies.

This book targeted the problems of history, writing with respect as to why the Libyan case became invisible. I fought to identify the consequences of this invisibility and silence over empire and colonialism, not only in the Anglo-American political and social theory of modernization, but in postmodernism as well. For example, it is troubling and also very clear that the most critical Western theorists of modernism and genocide, such as Michel Foucault and Giorgio Agamben, are silent on these questions. Colonialism, empire, and genocide outside Europe are absent histories in these theorists' critiques and theories. Foucault is the most influential philosopher and historian of the second half of the twentieth century. He theorized regarding the birth of the modern prison, the panopticon, the most central example of his critique, and the genealogy of power in modern capitalist society in nineteenth century. The birth of the modern prison is a case to illustrate the modern rupture of power and punishment which separated modern society from the middle ages. The modern prison functions as an example of disciplinary power which normalizes truth and presents itself as truth and right in all modern civic institutions. Foucault is surprisingly silent about the whole question of empire and French colonies, especially the most violent cases in Algeria in the nineteenth century.[1] When he wrote about non-Western cases such as Japan, Tunisia, and Iran he forgot his critical method and viewed these cases from a Western perspective. Yet, his most surprising silence in his critical scholarship is on concentration camps and especially the double cases of concentration camps and colony.[2]

Agamben, an Italian philosopher, has made the question of the concentration camp the center of modernity itself. He argued that the inhabitants of the Nazi concentration camp are not *the other* to modern society, but its dark symbol. For him, the camp replaced the city as the most significant feature of biopolitics in the West, and "in some way as the hidden matrix and nomos of the political space in which we are still living."[3]

As an Italian, one would expect him to confront the Libyan case and, perhaps, other colonial cases, but he chose instead to focus on the safe and familiar case of the Holocaust. Colonialism and capitalism are ignored in his analysis, despite the fact that Agamben teased Foucault for ignoring the concentration camps. Agamben is correct to argue that the camp replaced the city as a symbol of current world, postmodernism, but he is silent about which camps, and the colony itself, as if the non-Western world, especially the colonized people, do not exist! More troubling and scandalous is Agamben's use of the figure of "Muselmann" or Muslim as the most dehumanized, fatalist figure in the Holocaust concentration camp. He made the following argument:

> Now I imagine the most extreme figure of the camp inhabitants. Primo Levi described the person who in the camps jargon was called "The Muslim," der Muselmann – a being from whom humiliation, horror, and fear had so taken away all consciousness and all personality as to make him absolutely a pathetic, hence the ironic name giving to him.[4]

For Agamben, this extreme figure has lost all consciousness, because of fear and horror, to the point that he has lost his humanity and cannot even kill himself; he has become, in effect, a walking or a living dead person. Yet, this character for him became a symbol of the complete witness because he is nonhuman because of the horrors of the camp. Once again, Agamben primarily focuses on Nazi death camps. He is completely silent on the state of exception, emergency, and "bare life" in the Italian concentration camps in eastern Libya and one must conclude from this amnesia that Agamben, and before him Foucault, accept their disregard of Italian Fascist horrors. Like Foucault, this colonial silence is the common, traditional Eurocentric view of history; they should not escape criticism, because their Eurocentrism and silence on the record of crimes against humanity, as in the cases of mass killing and colonial genocides, including the Libyan case, is a glaring omission.[5]

Nor should it be acceptable to study modern Libya by perpetuating silence, failing to even mention the camps, or repeating the Neo-orientalist assumptions of approaching Libya through the lens of tribalism, through strongmen like Qadhdhafi, or by the recent media and scholarship focused on the assumption of anarchy fragmentation. The genocide that occurred in Libya between 1929 and 1934 represents the most inhumane and brutal genocide in Africa's history. It is a genocide that has had a significant consequence for the society, especially if one sees it through the victims' language, their subculture, their oral history, folk poetry, and the living culture as depicted in modern Libyan literature, poetry, and novels. Breaking the silence of Eurocentric scholarship not only reveals the history of genocide and its consequences that affected Libya, but, by extension, beyond Libya and its modern boundaries.

Italian military and colonial soldiers committed violence with clear and legal orders for extermination produced by the Fascist Italian state. They justified its order to starve and exterminate the resisting people of eastern Libya by using language similar to that used by German and Belgian colonial states such as "the right of empire, progress, racial superiority," but also by the claim of Roman destiny and history to not only kill but to also achieve colonial demographic dominance by Italians in Libya.[6] Italian Fascism was ideologically rooted in militaristic and racial superiority but cannot be understood without the knowledge that it had its own colonies, and like all settler colonies was the most violent. One cannot assume that all settler colonies are not only violent but also genocidal, as many scholars have shown over the ages from North and South America, Australia, and Africa.

That the fascist state used extermination is documented in the letters of the three generals in charge of the colony and the plan and who executed the killing in the punishment camps: De Bono, Badoglio, and Graziani. These letters discuss plans of extermination, deeply rooted in European science and studies. Yet, the difference in the case of Italy colonial violence was the absence of war crime trials and the continued survival of the fascist ideology, institutions, and mentality after the collapse of Italian Fascism in 1943. The politics of the Cold War further enabled the Italian elite to invent the myth of difference and the essentialist notion that fascism in Italy was moderate, there being no available records of genocide and anti-Semitism. Consequently, this led to a notion that Italians were good people, unlike the Germans. As the Holocaust case became more visible, this silence over the dark history of the Italian genocide in Libya was perpetuated and continued to remain hidden. As Stuart Hall argued, mass culture is an arena for struggle. Film, as a genre example, perpetuated and exposed colonial silence and myths regarding mass killing and atrocities.

Films that questioned the silence, such as *Lion of the Desert* (1981), and the BBC's *Fascist Legacy* (1989), were bought and then shelved, while others that reproduced the myth of moderate fascism and "human" colonization abound, including the films of talented leftist directors such as Pontecorvo, Visconti, and Fellini. Despite this silence and collective amnesia, the Libyan genocide is still with us inside Libya, and in Italy as well. In Libya, the graves and cemeteries are still reminders of the ghosts of the genocide, as I discussed when I did my fieldwork in the location of the four killing camps. Also, Italian Fascist monuments from colonial Libya and Ethiopia are still visible, honoring the colonial soldiers, and even the memory of General Rodolfo Graziani, who executed the genocide and is openly celebrated, has been honored in his home town using public tax funds. The genocide is indirectly present, and it defines both Libyans and Italians.

Hannah Arendt was right: the Holocaust is rooted in the racist and totalitarian institutions and ideologies of European colonialism in Africa, especially in the Belgium Congo and Central and East African colonial experiences. When I checked her references, I found a major source was Joseph Conrad's *Heart of Darkness*. This novel exposes the horrors and violence committed by European colonialists in Africa, especially in the Congo.[7] The question at hand is why Arendt's critique of imperialism and racism, and her visionary argument to link colonial genocide to the European Holocaust, which was written in

1951, was ignored for many decades. While she did not perhaps know about Libya, her silence on the Native American genocide is, however, troubling. The history of native people is of dispassion, military repression, and violation of treaties, confinement, and genocide. I have in mind her silence over the "Indian removal," "the Trail of Tears," of the massacres at Wounded Knee, and of the "Reservation" system. Native American historians have been producing a revisionist history that challenges the triumphant narrative reflected in schools, books, monuments, and films. Only in the last 20 years have we witnessed a revival of her argument by some postcolonial scholars at European and Australian universities.

We now have detailed and documented studies of the link between colonial genocide and the Holocaust, including the normalization of extermination ideologies and even the sciences, including eugenics, such as the fact that more than 40,0000 Germans either visited or lived in the colony of South West Africa and participated in the horrors and genocide there between 1904 and 1908. These settlers, soldiers, and scientists popularized racist and extermination ideologies through their memoirs and works which, in turn, influenced Nazi leaders. These future Nazi leaders, such as Hermann Göring, Franz Ritter von Epp, and Eugene Fisher, had connections with the German settler colony of South West Africa and General Carl Peters in German East Africa. Hermann Göring is directly linked to the Libyan case. Göring, a top military leader in the Nazi state, was in charge of the first concentration camp. Eugene Fisher was an anthropologist with a specialty in racialism and race relations. He justified killing mixed race and bastard children in the colony. Later on, he became a director of the Nazi Institute in Berlin, specializing in race and eugenics. One of his best students was Josef Mengele, who was behind the horror killings in the concentration camps.

Göring is the most relevant figure. As discussed in Chapter 4, he visited Libya in 1939, and there is even a film of this visit to Tripoli to learn about Italy's "successful" colonization of Libya, including cleaning the land of the indigenous people and settling thousands of Italian peasants, a key topic for Nazi leaders who had a plan to settle 15 million Germans in Eastern Europe. There were more Nazi delegates who visited Rome and Tripoli. This hidden German connection between Italian Fascism and Nazi Germany, and the use of the Libyan genocide as a model for the horrific genocide perpetrated by Germany, requires major consideration in studies by both the Italian and German regimes of modern genocide. This new evidence should prompt a rethinking of the Holocaust. Until now, the Holocaust has been viewed as an isolated and unique case of genocide. However, it should now be read as a colonial case rooted in the wider practice of European colonial genocide, such as in the Congo, South West Africa, and Libya. The German deep interest and extensive study of the case of Italian colonialization and genocide in Libyan shows a clear link between the two genocides and leaves no doubt that the Holocaust has a history rooted in Libya, Namibia, and the Congo.

The Nazis learned from the Italian Fascists about the use of concentration camps and how to defeat resistance through extermination and genocide. Muslim Libyans and European Jews have in common the fact that they were victims of genocide and fascism. The discovery of anti-Nazi and anti-fascist articles and books by the exiled Libyans in the 1930s and 1940s presents fresh new evidence of a significant anti-colonial struggle often overlooked in the Arab and African world. Genocide studies must not only must the colonial with the European mass killing but must reconceptualize the two as highly similar cases of genocidal regimes. I would argue that the Holocaust is a colonial case and that the Libyan case contributed directly to its making. Yet, for such a paradigm change to occur in genocide studies, one must decolonize the field and reconsider long-standing ways of thinking in modern Western political theory and international relations scholarship. This requires breaking the silence, rethinking areas studies, and recovering transnational diversity. This rethinking must first decolonize social sciences and the hegemony of the rise of the West, including fascism and "provincializing Europe." Also, it requires rethinking the nation-state and nationalism inside the Arab and African world. We must study Italy to understand Libya, and we must study Libya to understand Italy.

The production of scholarship whether Eurocentric, colonial, or nationalist took place within the historical context of the Cold War and shaped the views of people in Rome, London, and Washington DC after the defeat of fascism in 1943. Yet this Cold War scholarship, which produced silence and the view of a moderate Italian Fascism, has also been contested through African and Arab resistance. The Libyan elite that led the independent state in 1951 decided to overlook the genocide and instead focused on tacit forgiveness and development. That is why there was no official monument, collection of oral history, trials for Italian colonial generals, or reparations for the survivors of the concentration camps. King Idris I first spoke only in general terms of the anti-colonial Libyan Jihad and was silent on the concentration camps' brutal history. Consequently, the loyalists and Italian settlers who stole land from the indigenous people were untouched and faced no war crime charges. The monarchy's elite did its best neither to protest to the Italian government nor to challenge the Italian settlers. Instead, it assumed that independent Libya would forget the past atrocities and would not press for war crimes trials and justice. In Italy, there was neither a call for official examinations of the violence in Libya nor any attempt to teach the public about these colonial crimes through the media and public schools. Instead, there was widespread sympathy for colonial soldiers and officers who served under Italian Fascism. It should not be surprising that the files and records of the concentration camps were missing or classified. That is why we still have no precise record of how many died as a result of the deportation, internment, hard labor, starvation, and disease wrought by the genocide. This does not mean that we cannot think about the problem in a creative and critical way. We can make an estimate and rely on the survivors who gave us specific details and counts of the people who died, their approximate ages, and their causes of death. One has to admit that under Qadhdhafi's leadership there was a push for collecting the history of the genocide and pressure placed on the Italian government to admit its responsibility. Despite his airing of the genocide with the Italians, Qadhdhafi ultimately let himself be used by the Italians for economic and political gains, thereby undermining the legitimacy of his own regime. The result of his policy to press the Italians was therefore diminished following the 2008 apology and agreement.

There is no major change in Italian education, debates, and public opinion regarding the Libyan genocide. In Libya, despite the anti-colonial rhetoric of Libyan leadership, I found no major monuments or ongoing studies. Most of the camps have been lost to development and construction, with the exception of Agaila and, to a degree, Braiga. On a more positive note, the societal narratives and memories of the genocide remain alive and Libyan literature continues to contribute to the memory of the genocide. Whatsmore, the University of Benghazi and the Libyan Studies Center have collected rich volumes of oral history and poetry published over the past 40 years. The survivors told me time and time again that they are still poor and struggling, and some have demanded reparations. Most of them, however, solely want their history and their families to be recognized and the atrocities they faced to be made public. I promised many of them I would translate my book into Arabic and send them copies. However, many of them have died from poor health and old age. This book should be read as the story of these survivors and their descendants. Hopefully, it will be read not as the last word on the Libyan genocide, but as a call for more research and examination of hard questions, and perhaps a decolonization of colonial and fascist knowledge and a decentering of genocide studies.

Notes

1 See Michel Foucault, *Discipline and Punish: The Birth of Modern Prison* translated by Alan Sheridan, (New York: Vintage Books, 1995, 1997). Foucault is silent about empire and colony including French colonies such as Algeria and Haiti. See Michel-Rolph Trouillot, *Silencing The Past*, (Boston: Beacon Press, 1995), 26–27, 95–107.
2 See Foucault's summary of his critique of Western political theory of power, Liberal and Marxist, "Two Lectures" in Nicolas B. Dirks, Geoff Eley, and Sherry B. Ortner, eds, *Culture/Power/History: A Reader in Contemporary Social Theory*, (Princeton: Princeton University Press, 1994), 201–221.
3 Giorgio Agamben, *Homo Sacer: Sovereign Power and Bare Life* translated by Daniel Heller-Rozen, (Stanford: Stanford University Press, 1998).
4 Giorgio Agamben, *Remnants of Auschwitz: The Witness and the Archive*, (New York: Zone Books, 2002). See the recent critical collection on Agamben by Marcelo Suirsky and Simone Nignall, eds, *Agamben and Colonialism*, (Edinburgh: Edinburgh University Press, 2012).
5 Marina Lazreg, *Foucault's Orient*, (New York: Berghahn, 2017), 202.
6 On the history of European racism in Africa see Sven Linqvist, *Exterminate All the Brutes*, (London: Granta Publications, 1997), 72–73, 140–141, 172. Also see A. Dirk Moses, ed., *Empire, Colony, and Genocide*, (New York: Berghahn Books, 2008), and

A. Dirk Moses and Dan Stone, eds, *Colonialism and Genocide*, London: Routledge, 2007.
7 Arendt, *The Origins of Totalitarianism*, (New York: Harcourt, Brace and Jovanovich, 1973), 172, 189, footnote on 189and 193. Also see David Stannard, "The Dangers of Calling the Holocaust Unique," *The Chronicle of Higher Education*, 42:47 (August 2, 1996), 1–5.

APPENDICES

A.1 Statistics data on the people present in the detention colonies

Colony	31 Jan 1912	20 Mar 1912	30 Apr 1912	10 Jun 1912	20 Jul 1912	20 Aug 1912	30 Sept 1912
Gaeta	654	648	530	324	266	331	83
Ponza	136	105	115	125	144		
Tremiti	1,080	655	405	10			
Ustica	834	805	766	4			
Favignana	349	426	420	271	265	198	
Total	**3,053**	**2,639**	**2,236**	**734**	**675**	**529**	**83**

A.2 Relocation of the groups of Libyans employed in Italy

Groups	Destination	Number of Workers
No 1	Sampierdarena	500
No 2	Sesto San Giovanni	460
No 3	Piacenza	240
No 4	Bagnasco	388
No 5	Godrano	386
No 6	Brescia	500
No 7	Linate	200
No 8	Turin	500
No 9	Sesto San Giovani	200
No 10	Brescia	200
No 11	Montecelio	100
No 12	Capua	200
No 13	Piacenza	200
No 14	Milan	227
No 15	Dalmine	100
No 16	Castellammare di Stabi	200
		4,601

A.3A Libya's Governors

October 5, 1911–October 13, 1911	Rear-Adm. Raffaele Ricci Dolmo
October 14, 1911–August 28, 1912	Gen. Carlo Caneva
October 12, 1912	The sole governorship is substituted by two governorships in Tripolitania and Cirenaica

A.3B Governorships of Tripolitania

October 28, 1912–May 31, 1913	Gen. Ottavio Ragni
June 1, 1913–October 1, 1914	Gen. Vincenzo Garioni
October 2, 1914–November 16, 1914	Gen, Giorgio Cigliata
November 17, 1914–February 5, 1915	Gen. Luigi Duetti
February 6, 1915–July 14, 1915	Gen. Giulio Cesare Tassoni
July 15, 1915–August 1, 1918	Gen. Giovanni Ameglio
August 2, 1918–August 16, 1919	Gen. Vincenzo Garioni
August 17, 1919–July 10, 1920	Ch. Off. Vittorio Menzingher
July 11, 1920–July 31, 1920	Ch. Off. Ugo Piccoli
August 1, 1920–July 16, 1921	Min. Luigi Mercatelli
July 17, 1921–August 24, 1921	Ch. Off. Edoardo Baccari
August 25, 1921–July 2, 1925	Count Giuseppe Volpi
July 3, 1925–November 9, 1929	WO Emilio De Bono

A.3C Governorships of Cyrenaica

January 31, 1913–November 6, 1913	Col. Ottavio Briccola
November 7, 1913–July 6, 1915	Gen. Giovanni Ameglio
July 7, 1915–August 8, 1918	Gen. Giovanni Ameglio (regent)
August 9, 1918–July 1, 1919	Gen. Vincenzo Garioni
July 2, 1919–November 23, 1921	Sen. Giacomo De Martino
November 24, 1921–October 20, 1922	Ch. Off. Luigi Pintor
November 22, 1922–December 1, 1922	Ch. Off. Edoardo Baccari
December 2, 1922–June 6, 1923	Gen. Oreste De Gasperi
June 7, 1923–May 1, 1924	Gen. Luigi Bongiovanni
May 2, 1924–November 22, 1926	Gen. Ernesto Mombelli
November 23, 1926–December 11, 1928	Gen. Attilio Teruzzi

Vice-Governors in Cyrenaica

January 21, 1929–March 15, 1930	Col. Domenico Siciliani
March 16, 1930–May 31, 1934	Gen. Rodolfo Graziani
June 1, 1934–July 1, 1935	Gen. Guglielmo Nasi

A.3D General Governors of Libya

June 10, 1929	Sole governorship is restored
January 1, 1929–December 31, 1933	Marshall Pietro Badoglio
January 1, 1934–June 28, 1940	WO Italo Balbo
June 29, 1940–March 22, 1941	WO Rodolfo Graziani
March 23, 1941–August 5, 1941	Gen. Italo Gariboldi
August 6, 1941–January 22, 1943	Gen. Ettore Bastico

A.4 Questions on the History/Memory of Italian Concentration Camps 1929–1934

Name _____

Female _____
Male _____

Date and Place of Birth _____

Education _____
Major _____

Date _____

Have you heard of the Italian camps?
Yes _____

No _____

When and how did you first hear of them?

Parents _____

School _____

Have you seen the film *Lion on The Desert*?

Yes _____
No _____

What is your reaction to the film and the representation?
Positive _____
Negative _____

Of the camps?

Positive _____
Negative _____

What should be done to educate people about the camps?

A.5 University of Sabha, Libya: students' answers to survey questions on the Italian concentration camps, 1929–1934

College	Majors	Females	Males	Number
College of Arts and Science:	History	12	8	20
	Communications	6	6	12
	Language	3	7	10
	Arabic	3	2	5
	Sociology	10	5	15
	Psychology	3	2	5
College of Sciences:	Chemistry	3	4	7
	Physics	3	2	5
	Computer Science	1	3	4
	Anatomy	3	2	5
	Agricultural Science	2	3	5
	Medicine	7	5	12
	Engineering	5	6	11
	Law	2	3	5
	Total:	**63**	**58**	**121**

A.6 Poem by Fatima 'Uthamn (1928), translated by Ali Abdullatif Ahmida
Our Homeland Ruined Twice

Ruined twice, our homeland   خرابين يا وطن ما فيك والي
All are wandering, homeless   وذيلك جوّالي
some are hanging from the gallows, or killed   ولخرين في المشنقة والقتالي

We are ruined twice, our homeland   خرابين يا وطن ما فيك هل
Overwhelmed by tyranny   ركبك الذلّ
Those who did not flee were hung   اللي ما جلا، في المشانق حصل

They are gone, no one reached their destination   عدّوا ولا زول منهم وصلْ
Dead, hanging bodies,   وباتوا مدالي
Like the fruit of the date palm   مثيل العراجين في راس عالي

Ruined twice, our homeland, no work to be found   خرابين يا وطن ما فيك دايل
to take care of oneself   بجدّ الشغايل
Lives are lost for the pettiest excuses   وناسك غدوا من كلام السبايل

My tears continue to pour   يا دمع لنظار تذرف وسايل
Lament the loss of the dear ones who   على زول غالي
Are hanging from thin ropes   وعده حضر في رقاق الحبالي

And thick robes brought from beyond the sea   وعُده حضر ف امقاط البحر في يوم زرّ
by the infidel state of aggression on this horrible day   دولة العدوان همّ الكفر

I tried patience, but could not take it anymore صبرت يا خاطري ما صبر
Madness increased, became worse زايد هبالي
Oh, people to tell you what I have witnessed نا بعدهم يا عرب ماطرالي

ruined twice, our homeland, nobody is left behind خرابين يا وطن ما فيك حد
except our noble grief حزنك مُجد
and the feeble and the low ومن ما عقبْ فيك غير اللمد

Look at how many, honorable sons ها المشنقة ما هفّت من ولد
Like Hilalian Arab knights تحلف هلالي
Are now weightless on the gallows ولا خلفّت زول اللي ما يشالي

ruined twice, our homeland, our lights are gone خرابين يا وطن ما طاف ضّيه
darkness cover us كمل بالسوية
honest people, unjustly punished, eliminated وراحوا مظاليم من غير سيّه

I call upon you God, and the prophet's Hamshimites blessed ones ندهت يا رب يا هاشمية
Bring back our beloved ones جيب الغوالي
in a blessed day and end our pain and loss في يوم مبروك يخلص سوالي

Ruined twice, our homeland, nothings remains خرابين يا وطن من فيك باقي
to overcome the gloom يجلّي أنكادي
to bring light to my dark heart ويبيّض العقل بعد السوادي

I call upon you, our countries' saints' ندهتكم يا مشايخ بلاد
Come to me تجوا عند بالي
Come and rescue my sad heart في يوم حامي عليهم يكالي

Come on a hot, terrible day في يوم حامي عليهم يزرّ
Send a menacing, raging sand storm عجاجه كُبر
Bring waves of bullets like rain وتفاح لسلام كيف المطر

To knock down the infidels' heads يباتن مطاويح رُوس الكفر
send them into oblivion تحت النّعالي
That would bring me life and solace هاناك نزهى ويطمان بالي

Ruined twice, my homeland, all my family's gone خرابين يا وطن ما فيك عيله
All are gone, victims, عدّوا جزيله
I cannot find anyone to tell my deep pain ولا زول بمواجعي نشتكي له

My people, my inner pain, is like a lantern light لي جوف يا ناس مثل الفتيلة
Keeps me up all night سامر ليالي
But God, we have You, and only on You we can count ويارّب عطنا عليك التكالي

A.7 Poem by Rajab Buhwaish

I have no illness but this place of Agaila, translated by Khaled Mattawa

I have no illness but this place of Agaila,   مابي مرض غير دار العقيله
    the imprisonment of my tribe   وحبس القبيله
and separation from my kin's abode.   وبعد الجبا من بـلاد الوصيله

No illness but endless grief   مابي مرض غير حد النكاد
    meager provisions   وشوية الـزاد
and the loss of my black red-spotted steed   وريحـة اللي مجبرة بالسـواد

who, when strife broke, stretched her solid-flesh neck,   الحمرة اللي وين صـار العناد
    impossible to describe,   عناتها طويـله
her peer does not exist.   ها وصف ما عاد تـاجد مثيله

I have no illness except my threadbare state   مابي مرض غير واجد مرايف
    and this unbearable longing   والحال صايف
for Aakrama, Adama and Sgaif,   على عكرمة والعدم والسقايف

And for the pastures Lafwat, best of places,   وحومة لفاوات عز العطايف
    which, even when parched   حتى وهي محيله
bursts grass green for the herds.   تربي المهـازيل جلـة خويـله

I long for Aakrama and Sarrati,   . . مرايف علي عكرمة والسراتي
    I wish I were there now.   اللي هن مناتي
I'll be grateful to reach them alive.   انشكرن ان طلتهن في حياتي

When I remember those places I forget my misery—   علي وين يخطرن ننسى اوقاتي
    tears fall,   دمعي نهيله
storms drenching my beard, raging floods.   زواعب علي لحيتى سال سيله

I have no illness but the raining of spears,   . مابي مرض غير مطرى الحرابي
    best of friends   خيرة أصحابي
who keep on striking as bullets whiz past   لضرابين والمكوعظ ينابي

and who ride spirited red horses—whoever fall   ركابين كل حمرة دعـابي
    is promptly snatched up   الطـايح تشيله
by great companions who concede his love.   نضـيده رفاقاه قبلوا جميله

I have no illness but the loss of good men   مابي مرض غير فقد الرجال
    and all our possessions   وفنية المال
and the incarceration of our women and children.   وحبسة نساوينا والعيال

The horseman who once chased untamed camels,   والفارس اللي يقدع المال
    Now bows his head to the invaders   نهاره جفيله
like an obedient girl.   طايع لهم كيف طوع الحليه

He bows to them like a concubine طايع لهم كيف طوع الوليه
    who has made a mistake إن كانت خطيه
and must show deference morning and night. نرمي الطاعة صباح وعشيه

Carrying filth and wood and water, نشيل في الوسخ والمويه
    a low life indeed— معيشة ذليله
none but God can rise and lift this grief. مفيت ربنا يفزع يفك الوحيله

Bowing like a slave طايع لهم كيف طوع الوصيف
    forgetting my status نسيت الوظيف
having lived my life untainted, strong, بعد بقيتي كنت ظاري عفيف

I stand without vigor, light and useless, نصبي بلا حيل عندي خفيف
    a mere factotum نشيل الثقيله
carrying on as if healthy, free of disease. نزازي مزازاة من زين حيله

I have no illness except missing loved ones مابي مرض غير فقد الغوالي
    gentle, honorable folk أسياد المتالي
riding sturdy camels, prancing steeds. سماح العضادات فوق العوالي

They were lost for a trifle before my eyes راحوا حساب شي تافه قبالي
    and I've found nothing ولا لقيت حيله
to console me since they were laid to waste. نشالش بها نين راحوا دقيله

I have no illness except this endless aging مابي مرض غير طولة لجالي
    this loss of sense and dignity وضيعة دلالي
loss of good people who were my treasure, وفقدة أجاويد هم روس مالي

Yunes who rivals al-Hilali يونس اللي كيف صيت الهلالي
    throne of the tribe كرسي القبيله
Emhemed and Abdulkarim al-Ezaila . امحمد وعبد الكريم العزيله

And Buh'sein's sweet countenance and open hand وبو حسين سمح الوجاب الموالي
    and al-Oud and the likes of him, والعود ومثيله
lost without a battle to honor their parting راحوا بلا يوم ذايب ثقيله

I have no illness except the loss of young men مابي مرض غير فقد الصغار
    masters of clans سياد العشار
plucked out like dates in the daylight اللي لقطوا كيف تمر النهار

who stood firm-chested against scoundrels الضرابين للعايب صدار
    the blossoms of our houses نواوير عيله
whose honor will shine despite what the ill-tongued say. ما ينطروا ب ناسا ذليله

I have no illness except the dangers of roadwork   مابي مرض غير شغل الطريق
      my bare existence,   وحالي رقيق
returning home without a morsel to shove down a throat.   ونروح وما طاق البيت ريق

Whips lash us before our women's eyes   وسواطنا قبال النسا في الفريق
      rendering us useless   وقبينا زطيله
degraded, not even a match among us to light a wick.   ما طاقنا عود يشعل فتيله

Nothing ails me except the beating of women   مابي مرض غير ضرب الصبايا
      whipping them naked   وجلودهن عرايا
not an hour are they left in peace.   ولا يقعدن يوم ساعة هنايا

Not even a shred of regard for them,   ولا يختشوا من بنات السمايا
      calling them "whores'"   قول يارزيله
and other foulness, an affliction to the well-bred.   عيب قبح ما يرتضي للعويله

I have no illness except an inability to think straight   مابي مرض غير غيبة أفكاري
      my scandalized pride   وبينة غراري
and the loss of Khiyua Mattari's sons,   لسيد خيوة مطاري

Moussa and Jibril sweet companions of night-dirges,   موسى وجبريل سمح السهاري
      masters of horses   أسياد الخويله
unharmed by rumors calling them cowardly, meek.   ماينطروا بقول داروا عويله

I have no illness except this long homesickness   مابي مرض غير طولة ريافي
      my arms bound tight   ووثقة كتافي
my patience withered, no means to make a livelihood.   وصبري بلا كسب ميل الشعافي

And my stalwart mates who rescue in strife   وتريسي اللي ع السوايا يكافي
      best of the tribe   خيار القبيله
neighbors who nightly guard the camel herd.   عشا للجوارين يحموا كحيله

I have no illness except my far-flung kin   مابي مرض غير بعد العمالة
      imprisoned by thugs   وحبس الرزالة
and the lack of friends to grieve to when wronged   وقلة اللي م الخطا ينشكى له

the lack of those who rule with fairness,   وغيبة اللي يحكموا بالعداله
      justice nonexistent   النصفة قليله
evil dominant, crushing any grain of good.   والباطل على الحق واخذ الميله

I have no illness except my daughters' despicable labor   مابي مرض خدمة بناتي
      the lack of peace   وقلة هناتي
loss of friends death hurriedly took   وفقدة اللي من تريسي مواتي

and the capture of my firm-muscled Bu Atatti ووخذة غزير النصي بوعتاتي
    his likes desirable العايز مثيله
who sooths the heart in a forlorn hour. يهون علي القلب ساعة جفيله

No illness except the loss of my pasture مابي مرض غير فقدة نواجع
    and I'm not counting ونا مانراجع
even though the taker has no remorse, no pangs of guilt. اللي لفهن لاجفا لامواجع

They bring nothing except rule by torture ولا ينظروا غير حكم الفواجع
    long booming throats وريقة طويله
tongues tapered with pounding epithets. ولسان مر شر منضرب الثقيله

No illness except the lack of defenders مابي مرض غير قل المحامي
    frailty of my words ولينة كلامي
the humiliation of the noble-named وهينة أجاويد روس ومسامي

the loss of my gazelle-like unbridled steed وريحة اللي خايلة باللجامي
    swift-limbed غريمة الهميله
fine-featured like a minted coin of gold. منقودة التناسيب نقدة الريله

I have no illness except the hearing of abuse مابي مرض غير سمع السوايا
    denial of pleas ومنع الغوايا
and the loss of those who were once eminent. وفقدة اللي قبل كانوا سمايا

And women laid down naked, stripped وربط النساوين طرحى عرايا
    for the least of causes بسبله قليله
trampled and ravished, acts no words deign describe. يديروا لهن جرم مافيه قيله

No illness except the saying of "Beat them" مابي مرض غير قول اضربوهم
    "No pardon" ولا تصنعوهم
and "With the sword extract their labor," وبالسيف في كل شي خدموهم

thronged in the company of strangers, ومقعد مع ناس مانعرفوهم
    a base living— حياة عليله
except for God's help, my hands' cunning stripped. إلا مغير ماعاد باليد حيله

No illness but the swallowing of hardship مابي مرض غير زمط العلايل
    my imagination pining وديما نخايل
for our horses, sheep, beasts of burden. علي خيلنا والغلم والشوايل

Nothing but starving work under lashing wails— وخدمة بلا قوت والسوط عايل
    what a wretched life! معيشة رزيله
Then for tattered chattel they turn on the women. علي أثر الدباويش جوّا للعويله

No illness except the loss of good people—   مابي مرض غير فقد الملاح
   a government of imbeciles now   ودولة القباح
faces that bespeak calamity, others vulgar glare.   للي وجوهم نكب وأخرى صحاح

How many a child has fallen writhing to their whips   وكم طفل عصران م السوط ذاح
   his senses bewildered.   حاير دليله
O my conscience, an old man now among his peers.   يا نويرتي صاف من دون جيله

No illness except the breaking of wills   مابي مرض غير كسر الخواطر
   my tears pour and drip   ودموعي قواطر
herds let loose to no one's care.   ووشنات مادونهن من يساطر

Shepherds have roped their best studs   الراعـي معقل جمال القناطر
   letting unfit, measly males   فحولة كحيله
mate with their young dromedaries.   وطالق قعادين فوق الخويله

No illness except the capture of honored men   مابي مرض غير حبس المسامي
   the nullity of my days   وميحة أيامي
and the Capo who daily beats the kind-hearted.   وكابو علي ضرب لجواد دامي

He stands, calls you out with a burning tongue   يصبي يناديك بلسان حامـي
   spewing foulness.   ولغوة هزيله
You fear he'll kill you before you sound your grievance.   تخاف يعدمك قبل لا تشتكيلـه

Ill-bred imbeciles now rule. How could one sleep   وشوخة ردي لصل شوت منامي
   with them roaming about?   حتى وهو عزيله
They'll sell you out for the slightest of cause.   يبيعك علي شان حاجة قليله

I have no illness except shorn honors.   مابي مرض غير فوت الحدود
   Black guards standing   ووقاف سود
stiff with cruelty, barbed wire looped around poles.   وشبردق ملوي على رأس عود

No strength, will, or effort to lift these burdens—   لا حيل لا قادرة لاجهـود
   to lift these burdens   لشيل الثقيلـه
to ready to hand back our lives when the angel comes   زاهدين في العمر لوجا وكيلـه

No illness except the bad turn of my stars   مابي مرض غير برمة أفلاكي
   the theft of my property   وهلبة أملاكي
the tight misery of where I lie down to rest.   وضيق دار واشون قاعد متاكي

The fearsome horseman who on days of fray   الفارس اللي كان يوم الدعاكـي
   shielded his women folk   ذرا للعويله
now begs, straggling after a tail-less ape.   يساسـي ورا قرد مقطوع ذيلـه

Every day I rise complaining of subjugation وكل يوم الظلم نا نوض شاكي
my spirit disgraced ونفسي ذليله
and like a helpless girl I can't break my chains. وكيف المرا مانفك العقيله

I have no illness except the bent shape of my life مابي مرض غير ميلة زماني
my limpid, wilted tongue. وقصرة لساني
I never took to shame, and now shame overtakes me. وما نحمل العيب والعيب جاني

And my tribesmen of whom I used to boast وتريسي اللي قبل بيهم نقاني
beautiful in strength and poise جمال العديله
unshakeable when a day turns, disaster foretold— ثقال روزهم يوم ذايب ثقيله

When they fell, I was chased out of my home على أثر ياسهم روجتي من مكاني
a long night ليلة طويله
its darkness overpowered my lanterns' bright flames. ظلامها غطا ضي قاز الفتيله

I have no illness except missing my land مابي مرض غير فقدة بلادي
and longing for my home وشي من اريادي
the pastures out west towards Sa-aadi ... نواجع غرب في خيوط السعادي

I plead with the Generous one on whom I rely طالب الكريم اللي عليه اعتمادي
to swiftly lift this evil يعجل بشيله
before thirty nights pass. قبل لايفوتن ثلاثين ليله

Only God is eternal. The guardian of Mjamam— الدايم الله راعى المجمم
an oppressive light now shines طغى ضي ظلم
no daylight is safe from the wicked's dark. العاصي علي طول ما يوم سلم

If not for the danger, I would say what I feel— لولا الخطر فيه بيش نتكلم
I would raise him to noble heights ونعرف نشيله
expound my praise, sound my gratitude. ونعرف نبين ثناه وجميله

REFERENCES

Conferences

Tripoli, Libya, Libyan Studies Center, "Libyan Concentration Camps and the Study of Colonial Concentration Camps" (2006).

Siena, Italy "Colonial Camps in the History of Concentration Camps" (2008).

UC Berkeley, USA, "Writing and Speaking Libya's Histories" (2009).

Fieldwork oral interviews

Al-Abaidi, Haja Bahiya Hamad. August 24, 2008, al-Iziyyat.

Al-'Abaidi, Mtawal 'Atiyya. December 15, 2008, Slug.

Al-'Abar, 'Uthman, Al-Shilmani, Muftah, Al-'Amruni, Mabruk and Al-Fakhri, 'Abda-lalli. December 5, 2008.

Al-Agaila, and al-'Aquri, Mijdal. December 15, 2008, Slug.

Al-'Amrani, Jibril Ali. November 5, 2008. Agaila.

Al-'Aquri, Aziz 'Abdaljalil. December 15, 2008.

Ayoub, Abderrahman. March 6, 2007, Tunis.

Al-Bal'azi, Yusuf Sa'id. December 15, 2008, Magrun.

Al-Bal'azi, Um al-'Izz, Hania al-Lawati. December 15, 2008, Slug.

Burhana, Ali. December 30, 2003, Sabha.

Al-Fakhri, Abdal-Khaliq, Al-Shilwi, Idris, Al-Sha'ri, Hamad al-'Awami, and 'Usman al-Shami, Muhammad. June 13, 2007, Agaila.

Al-Fisi, Nuh Hamad. May 30, 2008, Rajma.

Jadallah, Khalifa interviewed by Yusuf Salim al-Barghathi, *Oral History Archives*, June 24, 1981. Tripoli: Libyan Studies Center.

Jarba', Zahra Ahmad. October 24, 2007, Benghazi.

Al-Lafi, Haj Sa'id Atiyya. November 1, 2008, Benghazi.

Al-Rifadi, Haj 'Abdalnabi 'Abdalshafi interviewed by Muhammad Mukhtar al-Sa'di, January 23, 2008.

Shalqam, Abdrahamn. May 15, 2012, New York.

Al-Shami, Muhammad 'Usman. June 13, 2007, Agaila.

Al-Shami, Muhammad 'Usman. Yusuf Sa'id al-Bal'azi. June 13, 2008, Agaila.

Al-Shami, Muhammad 'Usman. October 23, 2008, Benghazi.

Al-Shilmani, Idris. December 15, 2008, Slug.

Al-Shilmani, Idris. May 5, 2004, Slug.

Al-Shilmani, Muftah. May 23, 2009.

Al-Shilwi, Salim Muftah. Interviews 14–114 *Oral History Archives*, Tripoli: Libyan Studies Center.

Al-Shilwi, Salim Muftah interviewed by Yusuf Salim al-Barghathi, *Oral History Archives*, June 25, 1981. Tripoli: Libyan Studies Center.

Zagub, Abdallah. May 16, 2016.

Films and videos

Captain Corelli's Mandolin John Mellen, 2001.

Fascist Legacy Ken Kirby, BBC, 1989.

Lion of the Desert Mustafa Akkad, 1981.

Marshal Göring in Tripoli. YouTube. April and May 1939.

Mediterraneo Gabriele Salvatore, 1991.

Roman Holiday William Wyler, 1953.

Tea with Mussolini Franco Zeffirelli, 1999.

The Battle of Algiers Gillo Pontecorvo, 1966.

Newspapers, articles, and official statements

All articles published by *The New York Times* on Italian colonialism and Libya (1911–1943).

"20-Year War Ended by the Italians in Tripoli" *The New York Times*, (January 27, 1932).

"Arabs in Libya Bellicose" *The New York Times*, (November 23, 1914).

Al-Hrair, Jad al-Mawla, and al-Arabiyya, *Al- Jihad al-Libi fi Shu'ra al-Aqtar*, (Tripoli: Libyan Studies Center, 1991).

Al-Jabiri, Muhammad Salih, and Al-Tunisiyya, *Yawmiyat al-Jihad al-Libi Fi al-Sahafa*, (Tripoli/Tunis: Al-Dar al-Arabiyya Lil Kitab, 1982).

"Italy's Bloody Secret" *The Guardian* (June 25, 2003).

"Italy–Libya statement," BBC News (July 10, 1998).

Kilani, Muhammad Sayyid. Al- Ghazu al Itali 'ala Libia wa al Maqalat al lati kutibat fi a Suhuf al-Masriyya, 1911–1917, (Tripoli: Dar al-Fijani, 1996).

"Libya is Safe for White Settlers" *The New York Times* (November 1, 1938).

Meldrum, Andrew. "German Minister Says Sorry for Genocide in Nambia" *The Guardian* (August 15, 2004).

Motadel, David. "The United States Was Never Immune to Fascism, Not Then, Not Now" *The Guardian*, (August 17, 2017).

Povoledo, Elisabetta. "Anti-Fascist Protestors Rally in Italy as Mussolini Heirs Gain Ground" *The New York Times*, (June 20, 2018).

Povoledo, Elisabetta and Pianigiani, Gaia. "Italian Minister Moves to Count Roma, Invoking Memories of Mussolini" *The New York Times*, (June 20, 2018).

Websites

Ashcar, Gilbert. "Fascism in the Middle East and North Africa" The Oxford Handbooks online, (September 2015). www.oxfordbooks.com.

Pocock, David. "Sir Edward Evans-Pritchard 1902–1973, an Appreciation" www.Cam
bridge.org/.com.

Selected published material: books, articles, poems, and letters

Adams, H.C. "Cirenaic, Eastern Wing of Italian Libya" *National Geographic*, 57:6 (1930) 689–726.

Al-'Abar, 'Uthman 'Abdulsalam and Adham, Rabab ed., in *Oral History*, vol 29, (Tripoli: Libyan Studies Centre, 1991) 228.

Handbook of Cyrenaica, (Cairo: British Military Administration, 1947).

'Agaila, Ahmad Yusuf. *Sirat al-Naj'a [The Biography of The Camp]*, (Benghazi: Daral-Bayan, 2003) 60–62.

Agamben, Giorgio. *Homo Sacer: Sovereign Power and Bare Life* translated by Daniel Heller-Rozen, (Stanford, CA: Stanford University Press, 1998).

Agamben, Giorgio. *Remnants of Auschwitz: the Witness and the Archive*, (New York: Zone Books, 2002).

Al-Ahlafi, Hussain Muhammad. *Al-Ahlafi, Hussain Muhammad* (Benghazi: Mansharat Majlis al-Ibda'a al-Thawafi, 2004).

Ahmida, Ali Abdullatif. *Forgotten Voices: Power and Agency in Colonial and Postcolonial Libya*, (New York: Routledge, 2005).

Ahmida, Ali Abdullatif. *The Making of Modern Libya: State Formation, Colonialization and Resistance*, 2nd edition, (New York: State University of New York Press, 2009).

'Ajailla, Abdali Abu. *Um al-Khair: The Poet of the Braiga Concentration Camp*, (Benghazi: Al-Maktaba al-Wataniyya, no date).

Allan, J. A. *Libya: The Experience of Oil*, (Boulder, CO: Westview Press, 1981).

Altorki, Sorya and Fawzi El-Solh, Camila. *Arab Women in the Field*, (Syracuse, NY: Syracuse University Press, 1988).

Amin, Samir. *Eurocentrism*, (New York: Monthly Review Press, 1980).

ANA, Internal affairs Italy 130–139, Decimal 865, Roll 31.

Arendt, Hannah. *On Revolution*, (New York: Penguin Classics, 1951).

Arendt, Hannah. *The Origins of Totalitarianism*, (New York: Harcourt, Brace and Jovanovich, 1973).

Arendt, Hannah. *Eichmann in Jerusalem*, (New York: Penguin Books, 1994 [1963]).

Arielli, Nir. "Colonial Soldiers in Italian Counter-Insurgency Operations in Libya, 1922–32" *British Journal of Military History*, 1:2 (February 2015) 47–66.

Atkinson, David. "Embodied Resistance, Italian Anxieties, and the Place of the Nomad in Colonial Cyrenaica" in Charlotte Ross and Loredana Polezzi, eds., *In Carpore: Bodies in Post-Unification Italy*, (Farleigh, NJ: Dickinson University Press) 56–79.

"Arresting 'Umar al-Mukhtar the Leader of Rebels in Barca" *Bred Barca*, 346, (September 8, 1931).

Awagir Tribe to Slug by The Italian colonial Mutasarif of Benghazi ASAMI, vol. v, in ventari e, supplementi, Bacco 5, commissania to regional de Begnasi, Relazione Sloug, 28 Lunglio 1932. 4.

Awkali, Salim. "Abi," ["My Fathe"r]. Recived from: Fayruz Salim al-Awkali and Ahmad al-Fakhri, November 5, 2018.

Baldinetti, Anna. *Orieutalismo E Colonialismo La ricerca di cousenso in Egitto Per L'impesadi Libia*, (Roma: Insititutio Per L'Oriente "C.A. Nallino," 1997).

Baldinetti, Anna ed., *Modern and Contemporary Libya: Sources and Historiographies*, (Roma: Institito Italiano per L'Africa E L'Oriente, 2003).

Baldinetti, Anna. *The Origins of the Libyan Nation*, (London: Routledge, 2006).

Al-Barbar, Aghil ed., *'Umar al-Mukhtar, Nashatuhu Wa Jihaduh, 1862–1931 ['Umar al-Mukhtar, His Upbringing and Jihad]*, (Tripoli: Libyan Studies, 1983).

Al-Barghathi, Yusuf Salim. "Al-Mu'taqalat Wa al-Adrar al- Najma 'An al-Ghazwual-Itali" ("The Concentration Camps and their Impact on Libya") in Aghil al-Barbar ed., *'Umar al-Mukhtar*, (Tripoli: Center for Libyan Studies, 1983) 146–147.

Al-Barghathi, Yusuf Salim. "Al-Mu'taqalat wa al-Manafi" *Al-Shahid*, 10, (October 1989) 260–266.

Al-Barghathi, Yusuf Salim ed. *The Mawsu'at Riwayat al-Jihad. Volume 22, [The Encyclopedia of Jihad Oral History]*, (Tripoli: Libyan Studies Center, 1991).

Al-Barghathi, Yusuf Salim. *"Al-Mu'taqalat al-Fashistiyya bi Libia" [Italian Fasccist Concentration Camps in Libya]*, (Tripoli: Libyan Studies Center, 1993).

Ben-Ghiat, Ruth. "A Lesser Evil? Italian Fascism in and the Totalitarian Equation" in Helmut Dubiel and Gabriel Motzkin, eds., *The Lesser Evil: Moral Approaches to Genocide*, (New York: Routledge, 2004) 137–153.

Ben-Ghait, Ruth and Fuller, Mia eds., *Italian Colonialism*, (New York: Palgrave Press, 2005).

Ben-Ghait, Ruth. *Italian Fascism's Empire Cinema*, (Bloomington, IN: Indian University Press, 2015).

Ben-Ghait, Ruth. "Why Are So Many Fascist Monuments Still Standing in Italy" *The New Yorker*, (October 5, 2017).

Bernhard, Patrick. "Borrowing from Mussolini: Nazi Germany's Colonial Aspirations in the Shadow of Italian Expansionism" *Journal of Imperial and Commonwealth History*, 41:4 (2013) 617–643.

Bernhard, Patrick. "Re-narrating Italian Fascism: New Directions in the Historiography of European Dictatorship" *Contemporary European History*, 23 (2014) 151–163.

Bernhard, Patrick. "Hitler's Africa in the East: Italian Colonialism as a Model for German Planning in Eastern Europe" *Journal of Contemporary History*, 51:1 (2016) 61–90.

Black, Gregory Dale. *The United States and Italy*, (Lawrence, KS: University of Kansas Press, 1974) 13–14.

Borneman, John and Hammoudi, Abdellah eds., *Being There: The Fieldwork Encounter and the Making of Truth*, (Berkeley, CA: University of California Press, 2009) 259–292.

Bosworth, Robert. "Coming to Terms with Fascism in Italy" *History Today*, (April, 24, 2012) 4.

Bosworth, Robert. *Italian Dictatorship*, (London: Arnold, 1998).

Burhana, Ali ed., *Al-Shi'r al-Sha;bi*, (Tripoli: Al-Lajana al-Shabiyyia al-'Amma, 2000).

Bu-Rwais, Imran. *Waqi', 'Asr, Muhakamat, wa Shanq 'Umar al Mukhtar, [The Events, Trial, and Hanging of 'Umar al-Mukhtar]*, (Benghazi: Manshurat Solphyum, 2003).

Carney, John. *Rethinking Sartre*, (Latham, MD: University Press of America, 2007) 53.

Casserly, Colonial Gordon. "Tripolitania: Where Rome Resumes Sway" *National Geographic*, 48:2 (1925) 131–161.

Caton, Steven C. *Peak of Yemen I Summon*, (Berkeley, CA: University of California Press, 1999).

Céaire, Aimé. *Discourses on Colonialism*, (New York: Pantheon, 1988) 12.

Clancy-Smith, Julia. "Saints, Mahdis, and Arms: Religion and Resistance in Mid-Nineteenth Century North Africa" in Edmund Burke III and Ira Lapids, eds., *Islam, Politics, and Social Movements*, (Berkeley, CA: University of California Press, 1990).

Cohen, Jon S. "Was Italian Fascism a Developmental Dictatorship? Some Evidence to the Contrary" *Economic History Review*, 41:1 (1988) 95–113.

Cohen, William. "The Algerian War, the French State, and Official Memory" *Historical Reflections*, 28:2 (2002) 219–239.

Cowell, Alan. "The Ghost of Mussolini Keeps Rattling His Chains" *The New York Times*, (June 1, 1994), A3.

Cresti, Federico. *Non Desiderara la terra d'altri*, (Roma: Carlucci editore, 2011) 83–122.

Davis, John. *Libyan Politics: Tribe and Revolution*, (Berkeley, CA: University of California Press, 1991).

Davis, Mike. *Late Victorian Holocausts*, (New York: Verso, 2002).

De Felice, Renzo. *Interpretations of Fascism*, (Cambridge, MA: Harvard University Press, 1977).

De Grazia, Victoria. "Will IL Duce's Successors Make the Facts Run on Time?" *The New York Times*, (May 14, 1994) 21.

Del Boca, Angelo. *Gli Italinani in Libia: Dal Fascismo a Gheddafi*, (Roma-Barie: Laterza, 1988).

Del Boca, Angelo. *Gli Italiani in Libia II*, (Roma-Barie: Laterza, 1988) 175–232.

Del Boca, Angelo. "The Myths, Suppressions, Denials and Defaults of Italian Colonialism" in Patrizia Palumbo, ed., *A Place under the Sun*, (Berkeley, CA: University of California Press, 2003) 17–36.

Del Boca, Angeleo. *Mohamed Fekini and the Fight to Free Libya* translated by Anthony Shugbar, (New York: Palgrave Press, 2011), XV.

Dghaim, Muhammad ed., *Mahrajan Rafiq al-Adabi*, (Benghazi: Garyounis University Press, 1993).

Francesca Di Pasquale, "The 'Other' at Home: Deportation and Transportation of Libyans to Italy during the Colonial Era (1911–1943)" *International Review of Social History*, 63:26 (August 2018), 211–231.

Diggins, John P. *Mussolini and Fascism: The View from America*, (Princeton, NJ: Princeton University Press, 1972).

Dirar, Uoldelal Chelati. "From Warriors to Urban Dwellers" *Cahiers d'etudes africaines*, 175 (2004) 533–574.

Dirar, Uoldelal Chelati. "Truppe Coloniale e L'individuatione dell' Africa agency: Il Caso degli ascari eritrei" *A fricche e orienti. Il ritorno della memoria coloniale*, 1:1 (2007) 41–56.

Domenico, Roy Palmer. *Italian Fascism on Trial, 1943–1948*, (Chapel Hill, NC: University of North Carolina Press, 1991) 10, 114, 154, 160.

Dreschsler, Horst. *Let us Die Fighting: The Struggle of the Herero and the Nama People against German Imperialism (1884–1915)*, (London: 2ed Press, 1980).

"Duce with the Laughing Face" *People Magazine*, (April 27, 1992) 70.

Elkins, Caroline. *Imperial Reckoning*, (New York: Henry Holt and Company, 2005).

Elkins, Caroline. "Looking beyond Mau Mau: Archiving Violence in the Era of Decolonization" *American Historical Review*, (June 2015) 852–868.

Evans-Pritchard, E.E. *The Sanusi of Cyrenaica*, (Oxford: Oxford University Press, 1949).

Al-Fadi' al-Sud al-Humr: safahat min al-Isti'mar al-Itali fi Libia [The Black Red Horrors on [or of] Italian Colonialism in Tripoli and Barqa], (Damascus, Syria, 1932).

Fanon, Franz. *The Wretched of the Earth*, (London: Penguin, 1967).

Fanush, Yusuf and al-Hudhairi, Al-Hamali Sh'aib eds., *Diwan al-Sh'ir Fadhil Hussain al-Shilmani*, (Benghazi: Manshurat Majlis al-Iba'a al-Thawafi, 2004).

Al-Fatiuri, Haja Riqiyya, in Mawsucat Riwayat Al-Jihad, Interview, volume 37 (special volume on women) *Zainab Muhammad Zuhry*, (Tripoli: Libyan Studies Center, 1995).

Al-Fazani, Ali. *Death on the Minaret*, (Benghazi: Al- Makataba al-Wataniyya, 1973).

Feldman, Matthew. *Ezra Pound's Fascist Propaganda, 1935–45*, (New York: Palgrave, 2013).

First, Ruth. *The Elusive Revolution*, (London: Penguin, 1974) 87–98 and 99–118.

Fisher, Ian. "New Italian Minister Sheds Far-Right Image" *The New York Times*, (November 19, 2004).

Focardi, Filippo. "The Question of Fascist Italy's War Crimes: The Construction of a Self-Acquiring Myth (1943–1948)" *Journal of Modern Italian Studies*, 9:8 (2004) 330–348.

Forgacs, David ed., *The Antonio Gramsci Reader*, (New York: University of New York Press, 2000) 112–113, 149.

Foucault, Michel. "Two Lectures" in Nicolas B. Dirks, Geoff Eley, and Sherry B. Ortner, eds., *Culture/Power/History: A Reader in Contemporary Social Theory*, (Princeton, NJ: Princeton University Press, 1994) 201–221.

Foucault, Michel. *Discipline and Punish: The Birth of Modern Prison* translated by Alan Sheridan, (New York: Vintage Books, 1995, 1997).

Fuller, Mia. *Moderns Abroad*, (New York: Routledge, 2007).

Gellately, Robert and Kiernin, Ben, eds., *The Specter of Genocide: Mass Murder in Historical Perspective*, (Cambridge: Cambridge University Press, 2003).

Gewald, Jan-Bart. *Herero Heroes: A Socio-Political History of the Herero of Namibia, 1890–1928*, (Oxford: James Curey, 1999).

Gershoni, Israel ed., *Arab Reponses to Fascism*, (Austin, TX: Texas University Press, 2014).

Goffman, Alice. *On The Run*, (Chicago, IL: Chicago University Press, 2014).

Gran, Peter. *Beyond Eurocentrism: A New World View of Modern History*, (Syracuse, NY: Syracuse University Press, 1996) 88–121.

De Grazia, Victoria. "Will IL Duce's Successors Make the Facts Run on Time?" *The New York Times*, (May 14, 1994) 21.

Gazzini, Claudia. "Assessing Italy's Grand Gesto to Libya" *Middle East Report*, (March 16, 2009).

Graziani, Rodlofo. *Cirenaica PaCificata*, (Milano: Mondadori, 1932) 120.

Graziani, Rodolfo. *La Confraterra Senussita*, (Padava: Casa Edittorice Dott, 1932) V–VIII.

Gregor, James. *Italian Fascism and Developmental Dictatorship*, (Princeton, NJ: Princeton University Press, 1979) IX–IV.

Haddaadt, Said. *The Role of the Libyan Army in the Revolt against Gaddafi's Regime*, (Doha, Qatar: Al Jazeera Centre for Studies, March 16, 2011) 2–5.

Hamalainen, Pekka. "The Future of Native American History in The United States" http://historians.org/perspectives/issues/2012.

Hannoum, Abdealmajid. *Violent Modernity*, (Cambridge, MA: Harvard University Press, 2010).

Henneberg, Krystyna Von. "Monuments, Public Space and Memory of Empire in Modern Italy" *History and Memory*, 16:1 (2004) 37–85.

Herman, Edward and Chomsky, Noam. *Manufacturing Consent*, (New York: Pantheon Books, 1988, 1992).

Al-Hindiri, Sa'id 'Abdrahman and Al-Kubti, Salim Hussain eds., *Qusa'id al-Jihad Vol. I [Poems of the Jihad]*, (Tripoli: Libyan Studies Center, 1984) 180–181.

Ibrahim, Aballahi. "The Birth of Interview" in Luise White, Stephan Miescher, and David William Cohen, eds., *African Words, African Voices: Critical Practices in Oral History*, (Bloomington, IN: Indian University Press, 2001) 103–124.

Ignazi, Piero. "Legitimization and Evolution of the Italian Right Wing Social and Ideo-logical Repositioning of Alleanza Nazionale and Lega Nord" *South European Society and Politics*, 10:2 (July 2005) 313–349.

Iliffe, John. "The Social Organization of the Maji Maji Rebellion" *Journal of African History* 8:3 (1967) 495–512.

Iliffe, John. *Honour in African History*, (Cambridge: Cambridge University Press, 2005) 1–10.

Isenberg, Andrew C. *The Destruction of the Bison*, (Cambridge: Cambridge University Press, 2000) 12.

Jackson, James O. "Fascism Lives" *Time*, (June 6, 1994).

Jacoby, Russell. *Social Amnesia*, (Boston: Transaction Books, 1997) 1–18.

Kauffmann, Stanley. "Under Florentine Skies" *New Republic 2* 220:23, (June 7, 1999).

Kershaw, Ian. *The Nazi Dictatorship*, (London: Edward Arnold, 1993).

Khalidi, Ismail Raghib. *Constitutional Development in Libya*, (Beirut: Khayyat's College Books, 1963).

Khashiem, Mustafa A. "The Treaty of Friendship, Partnership and Cooperation between Libya and Italy" *California Italian Studies*, 1:1 (2010) 1–14.

Al-Kubti, Salim. *Wamid al-Bariq al-Gharbi, [The Shining of the Western Light]*, (Benghazi:: Maktabal al-Tumur 5, 2005) 21–28.

Labanca, Nicola. "Internamento Coloniale Italino" in Colstantino Di Sante, ed., *I campi di Concentratamento in Italia*, (Milan: Franco Angeli, 2001) 40–67.

Labanca, Nicola. *L'Oltremare: Storica dell'espansione coloniale italiana*, (Bologna: Societa editrice il Mulino, 2002).

Labanca, Nicola. "Colonial Rule, Colonial Repression and War Crimes in Italian Colonies" *Journal of the Modern Italian Studies*, 9:3 (2004) 300–313.

Labanca, Nicola. "The Embarrassment of Libya, History, Memory, and Politics in Contemporary Italy" *California Italian Studies*, 1:1 (2010) 1–19.

Laub, Dori. "Truth and Testimony: The Progress and Struggle" in Shoshana Feldman and Dori Laub, eds., *Testimony*, (New York: Routledge, 1992) 61–73.

Al-Lawatti, Idris Imghaib. "Ghaith al-Saghir" ["Little Ghaith"], (1937).

Lawson, Tom. *The Last Man*, (New York: I.B. Tauris, 2014).

Lazreg, Marina. *The Eloquence of Silence*, (New York: Routledge Press, 1994).

Lazreg, Marina. *Foucault's Orient*, (New York: Berghahn, 2017).

Lemarchand, Rene ed., *Forgotten Genocides*, (Philadelphia, PA: University of Pennsylvania Press, 2011).

Levy, Carl. "Fascism, National Socialism and Conservatives in Europe, 1914–1945" *Contemporary European History*, 8:1 (1999), 97–126.

Lewine, Annie Esme. "Ancient Rome in Modern Italy: Mussolini's Manipulation of Roman History in the Mostra Augustea della Romanita" *Studies in Mediterranean Antiquity and Classics*, 2:1 (2008) 1–10.

Lewis-Kraus, Gideon. "The Trial of Alice Goffman" *New York Times Magazine*, (March 17, 2018).

Libyan Anti-Fascist Committee, *Ha'iyat Tahrir Libia, Al-Fadi' al-Sud al-Humr: Min Safahat al-'Isti'imar al-Itali fi Libia [The Red Black Horrors: Pages of Italian Colonialism in Libya]*, (Cairo: Matba'at al-karnak, 1948).

Linqvist, Sven. *Exterminate All the Brutes*, (London: Granta Publications, 1997) 72–73, 140–141, 172.

Lutz, Catherine A. and Collins, Jane L. *Reading National Geographic*, (Chicago, IL: Chicago University Press, 1993) 10.

Lyttelton, Adrian. "What is Fascism" *The New York Review of Books*, (October 21, 2004) 33–36.

Al-Maimmuni, Ibrahim al-Ghmari. *Dhiqrayyat Mu'taqalat al-Agaila [Memoirs of the Agaila Concentration Camp]*, (Tripoli: Libyan Studies Centre), 1995.

Al-Maimmuni, Ibrahim al-Ghmari. *Dhikriyat Mu'taqal al-Agaila [Memoirs of the Agaila Concentration Camp]*, second edition, (Tripoli: Libyan Studies Center, 2006).

Malia Hom, Stephanie. *The Beautiful Country: Tourism and the Impossible State of Destination Italy*, (Toronto: University of Toronto Press, 2015).

Malia Hom, Stephanie. *Empire's Mobius Strip*, (Ithica, NY: Cornell University Press, 2019).

Al-Maliki, Hussain Nasib. *Sha'ir Mu'taqal al- Agaila [The Poet of the Agaila Concentration Camp]*, vol. 4, (Benghazi: no date) 10.

Mamdani, Mahmood. "Making Sense of Political Violence in Postcolonial Africa" *Identity, Culture and Politics*, 3:2 (2002) 1–23.

Mamdani, Mahmood. *Good Muslim, Bad Muslim*, (New York: Pantheon Books, 2004).

Mamdani, Mahmood. *When Victims Become Killers*, (Princeton, NJ: Princeton University Press, 2011) XIII–XV.

Marcus, George. *Ethnography through Thick and Thin*, (Princeton, NJ: Princeton University Press, 1998).

"Marshal Goerhing in Tripoli" *Libia al-Musawra [Illustrated Libya]*, 10 (Benghazi, 1939).

Al-Mahruq, Sa'id. *Poems that Silenced Voice*, (Tripoli: Al- Dar al-Arabiyya Lil-Kitab, 1987).

McLaren, Brian. *Architecture and Tourism in Italian Colonial Libya*, (Seattle, WA: University of Washington Press, 2000).

MDL, Shukri Faysal files, Arab documents, document November 27, 1934, from Arslan to Sa'dawi, 30, 31a collection.

Medley, Benjamin. "From Africa to Auschwitz" *History Quarterly*, 53:3 (2005) 429–464.

Mellen, Joan. "An Interview with Gillo Pontecorvo" *Film Quarterly*, 26:1 (Autumn, 1972) 2–10.

Moses, A. Dirk ed., *Empire, Colony, and Genocide*, (New York: Berghahn Books, 2008).

Moses, A. Dirk and Stone, Dan eds., *Colonialism and Genocide*, (London: Routledge, 2007).

Musa, Hussain Dafir Ben. *Mabruka*, (Damscus: Makatabat Dimashiq, 1937).

Ottolenghi, Gustavo. *Gli Italini E il Colonialiso I campi di detenzione italiani in Africa*, (Milano: Sugarco edizion, 1997) 149–182.

Palumbo, Michael ed., *Human Rights: Meaning of History*, (Lane/Malabar, FLLane/: Robert E. Krieger, 1982) 71–75.

Pankhurst, Richard. "Italian Fascist War Crimes in Ethiopia" *North East African Studies*, 6:1–2 (1999) 83–140.

Parry, Marc. "Colonial Atrocities and Academic Reputation on Trial in a British Courtroom" *Chronical of Higher Education*, (June 1, 2016) 1–10.

Patric, John. "Imperial Rome Reborn" *National Geographic Magazine*, 71:3 (1937) 269–325.

Pedaliu, Effie G. "Britain and the Handover of Italian War Criminals to Yugoslavia" *Journal of Contemporary History*, 39:4 (October 2004) 529.

Pelt, Adrian. *Libyan Independence and the United Nations*, (New Haven, CT: Yale University Press, 1970).

Pertrusewitz, Martha. "Hidden Pages of Contemporary Italian History: War Crimes, War Guilt and Collective Memory" Special Issue, *Journal of Modern Italian Studies*, 9:8 (2004) 269–270.

Peters, Emrys. *The Bedouin of Cyrenaica*, edited by Jack Goody and Emanuel Marx, (Cambridge: Cambridge University Press, 1990).

Portelli, Alessandro. "The Peculiarities of Oral History" *History Workshop Journal*, 2:1 (1981) 36.

Qanawi, Irwa'ii Muhammad Ali, *Bashir al-Sa'dawi wa Dawrah al-Haraka al-Wataniyya al-Libiyya [Bashir al-Sa'dawi and His Role in the Libyan Nationalist Movement]*, (Tripoli: Libyan Studies Center 2014). MDL Shukri file.

Rochat, Giorgio. *IL Colonialismo Italiano*, (Turin: Loescher, 1973).

Rochat, Giorgio. "IL genocide Cirenaico" *Belfagor*, 35:4 (1980) 449–454.

Salamh, Raja Ben. *Al Muwt wa Tuqusuh, [Death and its Rituals]*, (Tunis: Dar al-Janub, 1999) 94–116.

Salerno, Eric. *Genocido in Libia*, (Milani: Sugarco edizioni, 1979).

Salerno, Eric. *Genocide in Libya* second edition, (Roma: Manifesto Librio, 2009).

Salerno, Luigi. *Las Polizia dei costumi a Tripol, con cenni storici sulla prostituzione*, (Lugo: Tip. editorice trisi, 1922).

Samatar, Said S. *Oral History and Somali Nationalism*, (Cambridge: Cambridge University Press, 1982).

Santarelli, Enzo, Rochat, Giorgio, Rainero, Romain, and Goglia, Luigi. *Omar al-Mukhtar* translated by John Gilbert, (London: Darf Publishers, 1986).

Al-Sayyid al-Sharif, Miftah. *Masirat al-Haraka al-Wataniyya al-Libiyya [The Path of the Libyan Nationalist Movement]*, (Beirut: Dar al-Furat, 2011) 162–171.

Schmitz, David F. *The United States and Fascist Italy, 1940–1992*, (Chapel Hill, NC: University of North Carolina Press, 1988).

Scott, James. *Domination and the Arts of Resistance*, (New Haven, CT: Yale University Press, 1990).

Sha'ala, Saad Muhammad Abu. *Min Dakhil al-Mu'taqalat [From inside the Concentration Camps]*, (Tripoli: Al-Munshaa al-'Aamma Lilnshar, 1984).

Al-Sahli, Ali and al-Kubti, Salim eds., *Diwan al-Shi'r al –Sha'bi*, (Benghazi: The University Press, 1977) 76, 235.

Al-Sahli, Ali and al-Kubti, Salim eds., *Diwan al-Shi'r al-Sha'bi II*, (Benghazi: Garyounis University Press, 1998) 81.

Al-Sayyid Dughaim, Mahumd. "Jihad Bashir al-Sa'dawi Dida al-Fashiyya" *Jihad Bashir al-Sa'dawi against Fascism al-Hayat*, (February 27, 1995).

Al -Shinaty, Mahmud. *Qa'diyat Libya [The Libyan Question]*, (Cairo: Maktabat al-Nahda al-Masriyyia, 1951).

Shinib, 'Umar Fa'iq. "Libia Mahdal Butula wa'Arin al-Ausud" ["Libya Place of Courage and the Den of Lions"] *Majalat al-Ikhwan al-Muslimin*, 91–94 (February–March 1946).

Shukri, Muhammad Fu'ad. *Al-Sanusiyya Din Wa Dawla (The Sanusiyya: Religion and State)*, (Cairo: Dar al-Fikr al-'Arabi, 1948).

Shukri, Muhammah Fu'ad. *Libia al-Haditha wathi'q Tahrurha Wa Istiqlaluha, 1945–1947. [Modern Libya: Documents of its Liberation and Independence]*, (Cairo: Itihad Press, 1957) 157–164.

Al-Sa'dawi, Bashir. *Fadi' al-Isti'mar al-Itali al-Fashisti fi Tarabulus Wa Barqa [The Horrors of Italian Fascist Colonialism in Tripoli and Barqa]*, (Damascus: Manshurat Jam'iyal al-Difa' an Trabulus Wa Barqa, 1931).

Al-Sijil al-Qawmi. Qadhdafi Speeches, Libyan National Record.

Smith, Denis Mack. *Mussolini's Roman Empire*, (New York: Penguin Books, 1976) 37.

Spivak, Gayathri Chakravarty. "Can the Subaltern Speak?" in Cary Nelson and Lawrence Grossberg, eds., *Marxism and the Interpretation of Cultures*, (Urbana, IL: University of Illinois Press, 1988) 271–313.

Srivastava, Neelan. "Anti-Colonialism and Italian Left" *Interventions*, 8:3 (February 18, 2007) 427, 420, 425.

Stannard, David. *American Holocaust*, (Oxford: Oxford University Press, 1992).

Stannard, David. "The Dangers of Calling the Holocaust Unique" *The Chronicle of Higher Education*, 42:47 (August 2, 1996) 1–4.

Stone, Marla. "A Flexible Rome: Fascism and the Cult of Romanita" in Catherine Edwards, ed., *Roman Presences*, (Cambridge: Cambridge University Press, 1999) 205–220.

Sturgis, Amy H. *The Trail of Tears and Indian Removal*, (Greenwood Press: Westport, CT, 2007).

Suirsky, Marcelo and Nignall, Simone eds., *Agamben and Colonialism*, (Edinburgh: Edinburgh University Press, 2012).

Sulpizi, Francesco and Sury, Salaheddin Hasan eds., *Primo Convegno su gLi esiliate Libici nel periodo Coloniale 28–29 Otobre 2000*, Roma, 2002.

The Cherokee Removal: A Brief History with Documents, (Boston: Biddeford Books, 1995) 160–162.

Al-Tilisi, Khalifa. *Rafiq Sha'ir al-Watan [Rafiq Poet of the Homeland]*, third edition, (Malha: Malta Interunit Limited, 1976).

Todorov, Tzvetan. *The Conquest of America, The Question of the Other*, (New York: Harper & Row, 1984).

Trouillot, Michel-Rolph. *Silencing The Past*, (Boston: Beacon Press, 1995) 26–27, 95–107.

'Uthman, Fatima in 'Abdallah A. Zagub "Shahadat al-Mar'a Fi Zamin al-Harb," ["A Woman as an Eyewitness to War"] *Al-Thaqafa-al-'Arabiyya*, (1980), 85–117.

Vandewalle, Dirk. "The Libyan Jamahiriyya since 1969" in Dirk Vandewalle, ed., *Qadhdhafi's Libya*, (New York: St. Martins Press, 1995) 3–46.

Vansina, Jan. *Oral Traditions: A Study in Historical Methodology*, (Chicago, IL: Aldine Publishing Company, 1956).

Vansina, Jan. *Oral Traditions and History*, (Madison, WI: University of Wisconsin Press, 1985).

Volterra, Alessandro. *Sudditi Coloniali. Ascari eritrei, 1935–1941*, (Roma: Franco Angeli, 2014).

Williams, Manuela A. *Mussolini's Propaganda Abroad*, (New York: Routledge, 2006).

Wolf, Eric. *Europe and the People without History*, (Berkeley, CA: University of California Press, 1982).

Wolin, Sheldon. "Injustice and Collective Memory," in Sheldon Wolin, ed., *Presence of the Past*, (Baltimore, MD: John Hopkins University Press, 1989) 32–46.

Al-Za'idi, Muhammad Rajab. *Shakib Arslan wa al-qadiyya al-libiyya [Arslan and the Libyan Question]*, (Al-byada: Maktabat al-Wahda al-Arabiyya, 1964).

Al-Zawawi, Ali et al., "Deportees and Exiled Libyans to Southern Italy" *Mawusu'at Riwayat al Jihad*, Special Issue 7 (1991).

Al-Zawi, Tahir. *'Umar al-Mukhtar*, (Tripoli: Dar al-Fijani, 1970).

Zimmerer, Jürgen. "The Birth of the Ostland Out of the Spirit of Colonialism" *Patterns of Prejudice*, 39:2 (2005) 115–134.

INDEX

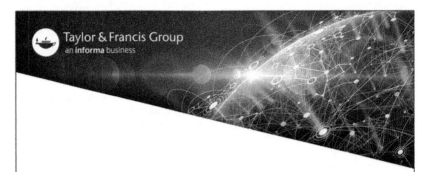